# DECISIVE FORCE

# DECISIVE FORCE

## The New American Way of War

### F. G. HOFFMAN

 PRAEGER

Westport, Connecticut
London

**Library of Congress Cataloging-in-Publication Data**

Hoffman, F. G.
    Decisive force : the new American way of war / F. G. Hoffman.
      p.  cm.
    Includes bibliographical references and index.
    ISBN 0–275–95344–0 (alk. paper)
    1. United States—Military policy.  2. United States—Strategic
aspects.  I. Title.
UA23.H5344   1996
355′.033073—dc20        95–22015

British Library Cataloguing in Publication Data is available.

Library of Congress Catalog Card Number: 95–22015
ISBN: 0–275–95344–0

First published in 1996

Praeger Publishers, 88 Post Road West, Westport, CT 06881
An imprint of Greenwood Publishing Group, Inc.

Printed in the United States of America

∞™

The paper used in this book complies with the
Permanent Paper Standard issued by the National
Information Standards Organization (Z39.48–1984).

10 9 8 7 6 5 4 3 2 1

The views contained herein are those of the author, and publication of this research by the Advanced
Research Program, Naval War College, does not constitute endorsement thereof by the Naval War
College, the Department of the Navy, or any other branch of the U.S. Government.

For Catherine and Claire

# Contents

# Acknowledgments

It is impossible to undertake a project of this scope without the guidance and support of many people. My words of appreciation cannot reward all of them appropriately; however, the following deserve formal mention.

Dr. Robert S. Wood, Dean of the Center of Naval Warfare Studies at the U.S. Naval War College, Newport, Rhode Island, who gave both permission and resources to undertake this project. To Dr. John B. Hattendorf, head of the Advanced Research Department at Newport, for his guidance and great support during the initial stages of the project.

To Colonel John E. Greenwood, USMC (retired), Colonel Mark Cancian, USMCR; Lieutenant Colonel Pat Garrett, USMC; and Mr. Matt Robinson of the Center for Naval Analyses, all of whom I owe both a personal and intellectual debt. Additionally, Mr. Andrew Hoehn has helped immeasurably in defining key elements of the strategy and policy debate, as well as identifying numerous useful sources. Recognition and appreciation must also be noted for the assistance of fellow historian Bruce Gudmundsson, founder of the Institute for Tactical Education. Special thanks are due Colonel Greenwood, the distinguished editor of the *Marine Corps Gazette*, who has mentored my writing for a decade with little reward.

To Dr. David E. Kaiser and Commander Daryl King, USN of the Strategy and Policy Department at the Naval War College, my sincere thanks for sharpening my many dull thoughts about strategy. To Professors John Waghelstein, Alberto Coll, Andrew Ross, and Michael Handel of the Naval War College, my appreciation for their collective insights and guidance. To Colonel John. B. Matthews, USMC, (retired), of the Marine Corps University, Quantico, Virginia, my gratitude for his personal insights about Marine operations in Beirut. Additionally, special thanks are due to Lieutenant General Bernard E. Trainor, USMC (retired), Director of National Security Programs at the John F. Kennedy School, Harvard University for his time and advice regarding senior-level decision making and military operations in Lebanon and Operation Desert Storm.

No author completes such a project without a very strong editing team. The professionals at Praeger steered me along the way throughout a long process.

Authors are always dependent upon many helpful hands who preserve and provide research materials and archives. I received timely support from Kerry Strong, chief archivist of the Marine Corps Research Center, and Benis Frank of the Marine Corps Historical Center. My strongest regards to Maggie Rauch and the assistance afforded me by the sterling professionals at Hewitt Library at the Naval War College.

Finally, to my principal advisor on this project, Dr. Mackubin T. Owens, of the National Security Decision Making Department at the Naval War College. Without Dr. "Mac" Owens, this project would not have been undertaken or finished. He has my unqualified gratitude for giving me the freedom to think, learn, write, and rewrite. Dr. Owens personifies a unique devotion to learning and academic inquiry. His unselfish assistance went far beyond duty, and is a credit to the renowned faculty at Newport.

Despite many helping hands and the excellent support I received, I ultimately followed my own reasoning. The conclusions herein and responsibility for the final product are completely my own. Any errors, omissions, and mistakes of fact are entirely mine.

# Introduction

For the past twenty years, ever since the last helicopter ignominiously left the rooftop of the American Embassy in Saigon, our country has debated how to use military force to serve the Nation's interests. This issue remains unanswered today. Despite a rich legacy of examples to draw from, our reluctance to conduct critical strategic studies limits our grasp of the problem and a deeper understanding of our own history.

In the immediate aftermath of Vietnam, there was a deeply emotional debate about the political, social, and moral aspects of the war. Many serving military officers participated in this debate, but the military as an institution pushed the memories of the Central Highlands and the Mekong Delta out of its consciousness. Instead the Armed Forces focused therapeutically on the threat the Soviet Union posed in Europe. Over time, the "lessons" of Vietnam passed implicitly into the military culture, into its doctrine, training and education, and thought process. The collective conclusion can be reduced to the simplistic cry of "No More Vietnams."

Most observers agree that Vietnam was lost at the political and strategic level of war. The existence of a national style of warfare, an American Way of War, was raised as a fundamental and immutable element of American strategy. The American Way of War is built around a strategy that employs the vast economic and technological base of the United States to grind down opponents with firepower and mass. Our style is built around economic production capacity and resources. Because of its costs, this style is predicated upon national mobilization and national commitment. This national style reflects both our comparative advantages and the limits of a democratic government.

The American Way of War has become a convenient and useful description to characterize our unique approach to warfare, an approach that reflects the collective history, attitudes, geography, and political culture of the American experience. It is admittedly somewhat of an overgeneralization, but it is a useful one. National styles do exist, and their study serves a valid analytical and practical purpose.

Regrettably, Vietnam was a scenario that did not match our national style. Yet many would argue that the American Way of War reflects the strategic culture of the United States, and that policy aims and strategies must be crafted consistent with this distinctive fundamental style or face the calamity of another Vietnam.

In the early 1980s this debate was renewed as the Reagan Administration sought to cast off the malaise of the 1970s and the reticence of the "Vietnam Syndrome." This condition supposedly restrained America from asserting itself as a global power. The Reagan Administration sought to "draw a line" against the Soviet Union somewhere, anywhere. Eventually, U.S. military forces were introduced into Latin America and in the Middle East. The tragedy of the Marine barracks bombing in October 1983 resurfaced the great debate of when, why, and how U.S. military might should be applied. Ultimately, a formula was generated by the Defense Department, and advocated aggressively by then-Secretary of Defense Caspar Weinberger in 1984.

This formula was phrased in a series of criteria that restricted the use of military forces to those situations where vital interests were at stake, where all other means had failed, where public support from Congress and the American people was assured, and with the wholehearted intent of winning. This set of guidelines, which eventually became known as the Weinberger Doctrine, was widely accepted in the military. It was castigated by some observers, including then-Secretary of State George Shultz, as utterly unreasonable and inconsistent with the country's standing as a world power.

In 1991, the rebuilt armed forces of the United States demonstrated which nation reigned supreme as the world's foremost military power in a most convincing manner. The stunning victory over Saddam Hussein seemed to finally bury the haunting memories and painful lessons of Vietnam. To those who had advocated an American Way of War, as the natural and unchangeable exposition of our national and strategic culture, Operation Desert Storm stood as vindication.

During his tenure as Chairman of the Joint Chiefs of Staff, General Colin Powell became the proponent for another strategic framework to guide the consideration of how military force should be used to support national policy objectives. General Powell brought a unique perspective to this task: a veteran of Vietnam, an Executive Assistant to Mr. Weinberger during the Beirut deployment, and a former National Security Advisor. His framework was reflected in the Chairman's National Miliary Strategy published in early 1992 in the warm afterglow of Desert Storm under a concept titled "Decisive Force." Decisive Force, in shorthand, means assembling the necessary forces and overwhelming an opponent swiftly and decisively. Implicit within the concept is the belief that long conflicts will bring out civilian micro-management, public dissatisfaction with the military, and a critical media. The concept was explained further, and better, in a series of speeches and articles in late 1992.

## PURPOSE AND SCOPE

The purpose of this book is to trace the development and evaluate the merits of a "New American Way of War" embodied in the Decisive Force concept. Military attitudes and lessons about the utility of force drawn from four different conflicts will be examined. The four examples include:

1. Vietnam
2. The U.S. intervention in Lebanon (1982-1984)
3. The invasion of Panama in 1989
4. The Persian Gulf Conflict in 1991

The examination of each conflict will include a four-stage assessment regarding military perceptions, attitudes, or lessons learned. The four elements of the assessment include; the objectives of each case: how force was used or limited; the relationships between policy makers and military leaders during the planning and conduct of the conflict; and finally, the degree of popular support for each intervention.

The focus of the effort is not to discern the correct "lessons" of each conflict from a policy or strategic perspective. The emphasis is on what the U.S. military absorbed from each conflict, and the pattern of these lessons over the course of two decades. These lessons the military believes to be legitimate will be evaluated, however. The research will highlight both the existence and limitations of a body of thought within the military about the use of force. The following questions have been used to frame the book:

1. What is the principle of Decisive Force?
2. What historical experiences lie under the principle?
3. Is it consistent with our strategic culture?
4. What are the advantages and disadvantages of Decisive Force in both strategic and operational terms?

Ultimately, this effort will explore the existence and limitations of a so-called New American Way of War. A chief concern in this endeavor is to establish and examine attitudes extant in the U.S. military about the conditions necessary for the successful employment of violent means in the service of the State. Another concern is the weak validity of these attitudes, and the potential for maldeployment of U.S. military force. Over the last generation, the country has moved towards a better understanding of exactly what it means to use military force. This has been a long journey. In many respects we are at an historic intersection about the use of military as an instrument of national power today. Tragic incidents in Somalia during the course of writing this book, and the debate about potential American intervention in Bosnia, bely any positive conclusions at this point.

## THESES

This book began with three explicit theses. The first concerns the existence of a New American Way of War, which reflects subtle changes from the traditional description made famous by Professor Russell Weigley in his seminal *The American Way of War*. Implicit in the definition of a national style of warfare is the delineation of cultural attributes and attitudes that constitute the preferred operational codes and methods of any given culture. The American military culture has been predisposed towards large and offensive methods of warfare, and has evidenced a lack of political dexterity in the conduct of military operations. A national style also implies a prescriptive manner to warfare. In this century, other countries have had serious problems resulting from fixed offensive doctrines ostensibly tied to strategic or operational paradigms. Fixed doctrines or prescriptive styles are not a useful guide to policy makers because inflexible approaches seldom satisfy the myriad complex situations faced in foreign affairs.

The second thesis concerns how the military came to the conclusions that shifted the operating code that functioned from the Civil War through World War II. Vietnam initiated the change, and subsequent conflicts in Lebanon, Panama, and Kuwait have locked in changes in the manner in which the American military views the employment of the military instrument to serve policy goals. The lessons learned from these conflicts are at best oversimplified. At worst they are erroneous.

The third thesis involves the present status of civil-military relations in this country. My thesis, simply stated, is that the relationship is in a state of subliminal crisis in the United States. This is the result of a long term deteroriation of communication and understanding between elements of our society and government. Civil-military relations have not had the degree of study and care that they should get, and the fault for this lies at the feet of civilian policy makers, including the most senior elected officials of the land. The necessary involvement of military leaders in the political aspects of decision making has drawbacks, and the increasingly narrow perspective about the utility of force in the U.S. military exacerbates a precarious problem. Serious reconsideration of a number of recent social trends and Congressional initiatives in Defense Department and Joint organizational relationships is sorely needed.

The decision to use force is a critical matter for any state. Military leaders make a major contribution to these decisions. Their professional advice is a crucial element of the policy decision making process. This expert input is founded on a number of their own attitudes and lessons from earlier conflicts. The lessons of these experiences are now buried into the institutional subconscious of the Armed Forces, for better or worse. These attitudes and lessons should be understood by those involved in making policy decisions. How these attitudes mesh with our strategic culture and the demands placed on the United States in the post-Cold War environment is crucial if effective civil-military relations are to be maintained in the years ahead. Such relationships produce effective strategies that best correspond to the desired ends of policy. Poor relationships, as exist today, result in poorly framed strategic decisions and ineffective military operations.

What Ernest May once called the "ultimate decision," the decision to use force to resolve conflict, is an act that defines a nation. No other decision raises so many factors and questions, or puts so much treasure and blood at risk. There is no greater measure of national leadership, on the part of politicians and military leaders, than the issue of war. Ultimately, the goal of this book is to contribute to ensuring that this decision is made wisely and well.

# Abbreviations

| | |
|---|---|
| BIA | Beirut International Airport |
| BUR | Bottom Up Review |
| CENTCOM | U.S. Central Command |
| CIA | Central Intelligence Agency |
| CINC | Commander-in-Chief |
| CINCCENT | Commander-in-Chief Central Command |
| CINCPAC | Commander-in-Chief Pacific Command |
| CJCS | Chairman of the Joint Chiefs of Staff |
| CONUS | Continental United States |
| DMZ | Demilitarized Zone |
| DOD | Department of Defense |
| EUCOM | European Command |
| FDO | Flexible Deterrent Options |
| FM | Field Manual |
| FMF | Fleet Marine Force |
| FMFM | Fleet Marine Force Manual |
| IDF | Israeli Defense Force |
| JCS | Joint Chiefs of Staff |
| LAF | Lebanese Armed Forces |
| LBJ | Lyndon Baines Johnson |
| MAU | Marine Amphibious Unit |
| MACV | Military Advisory Command Vietnam |
| MNF | Multinational Force |
| NATO | North Atlantic Treaty Organization |
| NBC | Nuclear, Biological and Chemical |
| NMS | National Military Strategy |
| NSAM | National Security Action Memorandum |

| | |
|---|---|
| NSC | National Security Council |
| NSDD | National Security Decision Directive |
| NVN | North Vietnam |
| OMC | Office of Military Cooperation |
| OSD | Office of the Secretary of Defense |
| PAVN | People's Army of Vietnam |
| PDF | Panamanian Defense Force |
| PLO | Palestinian Liberation Organization |
| PSP | Progressive Socialist Party |
| ROE | Rules of Engagement |
| SECNAV | Secretary of the Navy |
| SOF | Special Operations Force |
| SOUTHCOM | Southern Command |
| UN | United Nations |
| US | United States |
| USAF | United States Air Force |
| USMC | United States Marine Corps |
| USN | United States Navy |
| WPA | War Powers Act |

# DECISIVE FORCE

# 1

# The American Way of War

The "American Way of War" used in this book is somewhat different and more narrowly constructed than the phrase made popular by the eminent American historian Russell Weigley.[1]  Recent scholarship underscores the conclusion that culture is the prime determinant in how societies approach the nature of warfare.[2] The study of strategic culture, representing the nexus of many attitudes, beliefs, and values, is now a recognized area of strategic study.  The strategic culture of the United States is the combination of both its socio-political culture and our military sub-culture.  Strategic culture and its attitudes shape and drive the basic beliefs of social institutions, including branches of the government and the various Armed Forces.  These beliefs and behaviors constitute our national approach to war as a instrument of policy.[3]

Instead of a broad definition of a strategic culture comprising the geopolitical environment, and the political, social, economic, and military elements and ideology of the United States, the "American Way of War" employed here addresses the military's orientation and preferred operational style.  Dr. Weigley aptly described this style as it evolved from the American Civil War through the world wars of the twentieth century. The U.S. military shows a marked predisposition for strategic offensives supported by full national mobilization, employing the economic and technological assets of the nation, to bring to bear a preponderance of power in the most direct and decisive manner possible.

Strategic culture does not necessarily move institutions within a State in the same direction.  A frequent assumption is that the U.S. military's culture and approach to its profession is directly derived from the society it represents.  However, a brief review of history shows there are elements of contrast and conflict between the two.[4]  It may be more accurate to describe the military as a subset of a given society.  Thus, the military reflects the culture and population, but it is not a perfect reflection.

A corollary of this definition is that cultures are not necessarily perfect or correct. They are neither accurate nor incorrect; they exist as the learned, however imperfectly, distillation of experience. They are shaped by geopolitics, history, and myths. The most significant influences in the military culture are lessons drawn from the cauldron of war.

Culture also generates normative values and operational codes passed on to new members through socialization and education. Military cultures have effective socialization processes, such as professional schools and doctrine. The value systems inherent in cultures organize and filter information and may lead to preformatted or preconditioned responses. They also lead to predispositions about what is acceptable or not acceptable. Strategic culture can be "an indispensable but subjective guide" to the interpretation of facts, and the organization of choices, but it can be "the product of ambiguous sources, potentially a source of prejudice and self-deception."[5]

During periods of great pressures and tensions, such as those experienced by democratic governments in crisis situations, cultural differences between the political and military cultures come into play. The interchange is usually tense, and sometimes disruptive. What one element of the culture views as acceptable or desirable is not necessarily acceptable to the other. Successfully integrating the different perspectives, or resolving the "dichotomy between the demands of policy and the dictates of the battlefield" is an inescapable problem of armed conflict.[6] Strategic cultures that contain wildly divergent attitudes between policy makers and strategists contain fault lines that can be fatal.

While conflict is inherent, there are rules and bounds accepted by both sides for the proper exchange of views in a democratic society. In our society these rules are structurally institutionalized in our form of government, and in the laws legislating the organization and functions of the Armed Services. However, as in all social organizations, substantial interaction occurs in the form of internal and bureaucratic politics.[7] In the United States, the interchange between political and military considerations comes under the area of civil-military relations.

The interaction known as civil-military relations is the testing ground of "strategic acceptability" for the selection of policy aims and the use of military force. As Clausewitz forewarned, "purely military" viewpoints are not useful in this discourse, for politics is the controlling factor and the source of logic for the use of military means to satify political aims. Military actions are rarely executed without considering what some in the military refer to as "the distraction of politics" and ensuring that strategic options pass muster with the political culture. Because political considerations include a wide variety of factors, the process is not necessarily rational. Viewed in this manner, strategic culture is the domestic "equivalent of battlefield friction" and it can erode the cold or pure rationality of any strategic process.[8] Some strategic cultures contain more friction than others.

In sum, strategic culture is the resulting confluence of political, social, and military viewpoints. The exchange can cause sparks of friction, as well as sparks of inspiration. Cultures reflect deeply rooted beliefs that drive institutional preferences and perspectives. Such preferences and perspectives have great impact during the flux of emotions and options present during major policy decisions. There may be no more important policy decision than the decision to wage war.

We need to be aware of the influence culture plays when studying history and analyzing the actions taken by policy makers. Likewise, future decision makers and military professionals must be aware of the influence of strategic culture in national security problems. Our political and military cultures *do not* bring the same interests or influences to the table. Their interests and influences are not homogenous, but the final product must integrate conflicting values inherent in the strategic culture to produce a successful strategy. Thus, in the words of one group of strategists:

Americans must always be conscious of those distinct aspects of their strategic culture that both provide the undergirding strength of their policies and strategies and bias their perspectives of what is and of what is possible. Wise statecraft requires not only that external policies be shaped in terms of fundamental national character but that national predispositions be so understood as to allow compensation for the defects inherent in that character.[9]

Accordingly, a primary purpose of this study is to explore the experiences and hidden assumptions behind changes in American military strategy over the past two decades, to assess the validity of the perspectives and conclusions drawn by the military, and to come closer to fully understanding both the defects and strengths of our strategic culture. The end result should be a wiser and wider perspective regarding national and military predispositions and their defects.

## AMERICAN POLITICAL CULTURE

Our political culture is essentially bounded by the unique form of democracy perfected by the Founding Fathers two centuries ago. Ours is a liberal and pluralistic social order. It represents a sharing and distribution of competitive power centers, with an abhorrence of a centralized or overly strong source of power. This has generated a slight tinge of suspicion to large military institutions or military influence in politics.

Ours is an idealistic society, in many ways naive at best, or poorly informed at the other extreme, about the ways of the world. In many ways we are self-centered and chauvinistic about our values and political institutions. We are prone towards "mirror imaging" and overlooking key differences from the enemy's point of view.[10] We like to export our values and social systems, as well as economic mechanisms, for emulation throughout the world. When challenged we prefer lofty goals and moral crusades to galvanize our collective efforts towards a common objective.[11] We sometimes let idealism run to moralism in our external affairs.

Our political culture is heavily influenced by several social attitudes endemic to America. One major attitude is the American problem solving orientation, which is both pragmatic and relatively focused on short term fixes. We are an impatient people used to ready access to drive-through windows and guaranteed 30-minute pizzas. Our impatience to get things done is supported by our wealthy economic position and our capacity for innovation and technology.

Our naivete and problem solving habits combine to create a "can do" attitude about challenges. This is reinforced by an activist orientation and our emphasis on rationalism. We do not accept intractability—all problems have solutions. Our sense of activism is balanced by our disinterest in foreign entanglements, and suspicions about international affairs that do not directly affect us.

Another element of American culture is the manner in which our society looks at war. War is viewed as an aberration, and not as a normal or frequent occurrence in international relations. This is a product of our ahistoricism and our collective inability to see things the way other cultures and societies see them.[12]

Thucydides was probably the first to point out that the nature of democracies created great tensions during the conduct of foreign affairs, particularly during wars. The most distinguished of commentators on the nature of democracy in America also pointed out that democracies were inferior when it came to the design and execution of foreign policy. They find it hard to develop a plan and stick to it in the face of strife and internal debate. In de Tocqueville's words:

It is especially in the conduct of foreign relations that democracies appear to be decidedly inferior to other governments. A democracy can only with great difficulty regulate the details of an important undertaking, persevere in a fixed design, and work out its execution in spite of serious obstacles. It cannot combine its measures with secrecy or await their consequences with patience.[13]

De Tocqueville was critical about democracies in terms of their external relations, and believed they tended to follow their feelings instead of rational calculations. He also knew the strengths of a popular government based on the power in the people when he acknowledged that "democracy does not provide a people with the most skillful of governments," but properly aroused it can generate "a restless activity, superabundant force, and energy never found elsewhere."[14]

Popular support is normally considered a constraining factor in our political culture. One of the greatest paradoxes for democracies is that the coldly rational and often secretive nature of diplomacy and foreign relations is not consistent with generating the necessary amount of public support for a given policy. Hans Morgenthau has noted that a democratic government has two tasks: pursue policy objectives effectively and secure approval for the policies. However, the conditions for generating public support are not necessarily identical or conducive to achieving a given policy objective.[15] Yet, eventually all efforts will fail without the consent of the governed to any costly activity conducted in their name that the majority comes to believe is not conducive to their interests. This paradox is most acute during protracted conflicts that require sacrifice or heavy costs.

The challenge for democratic leaders in our strategic culture is to create and sustain public support for policies that are in the long-term national interest, especially when such policy aims are not apparent on their face value. In Edmund

Burke's harsh terms, leaders exist to maintain and serve the interests of the people and must "be a pillar of the state, and not a weathercock."[16] This is a demanding obstacle in a diverse culture, with many competing interest groups. This challenge is one that several of our leaders have met successfully, while others have failed to "prepare the battlefield" on the domestic front.

## AMERICAN MILITARY CULTURE

The culture of the American military maintains deeply held convictions and "myths."[17] In some ways the military culture is not completely representative of society. As noted earlier, its reflection is not a perfect representation. This distinction has become more clear now that we have implemented an all-volunteer force in place of conscription. The military's social and power structure is not egalitarian or pluralistic, but hierarchial and heavily biased towards a conservative realism.[18] As a social order, the military stresses the group over individualism. Elements of commonality within the strategic culture include a bias for action, an emphasis on technology, and a pragmatic approach to getting results.

Like the rest of the country, the American military is an impatient culture. Furthermore, our country has provided the resources and technology to apply decisive force for quick results. We prefer to overwhelm our opponents with mass and firepower. Our society has had a comparative advantage in resources to give us the wherewithal to do so. We are frustrated when political constraints or a lack of trust from civilians results in limitations on the use of force best suited to our technological and economic strengths. Such limitations are imposed often in small or limited conflicts.

Limited wars, while not preferred, are a frequent occurrence. We have had a long legacy of experience in such conflicts going back to the American Revolution, the Indian Wars, and various incursions in Mexico, the Philippines, and Central and Latin America.[19] But our cultural orientation is towards large scale, production line, conventional warfare. Some find this bias reduces the utility of the U.S. military in lesser contingencies where force or the threat of force could be used as a preventive option or low-cost problem solver.[20]

The U.S. military sees force more as a tool of last resort, rather than an aberration. The military recognizes the inherent risks and costs associated with its application. When politics and diplomacy fail, other instruments, such as economic sanctions, should be tested and found wanting before "the dogs of war" are unleashed. The military has internalized the basic truth that military power is a blunt instrument whose utilization cannot be entirely predicted or controlled with any degree of precision. Opening "Pandora's box" creates risks and a dynamic all its own.

There are three major elements within the American military culture that are relevant to the intended focus of this book.[21] All three elements raise conflicts within the strategic culture, and contain both myths and contradictions with each other. These include three central themes that cut across U.S. military history:

1. Autonomy
2. Apoliticism
3. Absolutism

## AUTONOMY AND PROFESSIONALISM

An especially vital element of American military culture is found in its adherence to a strong sense of professionalism. The professional ethic originated late in the eighteenth century after the Civil War and developed continuously until World War II.[22] Harvard's Samuel Huntington has delineated three distinct characteristics of professionalism within the American military: its specific expertise, its corporateness, and its sense of social responsibility.[23]

Expertise is the first element of military professionalism. Warfare is viewed as a complicated matter involving multi-disciplinary skills, special training, and technical knowledge. Like most professions, entry to the profession is barred by society, which mandates special qualifications and obligations to those commissioned into service.

The second aspect of professionalism involves the corporate nature of military life, particularly the officer corps. Like other professions, the military generates a degree of organizational and professional commitment, which results in a strong identification with the profession. This is reinforced by the nature of military life, its work routines, social life, and deployments. It is further reinforced by professional military associations and other forms of socialization.

The third element of professionalism deals with the social responsibility assigned to the military. Like other professions, the military provides a social service and evokes an ethic of social responsibility over personal gain. The military serves the State, and its status is afforded certain rewards and considerations in pursuit of this function.

All three aspects of professionalism have drawbacks when taken to extremes. With respect to expertise, an orientation on the purely technical side of the profession limits the deft use of power. By focusing solely on the military arts and sciences to the exclusion of the social, political, and economic nature of the culture it represents, any military can reduce its effectiveness, or challenge the State's civilian policy makers. Ignorance of the political objectives or conditions when employed in conflicts abroad can result in strategic defeats like Vietnam, or Pyrrhic victories. The military must understand both its own political environment and the political context in which it is employed.

The concept of social responsibility can also be taken to an extreme and can lead to the idea that loyalty and obligations are owed only to the State as opposed to elected civil authority. General of the Army Douglas MacArthur reflects this erroneous sense of duty. In his Congressional testimony, General MacArthur found curious the understanding that the military "owe primary allegiance to those who temporarily exercise the authority of the executive branch," and implied he had a higher duty to the country and its Constitution.[24]

MacArthur believed the idea that allegiance was owed to the State as a whole and that anything else was a dangerous proposition. Under our strategic culture, he was constitutionally and legally bound to obey the orders of those appointed over him. The Constitution clearly defines civilian control over the military. MacArthur represents a far more dangerous concept whereby the military interprets the Constitution and pursues policy aims independent of civilian control. While the "Man on Horseback" crossing the Rubicon (or the Potomac in our case) is not likely to occur in the United States, the subversion of the principle of civilian authority can occur in less overt ways.

The overarching element of professionalism is the concept of professional autonomy: Professions are normally seen as self-functioning and self-regulating. Autonomy is a classic characteristic of professions, but one that must be limited in the military to constrain its power in a pluralistic government and ensure its application in accordance with the principle of civil supremacy. The military naturally prefers to conduct military operations without strict oversight or interference from civilians. This aspect of the American military culture has been noted by one of the most respected military theorists in the area of civil military relations. Sir John Hackett acknowledges that in American circles "those who have accepted that they serve the state have not necessarily bought into the complementary idea that the statesman is the master."[25]

In a final assessment, several analysts believe that professionalism can be carried too far, resulting in a force "unresponsive to society, rationalizing its actions as servants of the state and cloaked in the barrier of military expertise, that is most dangerous to professional ideals and to professional compatibility with democratic society."[26] The conflicting pressures of professionalism, autonomy, and the need for extensive interaction in the American political process bear close watching.

## APOLITICISM

Another trend in American military culture is the relation of politics to the military institution. Apart from the interaction expected of the military in a pluralistic government, the armed forces are in theory an apolitical institution. As a firm rule it eschews any association with partisan politics, and historically has even avoided understanding the interaction of political factors with military implications in war and peacetime. At the individual level, it is operationalized in a completely neutral stance for military officers in political matters, to include not even exercising the right to vote.[27] This tradition has lessened considerably in the last few decades.

At the institutional level though is the false separation of political matters from war. Concomitant with the rise of professionalism was the distinct separation and isolation of the U.S. military from politics. This reinforces the separation of political matters from military operations in the American military culture. The origins of apoliticism can be traced back to General William T. Sherman and his lieutenant, Brevet Major General Emory Upton. Upton conducted a tour of European military establishments during the 1880s and came back with a series of recommendations to professionalize the U.S. military.

Upton's recommendations were largely lifted from the Prussian military establishment and focused on entry qualifications, promotion policies, professional education, and the establishment of the equivalent of a German general staff. Mostly unknown are several policy recommendations to separate the military from politics that reflected Sherman's distaste for partisan politics and Von Moltke the Elder's influence in Prussia.[28] Russell Weigley assesses Upton's overall influence on U.S. military policy:

Emory Upton did lasting harm in setting the main current of American military thought not to the task of shaping military institutions that would serve both military and national purposes, but to the futile task of demanding that the national institutions be adjusted to purely military expediency.[29]

Although struck down by his own hand, Emory Upton was a significant contributor to early U.S. military strategy and his ghost lives on. His place in American military history is well recognized by historians, and there are indications that his influence is alive and well today.[30]

Upton's influence was seen during the Second World War, where contrary to popular belief, President Roosevelt and his military chiefs had distinctly different approaches to war. General Marshall, despite holding several positions that required extensive exposure to political issues, believed that the military should stay away from political issues, in order to maintain its "sacred trust" from the American people.[31] Accordingly, Marshall failed to press several military proposals during the war, and reluctantly deferred many times to Roosevelt's political acumen.

Even General Eisenhower, a politically astute general, could succumb to a false separation of political aims and military efforts. Pressured by Churchill to press forward rapidly to seize Berlin before the Russians could get there, Eisenhower replied, "personally and aside from all logistical, tactical or strategical implications I would be loath to hazard American lives for *purely political purposes* [emphasis added]."[32]

Because of a preference for total war, our military leaders often forget that policy aims serve as guidelines for directing war and for rational calculations involving both the magnitude and duration of conflict. Clausewitz warned against subordinating policy to military expediency. "Wars cannot be divorced from political life; and whenever this occurs," he warned, "the many links that connect the two elements are destroyed and we are left with something pointless and devoid of sense."[33]

The stress generated by the view that war should be fought strictly according to military logic resulted in the famous Truman-MacArthur controversy during the Korean War. General MacArthur was a product of a culture that artificially separated policy aims from military means. He attempted to conduct the Korean war as a sphere apart from the basic policy aim of the U.S. government, and actually attempted to subvert the policy by his involvement in both domestic and international politics. After his relief, MacArthur sounded like Upton or Moltke. A theater commander, MacArthur claimed:

Commands the whole area, politically, economically and militarily. At that stage of the game *when politics fails and the military takes over*, you must trust the military I do unquestionably state there should be no artifice under the name of politics which should handicap your own men.[34]

Moltke, Upton, and MacArthur would have preferred leaving those decisions to the military, despite Clausewitz's warning. The many dictums of Clausewitz, extensively employed in the halls of erudition and higher learning, are often "shallowly comprehended and constantly forgotten" in the U.S. military.[35] While MacArthur represents a single case in U.S. military history, the desire to exclude politics from military operations is extant today. From one recent assessment of U.S. strategic culture:

The American military tends to view war and peace as sharply delineated activities rather than as a continuum. The use of force tends to be seen as a last resort, a response to the failure of politics or diplomacy rather than as an instrument of politics or diplomacy.[36]

## ABSOLUTISM

The most distinguishing characteristic of the American Way of War is the military's penchant for total warfare, its preference for a sweeping conception of victory. We prefer quick and decisive results as opposed to limited warfare, and see decisive military victories over the enemy's main force as the quickest road to that end. "There is no substitute for victory" is one of MacArthur's most often quoted expressions and an apt summarization of the American style.

This orientation towards total warfare in the U.S. military is well recorded. Professor Russell F. Weigley, the distinguished American historian, first documented our style of war. In his seminal *The American Way of War*, Weigley established a concise taxonomy of two basic approaches to warfare. He contrasted our preference for the strategy of annihilation, based on the destruction of the enemy's military capability, over the strategy of attrition. This preference was traced back to the early examples of Generals Grant and Sherman during the great internal cataclysm of the American Civil War.[37]

Our preference is for "winning victory by the means sanctioned by the most deeply rooted historical American conceptions of strategy, the destruction of the enemy's armed forces and his ability to wage war."[38] Our institutional preference, reinforced by both our national character and resources, is for total warfare fought for unlimited ends by the complete destruction of the enemy's capacity to resist, including both the enemy's military forces and war-making capability. America's vast economic base and advanced technological state have matched our preferred military strategy very well.

The preference for strategies of annihilation is not unique to the American military culture. Military organizations have historically preferred offensive strategies. Some research supports a finding that military organizations prefer offensive doctrines, regardless of political or technological circumstances, because it maximizes professional autonomy and minimizes civilian interference.[39] The institutional motivation for offensive warfare "to disarm the adversary quickly and decisively by offensive means" should be examined carefully in each context. Under conditions of weak civilian control, as occurred prior to World War I, the military's "purity in its devotion to victory" has not always served politicians or democratic states well.[40]

The major approaches to warfare are also represented in two major groupings of military officers. Morris Janowitz, the prominent sociologist and author, made a distinction between "absolutists" and "pragmatists" in categorizing professional soldiers in the U.S. military.[41] The former are military officers who believe in the traditional type of total military victory rather than the measured application of military force and its relative consequence to a specific situation. Pragmatists are more inclined to understand the utility of employing partial means for specified purposes when those ends are limited in nature.

Clearly, coming out of the Second World War, the absolutist tradition was firmly entrenched in the American Way of War. During the 1950s, some military officers and academics, particularly Army Chief of Staff Maxwell Taylor, developed a theory of "Flexible Response" to describe the need for a more flexible range of options than Armageddon and the over-reliance on nuclear retaliation contained in Eisenhower's low-budget New Look strategy.[42] Taylor's strategy was eventually adopted by the new Kennedy administration and was an underlying element in the Bay of Pigs, the Cuban Missile Crisis, and America's entry into Vietnam.

The scars of Vietnam reinforced the position and attitudes of absolutists, or Warrior Generals, who descend from a long lineage of great names in American military history, including Grant, Sherman, Pershing, MacArthur, Lemay, and perhaps now Schwarzkopf. This represents a long and proud pantheon in the American military culture. Pragmatists have their own luminaries, including Generals George Marshall, Matthew Ridgway, and Max Taylor, but they are significantly outnumbered by their fellow absolutists.

Absolutist attitudes have come into conflict with policy when America has pursued war for limited objectives with limited means. The first instance was during the Korean war, and resulted in the relief of General MacArthur. MacArthur never accepted the basic concept of limitations on means. War, he said, meant that all other means were exhausted, and "there is no alternative than to apply every available means to bring it to a swift end. War's very objective is victory not prolonged indecision."[43] MacArthur remains the most obvious representation of the American style, although admittedly at the extreme end. His public statements during the hearing following his relief reflect both the artificial separation of political and military considerations and absolutism.

To MacArthur anything less than a total approach introduced the "concept of appeasement, the concept that when you use force you can limit that force."[44] He expressly disagreed with a limitless extension of bloodshed without creating the potential for the decisive battle to destroy the enemy in the minimum amount of time and loss.

This does not suggest that the military is heavy handed or prone to military interventions. Quite the contrary, the U.S. military has been historically reluctant to recommend military action. This resistance to resort to force is largely based on the U.S. military's understanding of the dynamic and costly nature of war, in political, social, and military terms.[45] However, while reluctant to resort to arms, the military does not support limitations or restraints on the nature of force once the decision to employ military means has been made.

Over the past twenty years, American military experience has retained and even reinforced the absolutist tradition in the American military culture.[46] Our experience in the jungles of Vietnam, and limited excursions throughout the 1980s where U.S. forces were employed in ambiguous situations for limited purposes, was not accepted as consistent with the American Way of War. Restraints on the effective employment of the full panoply of American armed might was gravely frustrating.

The problem, however, is that prescriptions like absolutism do not match the contingent nature of warfare. The bias for short, intense, conventional, and total warfare creates conflict when the political situation does not permit the unlimited application of American force. A direct result of our preference for strategies of annihilation with maximum means for unlimited ends is a distaste and poor capacity for unconventional warfare or for messy protracted conflicts with extensive constraints or political oversight.

Our preferences and professional ethos have resulted in a poor track record in "small wars," which by their very definition are limited and often protracted in time. "Resistance to a central role for special operations forces or recognition of the importance of the low intensity challenge continue to be deeply rooted" in our culture and the senior leadership.[47] The central issue remains one of reconciling our need for effective intervention in situations not conducive to the organizational paradigms of our military culture, with the our status as a global power with global interests. It could be argued that our national or political culture places us at a disadvantage in such situations. It could be further advanced that our strategic culture precludes effective intervention in such conflicts, and thus, we should avoid them. Others, however, have concluded that our poor track record is more the function of the military's cultural distaste for less than clear-cut situations that are more conducive to their preferred operating style, concluding that:

The most substantial constraints on America's ability to conduct small wars result from the resistance of the American defense establishment to the very notion of engaging in such conflicts, and from the unsuitability of that establishment for fighting such wars.[48]

However, past history continues to reveal situations where civilian authority deemed intervention necessary under circumstances less than ideal in terms of how the U.S. military establishment looks at and conducts war. Can our strategic culture, particularly the military institution, be adapted to the peculiar requirements of limited war?

## CIVIL-MILITARY RELATIONS:
## THE MODERN PROFESSIONAL OFFICER AND THE STATE

Civil-military relations constitute the arena where political considerations and military viewpoints merge. It is also the area of national security policy where political and functional perspectives clash. Within the American Way of War, civil-military relations is where the tectonic plates between our political culture and the military culture grind into one another. The sole lubricant that reduces friction is the principle of civilian control of the military, which is embodied in both law and our professional ethic. This area of study is frequently overlooked in national security studies, although well recognized as one of the timeless dimensions of conflict.[49]

Within the literature on civil-military relations, there are two schools of thought about the maintenance of civilian control. The first school of thought emphasizes separation of military perspectives and the military from the political process entirely. This line of thought emphasizes that the military has little time to be involved in, nor is competent at, the intrinsically complicated matters of international and domestic politics. This school, most ably represented by Samuel Huntington, prefers a form of objective control over the military by keeping them in a neutral and isolated position from politics.[50] This form of control is consistent with the traditional and the absolutist approaches to military force. Civilian control is essentially maintained by excluding the military from inputs on anything other than an advisory role on technical matters.

The other school in civil-military relations theory holds that political factors must be integrated with military advice and military considerations to produce effective policy decisions. Thus, the subjective control form of civilian control argues for maintaining civilian control over the military by integrating the military as a representative into policy making decisions. The military's interests and advice become "fused" into the political and decision making process under this line of thinking. The "modern" general in this scenario reflects the Soldier/Statesman mold, vice the traditional, purely functional Warrior. The distinction to be emphasized in this alternative is that the military remains nonpartisan in domestic politics in this role. This view of the military's role is closer to Janowitz's pragmatist categorization.

Table 1 captures the two basic schools of civil-military relations and contrasts some differences in the interaction and focus of the military in policy making. The American Way of War was originally built around the traditionist, absolutist style and relied upon an objective form of control. This traditional approach may no longer hold.

Subjective control is frequently criticized on two bases. The first is the lack of time for senior military officials to pick up the necessary perspectives and knowledge to function and advise on political-military matters. The other more frequently cited observation is a concern over the politicization of the military, and the potential loss of an unvarnished military perspective on matters.[51] The Iran-Contra Affair of the 1980s is evidence of the dangers of politicizing the military.

However, there is an even greater danger than infusing the military into political matters and sacrificing their detached professionalism. This deals with the corruption of the professional ethos and the reduction of its social responsibility as an *unconditional* servant of the State. Infusing the military as a distinct institution in political discussions permits the military to represent itself, and inject its preferences and biases, as professional military advice. One finds that the professional sword cuts both ways.

**Table 1**
**Forms of Civil-Military Control and Military Roles**

| Traditional/Objective Control | Modern/Subjective Control |
|---|---|
| Apolitical/Neutral | Nonpartisan |
| Separation/Isolation | Integration/Fusion |
| Warrior General | Soldier/Statesman |
| Absolutists | Pragmatists |

Such a corrupted sense of professionalism would seriously undermine civilian control, and the effectiveness of civil-military relations, during a crisis. "The principle of civilian control requires not only that the military not be policy makers," notes one recent examination of the issue by a team of political scientists, "but also that they not be seen (nor see themselves) as a separate constituency whose interests are to be considered in policy debates."[52] This requires a delicate equilibrium, and a refined sense of professionalism.

However, the alternative, objective control, is an even greater sin. Politicization of the military must be avoided, but since the nature of war, and democracy, mixes political factors and military considerations, the military is and must be politically conscious. "To presume that military professionals should remain unconcerned about the political and social conditions of potential aggressors, and that the military should not be involved until the first shot is fired" is to neglect the lessons of modern war.[53] To extend Clemenceau's maxim, war is too serious to be left solely to generals or statesmen.

During the past two decades the rise of the modern soldier/statesman has been clearly ascendent in the United States. This is consistent with the operative mode of civil-military relations, but conflicts with the conclusion that absolutism remains the predominant view of force in the military culture. In the past generation, numerous military officers, many with advanced education and experience outside a traditional military career pattern, have emerged. Most of these officers have served in the White House in crisis management situations, involving extensive military and political decision making. The list includes Generals Haig, Powell, Scowcroft, Colonel McFarlane, and Admiral Poindexter. During one point during the late 1980s, four consecutive National Security Advisors were retired or active military officers. The military's political consciousness and influence have increased with this representation.

## SUMMARY

The foregoing review supports the conclusion that the American Way of War now includes extensive representation of the military in policy making circles, and the supporting contention that subjective control is the operative form of maintaining civilian control over the military today.

The difficulties of subjective control, particularly given the military's pervasive integration in the national security bureaucracy, needs to be underscored. Furthermore, the military's professional culture, absolutist preferences, and political presence could make for difficult times. We have taken the issue of civil-military relations for granted. In a period when the Cold War military establishment is being dismantled, and when extensive societal influences are being imposed by fiat over the advice of the professional military leadership, harmonious relations are at risk. While a crisis is not inevitable, the potential exists, and anyone who denies that "today's military shows symptoms of evident distemper," ignores grave risks.[54]

The potential for conflict between elements of our strategic culture are greatest during deliberations over the employment of military force to achieve policy objectives. Governments face nothing more serious than a decision to use violent means to resolve conflict. As stated very early in this chapter, wise statecraft requires that we understand the predispositions of our national culture, including the military element, to account for the defects and differences inherent in their character. Wise statesman will pay careful attention to "strategic culture" and the state of civil-military relations in these decisions. Professor Huntington has warned:

Nations which develop a properly balanced pattern of civil-military relations have a great advantage in the search for security. They increase their likelihood of reaching right answers to operating issues of military policy. Nations which fail to develop a balanced pattern of civil-military relations squander their resources and run uncalculated risks.[55]

The American Way of War has changed in subtle ways over the past two decades. The next four chapters will trace these changes and assess their implications on our search for security and a properly balanced pattern of civil-military relations.

## NOTES

1. Russell F. Weigley, *The American Way of War: A History of United States Military Strategy and Policy*, Bloomington: Indiana University Press, 1973, p. xxii.

2. John Keegan, *A History of Warfare*, New York: Knopf, 1993, p. 387.

3. Colin S. Gray, "National Style in Strategy: The American Example," *International Security*, Fall, 1981, p. 22. Carnes Lord, "American Strategic Culture," *Comparative Strategy*, Vol. 5., No. 3., 1985, pp. 269–291.

4. John Keegan has argued that the culture of the warrior can never be the same as the broader civilization it protects. Keegan, *A History of Warfare*, p. xvi.

5. Yitzhak Klein, "A Theory of Strategic Culture," *Comparative Strategy*, Vol. 10, Fall 1991, p. 8.

6. Ibid., p. 6.

7. Graham T. Allison, *Essence of Decision: Explaining the Cuban Missile Crisis*, Boston: Little Brown, 1971. See also David Kozak and James Keagle, eds., *Bureaucratic Politics and National Security*, New York: Reinner, 1988.

8. Frederick M. Downey and Steven Metz, "The American Political Culture and Strategic Planning," *Parameters*, September 1988, p. 34.

9. Earl H. Fry, Stan A. Taylor, and Robert S. Wood, *America the Vincible: American Foreign Policy in the Twenty-First Century*, Englewood Cliffs, NJ: Prentice Hall, 1994, p. 133.

10. Downey and Metz, "The American Political Culture and Strategic Planning," p. 39.

11. Donald M. Snow and Dennis M. Drew, *From Lexington to Desert Storm: War and Politics in the American Experience*, Armonk, NY: M. E. Sharpe, 1994, pp. xvii, 13, 332.

12. Robert E. Osgood, "The American Approach to War," in *U.S. National Security: A Framework for Analysis*, Daniel J. Kaufman, Jeffrey S. McKitrick, and Thomas J. Leney, eds., Lexington, MA: Lexington Books, 1991, pp. 98–99.

13. Alexis de Tocqueville, *Democracy in America*, Edward Lawrence, ed. and J. B. Mayer, trans., New York: Doubleday, 1969, pp. 228–229.

14. Ibid., p. 244.

15. Hans Morgenthau, *A New Foreign Policy for the United States*, New York: Praeger, 1969, pp. 150–151.

16. Quoted in Richard J. Barnett, *The Rocket's Red Glare: America Goes to War*, New York: Simon and Schuster, 1990, p. 16.

17. The use of the word "myth" reflects the irrational, historical, and experiences of institutions and why they act on what they "know" to be true. See William H. McNeill, "The Care and Repair of Public Myth," *Foreign Affairs*, Fall 1982, pp. 1–13; Andrew. J. Bacevich, "Old Myths, New Myths," *Parameters*, March 1988, pp. 15–24.

18. Samuel P. Huntington, *The Soldier and the State: The Theory and Politics of Civil-Military Relations*, Cambridge: Belknap/Harvard Press, 1957, p. 79.

19. Weigley, *The American Way of War*, pp. 18–39, 153–166; Samuel P. Huntington, *Soldier and the State*, pp. 193–220; and Samuel P. Huntington, "New Contingencies and Old Roles," *Joint Forces Quarterly*, Autumn 1993, pp. 38–41.

20. See Richard H. Shultz, "Low Intensity Conflict: Future Challenges and Lessons From the Reagan Years," in Robert L. Pfaltzgraff, Jr. and Richard H. Shultz, Jr. *U.S. Defense Policy in an Era of Constrained Resources*, Lexington, MA: Lexington Books, 1990. Drew and Snow, pp. 327–353.

21. These are drawn indirectly from Huntington, *Soldier and the State*, and from Morris Janowitz's sociological portrait *The Professional Soldier: A Social and Political Portrait*, New York: Free Press, 1971, pp. 257–281, 303–320.

22. Huntington, *The Soldier and the State*, pp. 222–269.

23. Ibid., pp. 7–18.

24. MacArthur quoted in John W. Spanier, *The Truman-MacArthur Controversy and the Korean War*, Cambridge: Harvard University Press, 1959, p. 235.

25. John J. Hackett, "The Military in the Service of the State," in Malham M. Wakin, ed., *War, Morality, and the Military Profession*, Boulder, CO: Westview, 1979, p. 110.

26. Sam C. Sarkesian, *Beyond the Battlefield: The New Military Professionalism*, New York: Pergamon Press, 1981, p. 37. See also the excellent historical assessment of military intervention in domestic politics by S. E. Finer, *The Man on Horseback*, Boulder, CO: Westview Press, 1988. Finer defines military intervention as the substitution of the armed forces' own policies for those of recognized civilian authorities, p. 20. Military involvement can occur through acts of omission or by commission. Finer's most pessimistic point is that professionalism leads to intervention, pp. 20–53.

27. Donald Bletz, "The Modern Major General," *Parameters*, Vol. IV, No. 1, 1974, pp. 20–32.

28. Moltke thought there was a strict separation between policy and war, and thus statesmen and generals, writing that "the politician should fall silent the moment that mobilization begins." Moltke put great faith in the technical and operational virtuosity of the military, preferring that "the direction of the military effort should be defined by the soldiers alone." As Moltke saw it, "Politics uses war for the attainment of its ends; it operates decisively at the beginning and the end of the conflict." In the middle, the military directs "its efforts towards the highest goal which the means available make attainable." In this way, it aids politics best, working only for its objectives, "but in its operations independent of it." See Gehard Ritter, *The Sword and the Scepter: The Problem of Militarism in Germany*, Coral Gables: University of Miami Press, 1969, Vol. 1. and Gordon A. Craig, *The Politics of the Prussian Army 1640–1945*, New York: Oxford University Press, 1955.

29. Russell F. Weigley, *History of the United States Army*, New York: Macmillan, 1967, p. 281.

30. Upton is extensively cited in numerous sources involving American strategic culture. See Downey and Metz p. 37; Harry G. Summers, *On Strategy II: A Critical Analysis of the Gulf War*, New York: Dell, 1992, p. 128; Weigley, *American Way of War*, pp. 171–172, 221–222; also the commentary by historian Charles Royster, *Journal of Military History*, October 1993, p. 61.

31. Forrest Pogue, *Marshall: Organizer of Victory*, New York: Viking Press, 1980, pp. 315, 458–459.

32. Kent Roberts Greenfield, *American Strategy in World War II: A Reconsideration*, Malabar, FL: Krieger Publishing, 1963, p. 19. Stephen Ambrose, *Eisenhower: Soldier and President*, New York: Touchstone, 1990, pp. 189–195. Eisenhower was actually more astute and was more concerned with the casualties such an offensive would generate, the short distance the Russians had to cover, and the fact that the U.S. government had already agreed that Berlin was 175 miles inside the Soviet occupation zone. See Russell F. Weigley, *Eisenhower's Lieutenants: The Campaign in France and Germany 1944–1945*, New York: Macmillan, 1978, pp. 684–687; Eric Larrabee, *Commander-in-Chief: FDR, His Lieutenants, and Their War*, New York: Touchstone, 1989, pp. 505–506.

33. Clausewitz, *On War*, p. 608.

34. MacArthur quoted in Spanier, p. 6.

35. Snow and Drew, p. 3.

36. Carnes Lord, "American Strategic Culture in Small Wars," *Small Wars and Insurgencies*, Vol. 3, No. 3, Winter 1992, p. 208. The same point is stressed by Downey and Metz, p. 38.

37. Weigley, *The American Way of War*, pp. 128–152, 467–477.

38. Ibid., pp. 464–465.

39. Jack Snyder, "Civil Military Relations and the Cult of the Offensive, 1914 and 1984," in *Military Strategy and the Origins of the First World War*, Steven E. Miller, ed., Princeton: Princeton University Press, 1985, pp. 108–144. See also Snyder's *The Ideology of the Offensive*, Ithaca: Cornell University Press, 1984, pp. 15–40.

40. Bernard Brodie, *War and Politics*, New York: Macmillan, 1973, p. 161.

41. Janowitz, *The Professional Soldier*, pp. 264–279, 305–320.

42. Maxwell Taylor, *The Uncertain Trumpet*, New York: Harper Row, 1958; John Lewis Gaddis, *Strategies of Containment: A Critical Appraisal of Postwar American National Security Policy*, New York: Oxford University Press, 1986, pp. 183, 198–236.

43. Spanier, p. 222.

44. Ibid., p. 6.

45. The military man rarely favors war, despite the stereotype of the "military mind." See Huntington, *Soldier and the State*, pp. 68–69. The work of Dr. Richard Betts is the classic assessment of this attitude in the post-World War II American military. Betts has recently completed a new chapter adding the post-Vietnam era to his original dissertation. His original thesis was that the military was more cautious about the use of force than civilian policy makers. His new extension only found this to be more obvious and extreme in the post-Vietnam era. Richard K. Betts *Soldiers, Statesmen, and Cold War Crises*, New York: Columbia University Press, 1991, pp. 214–236.

46. Snow and Drew, *From Lexington to Desert Storm*, pp. 325–326.

47. Lord, "American Strategic Culture in Small Wars," p. 210.

48. Eliot A. Cohen, "Constraints on America's Conduct of Small Wars," contained in Steven Miller, ed., *Conventional Forces and American Defense Policy*, Princeton: Princeton University Press, 1987, p. 291. For discussion of institutional constraints with regard to small wars and low intensity conflict, see Sam C. Sarkesian, *The New Battlefield: The United States and Unconventional Conflicts*, New York: Greenwood, 1986; Carnes Lord, "American Strategic Culture in Small Wars," pp. 206–208.

49. Andrew J. Bacevich, "Clinton's Military Problem—And Ours," *National Review*, December 1993, pp. 36–40.

50. Huntington, *Soldier and the State*, pp. 189–192, 260–263.

51. For an assessment of both schools see Jerome Slater "Military Officers and Politics I," and John H. Garrison "Military Officers and Politics II," in John F. Reichart and Steven R. Sturm, *American Defense Policy*, 5th ed., Baltimore: Johns Hopkins University Press, 1982, pp. 749–766.

52. Kenneth H. Kemp and Charles Hudlin, "Civil Supremacy Over the Military: Its Nature and Limits," *Armed Forces and Society*, Vol. 19, No. 1, Fall 1992, p. 9.

53. Sarkesian, *Beyond the Battlefield*, p. 171.

54. Bacevich, "Clinton's Military Problem," p. 36.

55. Huntington, *Soldier and the State*, p. 2.

# 2

# The Legacies of Vietnam

Over twenty years have passed since America's withdrawal from Vietnam in 1973, and yet no national consensus exists regarding what lessons should be drawn from that traumatic experience. The only common conclusion is the universal cry of "No More Vietnams," without any agreement on what that actually means in political or military terms. To members of Congress, it means that an Imperial Executive should not be given blank checks and permitted to let the nation "drift" into war. To civilian academics, the lessons deal with foreign policy and the inherent defects in the policy of containment. To the media it means not relying on the military or the government for the truth. To military officers, there are numerous meanings. It could mean the end of limited warfare, the end of civilian micro-management and systems analysis, or the demise of gradualism. One's view of the war in Southeast Asia literally is based on where one sat.

The U.S. government never conducted a comprehensive assessment of the failures of Vietnam.[1] If one had been attempted, the dichotomy in the views between civilians, academics, and the military would have been deafening. The ensuing debate would have rivaled the tenacity and chaos of the Battle of Ia Drang.[2] The debate still goes on today.

The following chapter will draw on the professional literature to determine the military's definition of "No More Vietnams." The major lessons have been organized into four separate areas: clarity of purpose; how force was used or "playing to win"; civil-military relations; and popular support.[3] These categorizations were deduced from the Weinberger Doctrine as the major focus areas for lessons derived from the Vietnamese conflict.

The lessons culled from the literature reflect only the positions and attitudes of the professional military. The principal interest of this book is assessing the internalized attitudes about the use of force that exist in the military culture. Thus, the views of civilian executives, strategists, and historians are noted, but are not immediately relevant.  The focus is on determining what the U.S. military has accepted as the truth, and how this is built into the institutional biases and preferences of that culture.  These will be assessed and compared with other views where appropriate to gauge the validity of the lessons.  In the end, the reader will be able to evaluate the summarization made by one officer who came to the "ineluctable conclusion that if the Army has learned any lessons from Vietnam, it has learned many of the wrong ones."[4]

## CLARITY OF PURPOSE

It is a fundamental principle of U.S. military doctrine that "every military operation must be directed toward a clearly defined, decisive and attainable objective."[5]  Many military writers have criticized the civilian leadership of the United States for never having established clearly defined objectives in Southeast Asia.

Not the least important or the most daunting of war's many tasks is the determination of exactly what purpose is to be secured by "unleashing the dogs of war."  "The essence of war," notes one strategist, "consists of the political decision that a given cause is worth killing and sacrificing for."[6]  No one, wrote Clausewitz, presuming he has any sense, starts a war without a clear picture of exactly what he wants to achieve by resorting to war, and generally how he intends to use military means in the conduct of the war.[7]  Clausewitz called this the first and supreme act of judgment during war.  However, this advice is frequently overlooked.  Still, "the supreme decision in war, the one that makes a conflict a war, is designating an objective as important enough to kill and die for."[8]

The American military exited from Vietnam with the conclusion that U.S. policy makers had violated Clausewitz's first dictum and had never made the first and most supreme judgment.  Colonel Harry G. Summers would have us believe that "American political objectives were never clear during the entire course of the war."[9]

This conclusion is supported by two research efforts.  The first was conducted by Nebraska professor Hugh M. Arnold, who examined official justifications and pronouncements regarding American political objectives in Southeast Asia from 1949 through 1967.  He found that the American leadership annunciated a total of twenty-two separate rationales for our involvement ranging from resisting communist aggression, conducting a counterinsurgency, and after 1968, stretching our position to preserving American credibility and commitments.[10]

A more focused effort targeted the attitudes of military officers.  Army General Douglas Kinnard conducted a formal survey in 1974 of 173 officers who had commanded brigades and above during the war.  "Almost 70 percent of the Army generals who managed the war were uncertain of its objectives," was his major finding.  To Kinnard and many others this reflects a major failure, "the inability of policy-makers to frame tangible, obtainable goals."[11]  This study is cited by many critics of the government's conduct of the war.

Another senior participant, Lieutenant General Phillip Davidson, the author of a massive history of the war, believes that up until the advent of the Nixon administration, the United States could never determine clearly its national objective in Vietnam.  However, it is not clear if such criticisms reflect a criticism of the objectives's ambiguity or if it was the goal itself that was not sufficient.  The one unequivocal statement of national policy is found in National Security Action Memorandum (NSAM) 288 dated March 17, 1964, which clearly states that our objective was "an independent, non-communist South Vietnam."[12]

Davidson finds the NSAM so broad as to be worthless, since it could be interpreted in a number of ways.[13]  Even worse, "the objective was essentially defensive in nature and did not define success or victory and lacked any appeal around which the American people could rally."[14]  Davidson's comments point to a different, more qualitative objection about objectives.  To the military, objectives need to define victory in military terms, require offensive means, and ensure public support.

Generals who fought in Vietnam were not the only veterans who complained about the lack of clarity of purpose. General Bruce Palmer, author of an excellent history of what he calls "the Incomprehensible War," uses an illustrative anecdote. He writes of Pittsburgh Steeler fullback Rocky Blier who, upon returning to the Steelers after his Vietnam tour, noted "no one told me what it was all about." "I wanted some reason for doing what I was going to do," he stated, "but I never got it."[15]  The general conclusion from the literature is that the U.S. government was peculiarly inept at making a convincing case about what it was trying to achieve in Vietnam, but not from lack of trying.[16]

## PLAYING TO WIN

The second lesson or legacy from Vietnam is that U.S. military forces should be employed decisively and be permitted to win.  The reverse corollary from this lesson is that U.S. forces were not permitted to win in Vietnam because of political constraints imposed by civilian authorities in Washington.  Deep in the minds of many military officers is the firm belief that the war was won on the battlefield tactically, but lost at the strategic and political level due to self-imposed limitations on force or strategic incompetence from micro-managing politicians and amateurs. The lesson is that in future wars limitations should be minimized and the American military should not have to "fight with one hand tied behind its back."  One can find vestiges, and counter-arguments, to this legacy in the professional literature from military writers in generally two phases.

In the early phase, the participants and the institutional defenders were the most vocal and voluminous (1978–82).  Later, in the second phase, a number of junior officers who did not serve in Vietnam have applied a degree of distance and objective analysis to the war, and have come to different conclusions.  Thus, the legacy of "playing to win" in the professional culture appears mixed.

The elements of this legacy can be seen in much of the Vietnam literature. The first vestiges began immediately after the war by the published memoirs of many of the senior military officers who led the military effort, including General Westmoreland, the Commanding General of U.S. forces in the Military Advisory Command Vietnam (MACV), in his memoirs *A Soldier Reports*. Similarly, Admiral U.S. Grant Sharp, Commander in Chief, U.S. Pacific Command (CINCPAC), criticized the management of the U.S. war effort in his post-war critique: *Strategy for Defeat*.

General Westmoreland identified himself with the MacArthur dictum that there is no substitute for victory. Writing from his retirement, he asserted that Vietnam had been a winnable war, particularly in 1968, and that MacArthur's words should have been heeded. "For all who would face reality," he noted, "the truth of those words was proven not only in South Vietnam but in all of Indochina."[17]

Looking back on his nearly five years in Vietnam, and his four years as Army Chief of Staff, Westmoreland laid America's defeat at the foot of our "ill considered policy of graduated response." To the former Commanding General of MACV, the war was still winnable after the defeat of the enemy Tet offensive. If President Johnson had permitted him to change our strategy and authorized operations into Laos and Cambodia, coupled with the intensified bombing and mining of Haiphong, "the North Vietnamese doubtlessly would have broken."[18]

Thus, General Westmoreland's assessment is that the war should have been expanded, despite the political ramifications from domestic and international sources. Implicit in his argument is the belief that the North Vietnamese would have been forced to the negotiating table by this sudden escalation and the realization we were willing to permit the military to decisively engage NVN forces wherever they took sanctuary. The strategy of attrition and gradualism doomed us to a prolonged endeavor. In this matter, General Westmoreland quoted Sun Tzu,"There has never been a protracted war from which a country has benefitted."

Admiral Sharp was equally critical of political limitations from Washington. In his caustic memoirs, he was particularly critical about the handcuffs that had been placed on the application of air power and the incremental manner in which air power was applied throughout the war.[19]

### The Institutional Defenders

The next element in the first phase in the literature begins with the publication of a book by Colonel H. G. Summers, Jr., which was appropriately titled: *On Strategy*. Colonel Summers is a veteran of both Korea and Vietnam, and is a decorated infantryman with a flair for strategic analysis. Colonel Summers arguments are wrapped into a Clausewitzian framework that is often as contradictory as the Prussian philosopher himself. Colonel Summers is perhaps the leading proponent of the "tactical victory, strategic defeat" school of thought on the Southeast Asia conflict. While many acerbic quotes can be taken from the book to criticize civilians,

Colonel Summers' assessment is far more balanced and is just as quick to blame senior military leaders for their share of the strategic errors of the war.

Colonel Summers believes that the fundamental error of the war was the failure to properly identify the nature of the war.[20] The author believes that the Army overconcentrated on the unconventional aspects of the war, and overinvested in counterinsurgency operations.

Summers argues that the U.S. military should have taken the tactical offensive to isolate the battlefield by employing the El Paso plans for a major incursion into Laos that he assisted in developing during his tour in Vietnam. This position is consistent with General Westmoreland and many other senior Army officers. By establishing a major Corps-level blocking forces across the DMZ and into the Laotian panhandle, the argument goes, we would have struck at the source of the war, the North's aggression and support to the Viet Cong. Instead, writes Summers, we turned to symptoms, the "simulated insurgency" in the South, rather than causes.[21]

The cardinal principle of war, according to Summers, is that offensive action is needed to achieve decisive results. This permits our forces to gain the initiative and facilitates the imposition of our will upon the opponent. Military force was employed defensively in South Vietnam, according to this line of reasoning, and military forces were maldeployed in many security operations, security assistance programs, and pacification efforts that should have been addressed by another agency. Summers adamantly holds this position, despite the many "search and destroy" operations mounted in the 1967–69 time frame.

Summers also argues that we essentially misemployed our military by concentrating on "the other war," the pacification effort. He underscores the need to understand the nature of the armed forces. "They are designed, equipped, and trained for a specific task," he wrote, "to fight, and win on the battlefield." They are a "battle ax," a crude instrument of national policy with only a singular purpose, "not a force for providing for nation-building activities."[22]

Underpinning this argument is the premise that the American Way of War is not only a function of our own unique strategic culture, but a fundamental and universal military principle. "Carrying the war to the enemy and the destruction of his armed forces and his will to fight through the strategic offensive is the classic way wars are fought and won."[23] Such arguments clash with advocates of limited war, whom Summers apparently takes great relish in castigating as "academic gurus" who never saw a battlefield.

This assessment has been very popular, and was distributed upon publication to the White House and to all serving Army general officers. It is required reading at most major institutions of professional military education, where Colonel Summers is an invited speaker on an annual basis.

### The Revisionists

A new set of lessons learned, or more accurately a new set of critics to the legacies of "playing to win," emerged in the mid-1980s. Two specific efforts are of note because of their superb scholarship and the authors' standing as military officers instead of political scientists or journalists. These two efforts are *The Army and Vietnam* by then Major Andrew F. Krepinevich, Jr., U. S. Army, and *The Limits of Air Power* by Major Mark Clodfelter, U.S. Air Force.[24] Krepinevich's book stands in stark contrast with those sympathetic to Colonel Summers' interpretation about the application of overwhelming force in Vietnam.

Krepinevich's argument is succinct. Instead of adapting its institutional mindset and capabilities to the war at hand, a largely unconventional conflict, the U.S. Army doggedly insisted on fighting the war consistent with the American Way of War as it understood it, the application of conventional forces and massive amounts of firepower to decisively engage and destroy the main battle force of the opponent.

Dr. Krepinevich accuses the Army of remaining fixated with its own institutional paradigms and of "refighting the last war" despite the dramatically different circumstances it found itself in Vietnam. When the Army came to Vietnam, it was neither trained nor equipped to fight effectively in an insurgency conflict, and stuck to what Krepinevich calls the Army Concept, a style of warfare consistent with the American Way of War deeply embedded in the service's psyche or memory. The Concept reflects the Army's precepts on how war's ought to be fought, short wars with decisive military battles relying on technology and firepower.

This says little for the institutional agility of the U.S. Army in particular and the American military as a whole. Moreover, Dr. Krepinevich, who has retired from active duty but who is still deeply engaged in the study and assessment of U.S. national security, thinks that the Army still lacks the ability to adjust its organization, tactics, and doctrine to properly counter its opponent in an unconventional conflict:

For the Army, the Vietnam War still represents a series of unanswered questions, the foremost of which is: How could the army of the most powerful nation on earth, materially supported on a scale unprecedented in history, equipped with the most sophisticated technology in an age when technology has assumed the role of a god of war, fail to emerge victorious against a numerically inferior foe of lightly armed irregulars?[25]

Contrary to the positions of the participants or the institutional defenders, the revisionists and a number of Service unconventional warfare experts feel that the U.S. Army persistently ignored counterinsurgency warfare. According to Summers, the internal guerrilla threat was ignored because it would "wither on the vine" if external logistics support and infiltration from North Vietnam were eliminated. The People's Army of Vietnam (PAVN) and the support of the North were seen as the center of gravity. This permitted us to focus on the war that we were best prepared for, both in material and doctrinal terms. The revisionists feel that we under-resourced the internal threat defense and the pacification program, a point supported by several government officials who served in Vietnam during this time.[26]

Thus, Krepinevich's argument runs directly counter to Summers' assessment that we lost the war by our distraction with civilian strategists and guerilla warfare. The revisionist argument is that we lost the war because the military ignored the revolutionary and political aspects of the war. Our only lens of looking at the war made it seem a conventional military problem. Thus, "with its perspective on counter-insurgency distorted by its Concept," writes Krepinevich, "the Army convinced itself that airmobile forces provided the ability to conduct counter-insurgency operations using traditional operational doctrine."[27]

Thus, to the new school, the war was lost not by the fact that we were not permitted to win, but that the American military remained true to its own operational concepts about conventional war, based on firepower and technological and logistical dimensions of strategy while ignoring the political and social dimensions that formed the foundation of an unconventional war. Taking the argument to its conclusion, Krepinevich feels the Army failed because, "It expended human resources at a relatively high rate and material resources in a profligate manner as part of a strategy of attrition." The goal was to win a quick victory. Yet the United States achieved neither a quick victory nor the maintenance of support on the home front for a continued U.S. presence.[28]

The disproportionate emphasis on the external threat made the war more manageable in terms of the American Way of War. Yet, it turned out to be the wrong strategy according to the unconventional war school. "The tragedy is," writes Krepinevich, "that the nature of the war required that emphasis be placed, first and foremost, on the internal threat to the stability and legitimacy of the South Vietnamese government."[29] This is again in direct opposition to Colonel Summers' views that the war was lost because we dissipated our attention on "the other war" and failed to see the conventional threat presented by the PAVN in the North.

### Air Power Revisionism

Like the Army, the U.S. Air Force was anxious to put Vietnam behind it and thus failed to learn anything from it.[30] Whatever it did gain dealt with strategic bombing, tactics, or technology. Strategic lessons or errors were quickly phased out by a selective sorting of history. Like the Army, the Air Force did not teach anything about Vietnam in its professional schools, and it was not mentioned in their doctrinal manuals.[31]

Air power was a significant element in the war against North Vietnam. A total of 8 million tons of bombs were delivered, with over 6 million tons by the Air Force alone. The Air Force lost 617 fixed-wing planes, and the United States lost a total of 8,588 fixed and rotary-wing aircraft.[32] Air power enthusiasts almost universally concluded it was the limits *on* air power not the inherent limitations *of* air power that failed to bring the war to a conclusive ending in short order.[33]

Like the Army, the Air Force's "unhealthy myths" resulted in what air power historian Dr. Earl Tilford calls a subtle "stab in the back" thesis.[34] The myths resulted in an institutional form of self-delusion about the efficacy of air power in Vietnam. The most pervasive of these myths is that air power, specifically the Linebacker II campaign, won the war in 1972 by forcing the North Vietnamese to agree to our terms in Paris. The contention is that if air power had been employed unfettered earlier, in 1965, the war could be terminated quickly and more favorably. In Admiral Thomas Moorer's words, "Gradualism forced airpower into an expanded and inconclusive war of attrition."[35]

To subsequent air power scholars the Air Force developed a series of "unhealthy myths" that prevent it from learning anything from the war and from looking at it uncritically.[36] The military's professional advice for a decisive and massive air campaign was rejected, by the "flagrant arrogance or naive wishful thinking" of a few civilians.[37] Instead of a crushing "quick squeeze," the civilians tried their own form of political signalling and gradualism. The result was the incremental "on again, off again" approach of Rolling Thunder. This three-year campaign was a bust. With targets picked by the President, and additional restrictions placed on mission size, collateral damage, and routes, both Air Force and Navy aviators felt that the time–honored principles and concepts of strategic bombing had been utterly misused.[38]

Strategic bombing is close to the central operational values of the U.S. Air Force. According to Dr. Caroline Ziemke of the Institute for Defense Analyses, it is as central to the identity of the Air Force as the New Testament is to the Catholic Church.[39] Without strategic bombing, there is no need for an air force. Thus, it was impossible for the Air Force to seriously reconsider its organizational *raison d'etre*.

Yet this strategic bombing doctrine was the root problem in how the Air Force approached the air campaign over North Vietnam. Largely drawn from the lessons of the Combined Bomber Offensive of World War II, the Air Force applied what it knew to be the central truths about air power. This strategic bombing doctrine "led Air Force leaders to believe that North Vietnam, a preindustrial, agricultural nation, could be subdued by the same kind of bombing that helped to defeat industrialized Nazi Germany and Imperial Japan."[40]

In the same way that Krepinevich's argument represented a contrarian view, a number of Air Force officers and air power historians began to dismantle the scaffolding of myths surrounding the Rolling Thunder and Linebacker bombing campaigns. The best of these is Major Mark A. Clodfelter's *The Limits of Airpower: The American Bombing of North Vietnam*, which rejects the "we had our hands tied" theory. Clodfelter's major argument is that the Air Force misapplied its European war doctrine to the Vietnamese conflict without any thought. In effect, the Air Force followed its preferred concept just like the Army. Clodfelter's thesis is that the failure of U.S. airpower in Vietnam cannot be blamed entirely on a lack of resolve by civilian politicians, micromanagement, constraints, or a myopic media. The problems experienced by the Air Force were caused as much by poor strategy, lack of targets, undeveloped technology, and poor coordination between Services, as by civilian oversight.[41]

Clodfelter shows persuasively that any significance between the effects of the different bombing campaigns had less to do with the efficacy of air power or civilian mismanagement and more to do with the changes in technology, and the differences in available targets when the North converted from guerrilla to a more conventional military strategy in preparing to invade the South. Clodfelter's superlative scholarship and position at the Air University show that the Air Force, like the Army, has passed into a new phase in assessing the lessons of Vietnam.

The legacy of Vietnam remains mixed when it comes to how force should be applied. The veterans of Vietnam claim the war supports the absolutist position about using force quickly and decisively. The argument still goes on today:

No More Vietnams means to me that when we do launch military forces in that noble cause of freedom we must do so with an absolute desire to win. When we go to war, we must go to win, that or stay at home.[42]

The revisionists counter that the military had no effective strategies for winning and ignored the contingent aspects of the war. Dr. Ronald Spector, a historian who served in Vietnam in 1968 as a Marine, feels the root cause of the military's failure was its fixation on its traditional style of warfare, which proved pointless and ineffective. Based on a position developed two decades after the war, Spector insists the failure to adapt to the situation contributed to the stalemate and indecision that was the war's primary characteristic.[43]

Which school of thought is now operational among the officers who comprise today's officer corps? Recent research on the issue has concluded that the Army has no institutional critique of the Vietnam war.[44] An assessment of "America's Longest War" eludes consensus, a dubious distinction for an organization planning on prosecuting future low-intensity conflict situations. But the same research disproves the hypothesis that the U.S. Army specifically, and the Officer Corps in general, have internalized an "all or nothing" approach based on Vietnam. In a survey of nearly 200 Army Officers attending the U.S. Army Command and General Staff College course at Leavenworth, the following question was asked, "Which statement below comes closest to characterizing your overall views on the lessons of Vietnam?" A narrow majority supported the view that the United States did not have the right strategy to win the war and overlooked key elements of the strategic situation.[45] This pre-Desert Storm attitudinal survey suggests that the military culture has eventually moved away from Colonel Summers' view of the war and accepted something closer to the conclusions of the revisionists. However, a broader survey with greater participation of Officers from other Services, involving more than just Vietnam is necessary in order to draw more definitive conclusions.

## CIVIL-MILITARY RELATIONS

The area of civil-military relations remains one of the least conclusive legacies from Vietnam. Much of the literature from the military perspective resents the impression that the military's performance was less than adequate, and the general opinion exists that the military was cast as the scapegoat.[46] The participants hoped that history would eventually become more favorable to the military than to the politicians and policy makers who called the shots.

As one author has noted, Vietnam painfully reminded the U.S. military that under the U.S. constitutional form of government, they, not the temporary occupants of public office, bear the heaviest burden during war.[47]  The Vietnam experience reinforced the military perception that it was they who would bear the burden of blame in the policy post mortems.  As one Army general quipped, "Those who ordered the meal were not there when the waiter brought the check."[48]

Regrettably, one of the lessons learned and institutionalized by many of the senior level participants is that civil-military relations were largely satisfactory.  In the very last paragraph of his memoirs, General Westmoreland proudly observes, "The American people can be particularly proud that their military leaders scrupulously adhered to a basic tenet of our Constitution prescribing civilian control of the military."[49]  General Westmoreland may be proud, but the American people should not be.  The Vietnam War was fought employing a narrow interpretation of the proper interplay between policy makers and military men, and the end result speaks for itself.  We can be satisfied that the principle of civilian control was maintained, but it is pretty clear that effective interaction between the Statesmen and the Generals was far from satisfactory.

One Army general, in an understatement, wrote after the war that "civil-military relations in the United States, especially at the highest levels where political and strategic issues become entwined, have not always been close and harmonious."[50]  General Palmer disagrees with the premise that the military had its hands tied and can pass off all blame.  The military must share the onus of failure as well, he insists.  He is especially critical of the senior military leaders in Washington for being unable to articulate their misgivings and communicate effectively to the policy makers.  "The central point is that U.S. military leaders failed to get across the point that our strategy was not working," and that it would achieve U.S. policy objectives within a reasonable cost.[51]

The poor interaction between civilian policy makers and the Joint Chiefs of Staff began with Kennedy's assessment of the decision making process and inputs that led to the Bay of Pigs debacle.  The general conclusion drawn by President Kennedy and his advisors was that the military's viewpoint was excessively narrow and the military lacked the ability to integrate social, political, and economic factors into its assessments and advice.

This conclusion was immediately reinforced by the events surrounding the Cuban missile crisis.  Kennedy took away several negative lessons about the flexibility and depth of recommendations from the Joint Chiefs.  Eventually he felt compelled to issue a national security action memorandum to the Joint Chiefs charging them to include political and economic factors into their recommendations.[52]  Then Vice President Lyndon Johnson apparently picked up the same perspective on the quality and clarity of advice given by the Pentagon during these same crises.  This fostered a degree of mutual distrust manifested when LBJ decided to control target selection and rules of engagement from the Oval Office itself.  Likewise, the Secretary of Defense, in a often-cited example, had a clash with the then Chief of Naval Operations over operational details during the Cuban missile crisis, which did not increase his confidence that the U.S. military would remain, in the midst of super-heated confrontations with other nuclear powers, a responsive instrument of national policy.[53]

During the war, LBJ was particularly harsh on his military advisors.  He dressed down the Army Chief of Staff for "not giving me any solutions to this damn little piss-ant country.  I don't need ten generals to come in here and tell me to bomb.  I want some solutions, some answers."[54]  During the war, LBJ decried the overreliance of American military leaders on strategic bombing.  He was also worried about controlling the generals, and warned Westmoreland, "Don't pull a MacArthur on me."[55]  His solution was to retain control of the targeting process to preclude inadvertent or deliberate bombing missions from escalating the war.

For their part, the military leaders were critical of the intensive micromanagement they received at the Pentagon and from the White House.  The literature is replete with strong criticisms of "McNamara's Whiz kids," the arrogance of Ivy League political scientists,  the pipe-smoking professors with "tree full of owls" ideas.  Nothing more grated the professional military establishment than the rise of the ubiquitous systems analysts who introduced the overly quantitative and mechanistic Planning Programming and Budgeting System into the art of war.  "By default," insists Colonel Summers, "the military had allowed strategy to be dominated by civilian analysts, political scientists in academia and systems analysts in the defense bureaucracy."[56]

Yet when given a chance by the new administration in 1969, Dr. Henry Kissinger claims the military never offered useful strategic recommendations when Nixon came in and was eager for fresh military advice.[57]  Clausewitz warned that policy cannot be a tyrant and cannot get involved in tactical and operational details.  Policy, he said, does not deal with the posting of guards and the sending of patrols.  Yet during Vietnam, policy makers did post guards and send patrols.  But the military never forcefully put its foot down and insisted on the proper division of labor between policy makers and military professionals.

The lesson learned was that politicians would hold the military responsible for policy failures even when politicians imposed limitations, failed to heed professional advice, or ignored the costs and risks inherent in using force.  The senior military closed ranks after Vietnam and became even further reluctant to recommend the use of force.


## POPULAR SUPPORT

Another popular conclusion about Vietnam among the military is the belief that the war was lost at home because we violated Clausewitz's dictum "the people provide the passion and the motivation for war."[58]  Explicit among various commentators is the belief that the civilian leadership made several key strategic errors during the course of the war to maintain public support. Within this line of reasoning are complaints about our:

1. Failure to formally declare war
2. Failure to mobilize the reserves
3. Failure to ensure the draft was equitable
4. Failure to rally public support[59]

The lesson learned by the American military in Vietnam involves the third leg of Clausewitz's "remarkable trinity," the people. The consensus, particularly acute among Army officers, seems to suggest that the American people have a duty and a role in the authorization of military force, beyond that delegated to their elected representatives in the Congress and the President. This conviction can be summed up by the statement that war is a shared responsibility between the people, the government, and the military.[60]

Such a conclusion from Vietnam also reflects a popular assessment of the capacity of democracies to effectively wage war that dates back to Thucydides and runs to de Tocqueville. In the American military experience, this has been captured by General Marshall's oft-quoted comment that "democracies cannot fight a Seven Year's War."[61] To many military officers, the Vietnam conflict reinforced this conclusion. The social unrest and turmoil generated by opposition to the war, the fragging of officers, resistance to conscription, and widespread drug abuse throughout our society reflected the disintegration of a social system cracked by pressures beyond its capacity to withstand. This is traced back to a failure to unite the American people behind a war effort requiring social and personal sacrifices. To several prominent analysts, the solution is the promulgation of a declaration of war to validate the support of the people and the employment of the people's Army. As Colonel Summers has noted:

If Vietnam proved nothing else, it proved that the equivalent of a declaration of war, that is, the fixing of public will and the sharing of the responsibility for the war among the American people and the Congress and the Executive is absolutely vital for any future war of the United States.[62]

Military writers have concluded that the failure to marshal the nation's will behind the effort in Southeast Asia was a major strategic error.[63] To such officers, the national will is generated by mobilization and a formal declaration of war. The same writers are quick to criticize limited war theorists for excluding the American people from the strategic equation. "Public support is an essential precondition for the conduct of military operations," is how Colonel Summers wraps it up.[64] Such arguments find support in the interpretation that the framers of the Constitution intended all military excursions to be supported by popular acclaim via formal declaration from Congress.

The common position developed by military authors is once again best captured by Summers and Palmers. To both authors, the blame belongs to President Johnson for attempting to fight the war without raising the ire or the passions of the American people. In Dean Rusk's words, we tried to fight the war as a police action rather than a full scale war, in effect fighting a war "in cold blood" when what was required was the stirring of the passions of the people.

The Commanding General of all American forces in Vietnam, General William Westmoreland, agreed with this argument. "President Johnson should have forced Congress to face its constitutional responsibility for waging war" and had the legislature publicly declare war.[65] Another officer, General Palmer agrees:

Our government, itself lacking a clear understanding of what it means and what it takes to commit a nation to war, failed to persuade the public that it was necessary for us to fight in Vietnam. This was a fatal weakness, and a result of it the American people did not lend their whole hearted support to the war effort. This might have been obtained had the Congress been deeply involved in the decision to commit our forces to battle and been persuaded that a declaration of war was in the national interest.[66]

Such assessments are well embedded in the American military psyche. The declaration of war "legitimizes" the relationship between the people and what the Army is doing in the eyes of the world, provides certain responsibilities, and creates impediments to dissolution, according to these strategic analyses. Impediments to dissolution are important, because the U.S. military does not want their support cut out from under them after they have been introduced into a conflict. This point of view also ensures that the Army retains its relationship with the people it sees itself as serving. As General Westmoreland put it, "If a war is deemed worthy of the dedication and sacrifice of the military services, it is also worthy of the commitment of the entire population."[67] Without some form of visibly manifested support, the Army would prefer not to be deployed or employed at all.

Another reason that military officers frequently see mobilization as useful has nothing to do with Constitutional prerogatives of the Legislature or supporting the will of the people. One prominent author sees mobilization as a cure for emasculating the troublesome media, which "demolished popular support by misreporting the war, sometimes intentionally." "Not only does such a declaration commit the Congress and the people," so the argument goes, "but it brings into force other laws, regulations, and executive orders needed to fight a war (censorship for example)."[68]

This brings up the issue of rallying public support, and the role of the media in reducing public support during the war. The overall feeling in the Services is that the media contributed to ruining public support at home and weakened the morale of the Armed Forces in Vietnam. General Westmoreland was critical of the press, and General Kinnard's research showed that over 90 percent of the generals felt that the press had been irresponsible in Vietnam. Without any doubt, the U.S. military came out of Vietnam convinced that the press had undercut their efforts and morale on the homefront.[69] The wounds from this aspect of the Vietnam war have not healed.

Looking back on the discussion of the purported necessity of public support, it appears that such conclusions are warranted when the United States intends to fight major conflicts to which significant forces and resources are being applied. This is of course axiomatic of the American Way of War as seen by the U.S. military. But the lesson to draw is not that democracies cannot fight long wars, but that popular support is difficult to maintain during stalemates or protracted struggles with little apparent progress.

Former CIA Director, and a former pacification program participant, William Colby argues, "The real lesson is not that Americans cannot fight a long war or that we should eschew revolutionary conflicts because we found ourselves at a cultural disadvantage."[70] The real lesson from the war is more accurately reflected in a general proposition that protracted and inconclusive ground warfare will not command public support indefinitely.[71]

Above all, Americans remain pragmatic. To provide support, Americans must sense that the results are commensurate with the costs of involvement. They must perceive some sense of reasonable benefit, derived from a fairly general cost-benefit analysis. The general population seems to be willing to sustain major involvements over a short term, or a minor involvement over a longer term, if convinced that the results are worth the effort. What pragmatic Americans cannot support is a major involvement over a long term without results. If a minor conflict is going to be extended in terms of time, the military strategy and political leadership will have to provide the American people "incremental dividends" that indicate some progress towards a reasonably clear goal.[72] In the absence of such dividends, few investors are ever willing to pay into any endeavor for long.

Long wars or unconventional conflicts are not an inherent weakness of democracy itself. The Soviet Union's experience in Afghanistan showed that neither totalitarian regimes or democracies can long endure "a long, unfocused, inconclusive, and bloody war far from home, for unidentified or ill-defined national objectives."[73] Additionally, both the Israelis and the British have had long experiences with low-intensity conflicts.

## SUMMING UP

The American military in the decade after Vietnam fervently believed that the war was lost in Washington at the strategic and political level. The civilians failed to define clear objectives, overrode professional advice, and hamstrung the military in the execution of the war. This line of thought ignores the fact that the basic policy aim of the United States was both clear and consistent in the form of NSAM 288. The overall goal did change over time with new stages of the war. The major policy aims changed from the nation-building era (1955–64), the post-1965 period of conventional defense, and the post-Tet disengagement and Vietnamization phase. What never seems to have been clear was how the military strategies would achieve the desired policy aims within the limits and resources available.

The lack of clarity between military objectives or political objectives is also a criticism of the military's leaders. It does not speak well of the military if over 100 generals admit to having sent 500,000 men to combat in a sense of confusion. Nor does it say much for the leadership to have fought a conflict that claimed 58,000 lives, without any clear sense of purpose.

No one has satisfactorily proven that their alternative strategies would produce a decisive victory. Colonel Summers' thesis that a massive defensive barrier in Laos and Cambodia is predicated on an assumption that such a force would elmininate support from the North for the Viet Cong. How such a defensive and passive effort, not to mention costly and protracted program, would achieve U.S. aims is problematic. No one has yet offered a plan for "playing to win" aside from full scale invasion options, which clearly exceed the policy limits of the Administration and the international political context of the Cold War.

Civil-military relations were marginal because the military submitted passively to the decisions made by the President and the Secretary of Defense. More effective relations would have resulted in a better integration of political and military perspectives and helped the President understand the costs and risks of the decisions he made in 1965. The military properly learned that it would have to be more vocal and that its voice would have to integrate military and political considerations.

The military feels that public support is crucial to the war. The failures of the civilian leadership to generate and sustain this support via mobilization generated a subtle "stab in the back" syndrome. American policy makers should get the primary credit for losing the war, but not on the basis of poor maintenance of the home front. Krepinevich finds that the U.S. military is "perpetuating the fiction that its Concept of war remains valid in all conflict environments" and that future problems can be solved by staying the course with national consensus from the President, Congress, and the American people and by acceding execution of the war entirely to the military. This is the most significant lesson learned, and the most erroneous, since the U.S. military never had an effective strategy for "playing to win" in Vietnam. What might be a more appropriate lesson is the conclusion that public support is a product of success, not a precondition.

Thus, the military moved into the 1980s convinced that a vocal insistence for clear objectives (spelled out in military terms), sufficient troops and resources to accomplish the mission, with few constraints or interference, and an assurance of public support was a reasonable and justifiable set of conditions to be met for the military to accept another U.S. intervention. These lessons were carried forward into the next decade by a new generation of generals.

## NOTES

1. The Pentagon Papers constituted an attempt to pull together all the documentation related to the decisions made during the course of the war, but it is not an assessment and it is incomplete. The Army commissioned a study of the war, which the BDM Corporation

completed in 1980. The eight-volume effort is largely ignored, perhaps because it criticizes the Army for approaching the war consistent with its conventional American Way of War style. The BDM study also disputes the myth that the Army won every battle. BDM Corporation, *A Study of Strategic Lessons Learned in Vietnam*, 8 vols., McLean, VA: BDM Corporation, 1990.

2. The Battle of Ia Drang is considered a seminal event in the Vietnam war, where U.S. forces met NVA regulars in combat for the first time. The battle saw the first employment of the "air cavalry" concept and extensive use of helicopter mobility. Many reports cite this battle as the origination of General Westmoreland's strategy of attrition and the emphasis on fighting the North in conventional terms using American firepower and technology consistent with the American military culture. Harold G. Moore and Joseph L. Galloway, *We Were Soldiers Once. . . And Young*, New York: Random House, 1992.

3. This term was lifted from an article written by Samuel Huntington in 1986 by the same title, *National Interest*, Spring 1986, pp. 13–20.

4. Andrew F. Krepinevich, *The Army and Vietnam*, Baltimore: Johns Hopkins University, 1986, p. 269.

5. Field Manual 100–5, *Operations*, 1962, p. 46. The principle of the objective has been the first principle of war for the American military since such principles have been formally established.

6. Paul Seabury and Angelo Codevilla, *War, Ends and Means*, New York: Basic Books, 1993, p. 12.

7. Carl von Clausewitz, *On War,* Michael Howard and Peter Paret, eds. and trans., Princeton: Princeton University Press, 1976, p. 88.

8. Seabury and Codevilla, p. 161.

9. Harry G. Summers, *On Strategy: A Critical Analysis of the Vietnam War*, New York: Presidio, 1982, p. 98.

10. Hugh M. Arnold, "Official Justifications for America's Role in Indochina," *Asian Affairs*, September–October, 1975, p. 31.

11. Douglas Kinnard, *The War Managers*, Hanover, NH: University Press of New England, 1977, pp. 160–163.

12. Quoted from George C. Herring, *America's Longest War: The United States and Vietnam 1950-1975*, New York: Wiley, 1979, p. 116.

13. Phillip B. Davidson, *Vietnam at War 1945-1975*, London: Sidgewick & Jackson, 1988, p. 799.

14. Ibid.

15. Dave Richard Palmer, *Summons of the Trumpet: U.S.–Vietnam in Perspective*, San Rafael, CA: Presidio, 1978, p. xvii.

16. Ibid., p. xx.

17. William C. Westmoreland, *A Soldier Reports*, New York: DeCapo, 1989, p. 416.

18. Ibid., p. 410.

19. U.S. Grant Sharp, *Strategy for Defeat: Vietnam in Retrospect*, San Rafael, CA: Presidio, 1978, pp. 267–268.

20. Summers, *On Strategy*, p. 83.

21. Norman Hannah quoted by Colonel Harry G. Summers in "A Strategic Perception of the Vietnam War," in Lawrence E. Grinter and Peter M. Dunn, eds., *The American War in*

*Vietnam: Lessons, Legacies and Implications for Future Conflict*, Westport, CT: Greenwood, 1987, p. 92.

22. Ibid., p. 184.

23. Ibid., p. 187.

24. Andrew F. Krepinevich, *The Army and Vietnam*, Baltimore: Johns Hopkins University Press, 1986; Mark A. Clodfelter, *The Limits of Airpower: The American Bombing of North Vietnam*, New York: Free Press, 1989.

25. Krepinevich, p. 4.

26. See Robert W. Komer, *Bureaucracy at War: U.S. Performance in the Vietnam Conflict*, Boulder, CO: Westview Press, 1986; and Leslie H. Gelb and Richard K. Betts, *The Irony of Vietnam: The System Worked*, Washington, DC: The Brookings Institution, 1979. Ambassador Komer's views must be granted great credibility, as he was responsible for pacification programs in Vietnam once they were consolidated.

27. Krepinevich, p. 127.

28. Ibid., p. 259

29. Ibid, p. 268.

30. Earl H. Tilford, "Setup: Why and How the U.S. Air Force Lost in Vietnam," *Armed Forces and Society*, Vol. 17, No. 3, 1991, p. 328.

31. Earl H. Tilford, "Air Power in Vietnam: The Hubris of Power," in Lawrence E. Grinter and Peter M. Dunn, eds., *The American War in Vietnam*, Westport , CT: Greenwood, 1987, p. 69. Tilford is a graduate of the Air Force Academy and has taught at the Air University. He recounts that the word Vietnam does not appear in either the 1979 or 1984 updates to Air Force Manual 1–1, *Basic Aerospace Doctrine of the United States Air Force*. The Air University did not have a course on Vietnam until 1983, and the first course was eventually canceled due to lack of interest. See Tilford, "Setup," *Armed Forces and Society,* p. 341.

32. Earl H. Tilford, *Setup: What the Air Force Did in Vietnam and Why,* Maxwell Air Force Base: AL: Air University Press, 1991, p. xvii.

33. Richard P. Hallion, *Storm Over Iraq: Air Power and the Gulf War*, Washington, DC: Smithsonian Institution Press, 1992, p. 19.

34. Tilford, "Setup," *Armed Forces and Society*, p. 341.

35. Quoted by Guenter Lewy, "Some Political-Military Lessons of the Vietnam War," *Parameters*, Spring 1984, p. 8.

36. Earl H. Tilford, "Setup," *Armed Forces and Society*, p. 335.

37. Sharp, *Strategy for Defeat*, p. 268.

38. The official air proponent view is found in William W. Moymer, *Air Power in Three Wars*, Washington, DC: Department of Defense, U.S. Air Force, 1978; as well as Alan Gropman, "Lost Opportunities: The Air War in Vietnam," Grinter and Dunn, pp. 49–67.

39. This quote was extracted from Zeimke's foreword to Earl H. Tilford, *Setup: What the Air Force Did in Vietnam and Why*, p. ix.

40. Tilford, "Setup," *Armed Forces and Society*, p. 330.

41. Clodfelter, *The Limits of Airpower*, pp. 185–210. Two recent assessments support Clodfelter's interpretation. See Kenneth P. Werrell, "Air War Victorious: The Gulf War vs. Vietnam," *Parameters*, Summer 1992, pp. 41–54.

42. Raymond G. Davis, "Politics and War: Twelve Fatal Decisions That Rendered Defeat in Vietnam," *Marine Corps Gazette*, August 1989, p. 78. General Davis was a Marine Division Commander in I Corps in Vietnam. For another recent example see Oliver L. North and David Roth, *One More Mission: Oliver North Returns to Vietnam*, New York, Zondervan/Harper Collins, 1993, p. 47. Lt.Col. North makes the statement, in his recent semi–autobiographical account of a trip to Vietnam, that the United States did not intend to "win" in Southeast Asia, and that the military fought "with one hand tied behind their backs."

43. Ronald H. Spector, *After Tet: The Bloodiest Year in Vietnam*, New York: Free Press, 1993, p. 313.

44. Michael J. Brady, "The Army and the Strategic Military Legacy of Vietnam," unpublished Master's Thesis, U.S. Army Command and General Staff College, Fort Leavenworth, KS, 1990, p. 222.

45. Ibid., pp. 262, 282.

46. For example see Westmoreland, *A Soldier Reports*, pp. 424–425.

47. David H. Petraeus, "The American Military and the Lessons of Vietnam: A Study of Miliary Influence and the Use of Force in the Post–Vietnam Era," unpublished Ph.D. Dissertation, Princeton University, 1987, pp. 116–117.

48. Quoted in Petraeus, p. 117. Original source is from William A. Knowlton, "Ethics and Decision–Making," an address given to the Army War College, October 22, 1984.

49. Westmoreland, *A Soldier Reports*, p. 425.

50. Bruce Palmer, *The 25-Year War: America's Role in Vietnam*, Lexington: University Press of Kentucky, 1984, p. 200.

51. Ibid., p. 191. Admiral Sharp suggests that military leadership was not forceful enough. Sharp, *Strategy for Defeat*, p. 278.

52. Robert F. Kennedy, *Thirteen Days*, New York: Norton, 1969, pp. 97, 119. Kennedy noted after hearing yet again another suggestion from the Joint Chiefs of Staff on the use nuclear weapons, "I thought, as I listened, of the many times that I had heard the military take positions which, if wrong, had the advantage that no one would be around at the end to know."; Mark Perry, *Four Stars*, pp. 110–151; Betts, *Soldiers, Statesmen, and Cold War Crises*, pp. 8–12, p. 35; Stephen P. Rosen, "Vietnam and the American Theory of Limited War," in *American Defense Policy*, 6th ed., Schuyler Foerster and Edward N. Wright, eds., Baltimore: Johns Hopkins University Press, 1990, p. 314. Kennedy's instructions to the Joint Chiefs were contained in National Security Action Memorandum (NSAM 55), dated June 28 1961. This NSAM was titled "Relations of Joint Chiefs to the President in Cold War Operations." See Douglas Kinnard, *The Certain Trumpet: Maxwell Taylor and the American Experience in Vietnam*, Washington, DC: Brassey's, 1991, pp. 54–57, 226.

53. Graham Allison, *Essence of Decision*, p. 130–131.

54. David Halberstam, *The Best and the Brightest*, Greenwich, CT: Fawcett Crest, 1972, pp. 682–683.

55. Westmoreland, p. 270.

56. Summers, *On Strategy*, p. 43.

57. Henry Kissinger, *The White House Years*, Boston: Little Brown, 1979, pp. 35–36.

58. Clausewitz, *On War*, p. 89.

59. Geoffrey G. Prosch and Mitchell M. Zais, "American Will and the Vietnam War," *Military Review*, March 1990, pp. 71–80.

60. Harry G. Summers, *On Strategy II: A Critical Analysis of the Gulf War*, New York: Dell, 1992, p. 22.

61. Cited by Petraeus, p. 106. This widely cited maxim is found in Maurice Matloff, *Strategic Planning for Coalition Warfare, 1943–1945*, Washington DC: Department of the Army, 1959, p. 5.

62. Harry G. Summers, in Peter Braestrup, ed., *Vietnam as History: Ten Years After the Paris Peace Accords*, Washington, DC: University Press of America, 1984, p. 147.

63. Summers, *On Strategy*, p. 19.

64. Ibid., p. 13.

65. Westmoreland, p. 412.

66. Bruce Palmer, p. 191.

67. Westmoreland, p. 411.

68. Davidson, *Vietnam at War*, p. 810.

69. See Westmoreland, *A Soldier Reports*, pp. 419–422; Kinnard, *The War Managers*, pp. 124–135.

70. William Colby with James McCargar, *Lost Victory: A Firsthand Account of America's Sixteen-year Involvement in Vietnam*, New York: Contemporary Books, 1989, p. 367.

71. Earnest May, in "Vietnam Reappraised," *International Security*, Summer 1981, p. 4. This is also Dr. Spector's conclusion, *After Tet*, p. 313.

72. I am indebted to Professor David E. Kaiser, of the Strategy and Policy Department of the U.S. Naval War College, for this concept and conclusion.

73. Davidson, *Vietnam at War*, p. 798.

# 3

# Babes in Beirut

The introduction of U.S. forces to Lebanon in 1982 was the next event in the development of institutionalized attitudes about the proper use of force. It was not a pleasant experience. In many ways it was "Deja vu, all over again," to borrow an aphorism from Yogi Berra. Ambiguous missions, political interference, constraints, and interaction in a messy political situation were all associated with Vietnam and were seen again in Lebanon.

It was not a situation conducive to the American Way of War—military victory was not sought nor defined in terms the U.S. military could understand. Vietnam's bitter lessons were reinforced and hardened by the loss of 241 warriors. Post-conflict analyses, in the form of commissions and hearings, sought convenient answers, clouding the adoption of useful lessons out of the experience. The lessons that did evolve sought to reduce the reliance on military force as an instrument of U.S. foreign policy. These lessons established guidelines for when and how the harsh cutting edge of military force could be best employed. These guidelines mirrored the military culture's operational code.

Yet the record has been subjected to erroneous revisionism and distortion. It is difficult to determine if the military has learned lessons at all. In the words of one major participant, writing to help set the "distorted" record straight, "The Marines will surely have died in vain if we do not learn the right lessons."[1]

The U.S. military did not escape the fallout from the policy failure. Nor did it sit still in the aftermath and stoically accept blame. In many ways, Beirut reinforced the lessons of Vietnam about politicians, and the irresponsible actions of a Congress more concerned with partisan advantage and eluding responsibility than fulfilling a meaningful role in foreign policy. Like Vietnam, the military failed to accept any of its own shortfalls, either in the policy making arena, or on the ground in Lebanon. In the words of one observer of the Joint Chiefs and military influence in policy circles:

The U.S. intervention in Lebanon was the most crucial of the 1980s. Both phases of U.S. participation were opposed by professional military leaders, and when the venture ended grimly it thoroughly reinforced the lessons of Vietnam to them.[2]

A detailed overview of the events leading up to the tragedy in Beirut is necessary to come to grips with an assessment of military lessons learned and institutional myths surrounding the Marine deployment to what was once the Paris of the Middle East.

## THE MARINES IN LEBANON: 1982-1984

U.S. policy objectives in the Middle East must be clearly understood to evaluate the Reagan administration's policy aims and the means it chose to achieve them. Stability in the Middle East was an overarching strategic requirement for the United States. Events in Lebanon threatened both peace in the region and U.S. interests. American prestige and policy for the region was tied to the Camp David accords arranged by the Carter Administration. The accords were stalled in 1982, and PLO-generated violence against Israel's northern borders was not conducive to regional deals. Syrian hegemony into Lebanon was seen as a projection of Soviet influence to be blunted. Thus, U.S. influence in the region had to be preserved, wider conflagrations avoided, and access to oil maintained.[3]

Israel's Operation Peace for Galilee in June 1982 threatened those goals. A major clash between the Arab nations and Israel was at risk. The Israeli Defense Force (IDF) had already tangled with Syrian armored forces in Lebanon, as well as seriously bloodying the Syrian Air Force in the Bekka Valley. As the IDF invasion force closed on Beirut, an expansion of the conflict was feared. The U.S. dispatched Philip Habib to negotiate a cease fire and to try to arrange a permanent cessation of hostilities. The worst-case scenario for the U.S. was to get dragged into a Cold War conflict with the Soviets. If the Syrians and Israelis went at each other's throats, just such a scenario could evolve.[4]

Despite these critical interests, the U.S. ventured forth into a volatile region with no game plan. The players were suited up and sent to the arena, but no one really knew who the opponents were and what the rules of the game applied.

### Phase I—The PLO Evacuation

The Marine odyssey in the Levant began on June 24, 1982 when the 32nd Marine Amphibious Unit (MAU) docked at Juniyah to evacuate U.S. citizens from strife-torn Lebanon. Because of the deteriorating situation, violence in Beirut was unchecked and American lives were at risk. The nearby Navy/Marine task force afloat in the Mediterranean was ordered to proceed to Beirut immediately and evacuate U.S. citizens.

The Marines were given the execute order to land at Juniyah, five miles north of Beirut to avoid the heavy shelling and indiscriminate violence in downtown Beirut. The Marines successfully evacuated 580 U.S. nationals back to U.S. Navy ships afloat off the coast. After transporting the evacuees to Cyprus, the naval task force remained off the coast near Beirut and provided support to U.S. diplomatic efforts headed by special envoy Philip Habib, who was seeking a compromise to get the PLO out of Lebanon.

Back in Washington, Mr. Weinberger fought to limit the deployment of U.S. forces into the region.[5] He was purportedly vehemently opposed to using Marines to assist in the PLO evacuation. He strove to limit the time the force was deployed to the absolute minimum. The State Department and the National Security Council (NSC) wanted a 60-day deployment, but compromised on a 30-day maximum. Instead of deploying the Marines as an interpositionary force along Beirut's infamous Green Line, Weinberger successfully limited the Marines to the port area, with no authority to venture further than the limited facility.[6] Additionally, the Pentagon resisted establishment of UN mandates or a formal international military force. The result was that U.S. military forces remained responsive solely to Weinberger and the JCS, and precluded any U.S. diplomat on the scene from exercising any direct command authority over the force. DoD's express purpose was to resist becoming an instrument of any bargaining strategies by the State Department inside war-torn Beirut.[7] The Reagan cabinet debated the matter, and a National Security Decision Directive (NSDD) was signed by the President ordering the use of U.S. forces.

Mr. Habib began political-military planning to use a multinational force (MNF) to support the disengagement of the antagonists in and around Beirut and to support the evacuation of the PLO. Habib established a formal committee to facilitate planning comprised of U.S. military and diplomatic representatives, as well as military officers from the Italian and French forces. The technical problems and operational risks of the MNF were not overlooked. In the words of the MAU commander, Colonel James Mead, "The obvious concerns of inserting some portion of this force between 30,000 Israelis and 15,000 PLO and Syrian fighters were well recognized."[8]

The size of the force was limited to 800 French, 800 U.S. Marines and 400 Italians. The role of the MNF was to support the Lebanese Armed Forces (LAF) at checkpoints between the PLO and Syrian forces in West Beirut and the Israeli forces and the Christian allies in East Beirut. The Marine commanders understood the task was to be delicate.[9]

The first troops went ashore August 25, where they were met by Habib and all the diplomatic and press corps of the area. The role of the MNF as a neutral peacekeeping body was quickly established. Upon securing the port area, the Marine commander ran up the Lebanese flag, instead of hoisting the American colors. This distinction was duly noticed in the Arab press.[10] Marine forces went ashore with only personal weapons and light crew-served machine guns. No weapons were loaded, except for several designated marksmen standing by prepared to engage targets at the discretion of commissioned officers.[11]

Evacuation of the PLO began that morning as 1,066 Palestinian fighters loaded onto the Greek vessel *Sol Georgious*, and by the end of the evacuation a total of 6,436 Palestinians had been withdrawn. By September 3, all PLO and Syrian forces had been evacuated.

In Washington, Mr. Weinberger insisted that the MNF had now achieved its purpose and that it should be withdrawn at once.[12] The President agreed, and on September 10, the MAU was ordered to withdraw from Beirut only 16 days into its 30-day mission. That day Colonel Mead received calls from both President Reagan and the Secretary of Defense complimenting him and his Marines on a job well done.[13]

The early departure created severe problems, however, on the political level. Ambassador Habib had given assurances to the PLO leadership that the U.S. force would stay for 30 days, the IDF would withdraw, and the remaining refugees would be protected. Both the Lebanese Government and the United States provided these assurances.[14] The Pentagon's conclusion that their mission was complete would prove fatally unfounded.

### Phase II—The Peacekeeper's Return

Before long the 32nd MAU learned of the assassination of Lebanon's charismatic President-elect Bashir Gemayel. Despite the Israeli pledge during the evacuation negotiations, the IDF rushed back into Beirut in the aftermath of the bombing. Under the watch of senior IDF officers, the Christian Phalangists took their revenge immediately over two days, September 16 and 17, by systematically killing about 700 refugees, largely women and children, left behind by the PLO fighters. The savage massacres of Shabra and Shatila stunned the world.[15]

With little discussion, but with an obvious sense of guilt, President Reagan next ordered the reintroduction of U.S. forces to the area. Although the situation was now significantly altered from the previous commitment, the Marines were reintroduced with the same mindset, same mission, and the same peacetime rules of engagement they had operated under during the PLO evacuation.

President Reagan convened a meeting of the NSC over a weekend in September to discuss the deployment. The Pentagon still had problems with reintroducing forces.[16] Weinberger states he was urged by the NSC to send in a multi-division contingent to enforce a separation between Syria and Israel. Such a proposal was put together by the NSC, but it was opposed by both Weinberger and Shultz.[17] In little mood to broker between the dissenting elements in his own Cabinet, Reagan communicated clearly that he wanted something done.[18] Mr. Weinberger was silent, but according to Shultz resisted implementing actions during subsequent meetings between the State Department and the Office of the Secretary of Defense.[19]

An officer familiar with this momentous decision and the continued resistance from Weinberger and the Pentagon noted that they "had not been able to avoid a deployment into Lebanon, but they did ensure that any deployment would be kept small, militarily noncommittal, and ready to be withdrawn as soon as politically possible.[20]

"Cribbing" off the NSDD that directed the deployment, the crucial mission statement for the MAU was largely written by the European Command (EUCOM) staff itself, and was closely reviewed by senior officers including General Rogers.[21] The mission statement was closely coordinated with the Joint Staff and the Secretary of Defense. The mission was detailed as follows:

To establish an environment which will permit the LAF to carry out their responsibilities in the Beirut Area. When directed, USCINCEUR will introduce U.S. Forces as part of a multinational force presence in the Beirut area to occupy and secure positions along a designated section of the line from south of the BIA to a position in the vicinity of the Presidential Palace; be prepared to protect U.S. Forces; and on order, conduct retrograde operations as required.[22]

The Marines landed in Beirut on September 29, 1982. They were assigned positions in and around the Beirut International Airport (BIA), which was specifically selected by the Defense Department because it presented the least exposed of the military sectors being allotted to the MNF. The French took up positions in downtown Beirut and its labyrinth of streets and alleys. The French had a different perception of their mission, they "kicked ass" when they arrived and maintained a firm posture that brooked no nonsense in their sector. As Eric Hammel wrote later, "They were never loved nor even admired, but they were respected."[23] The Italians got the worst of the lot and were assigned the slums and three major refugee camps.

The Marine position at the BIA was hardly a resort. It was an area visited by extensive fighting during the past several years. Buildings around the airport had been used by fighting forces from both sides during the combat operations of the previous year. Many destroyed vehicles and numerous minefields would have to be cleared to make the area usable.

During the month of October, the Marines stayed busy with their internal guard requirements and local security patrols. Reaction from the Lebanese populace was generally favorable, and several MNF intramural sporting events were staged. There were little official MNF interaction and little political-military coordination in the absence of Ambassador Habib as the tour of the 32nd MAU came to a close. Colonel Mead and his 32nd MAU, properly proud of their role in providing for a measure of stability, were relieved by Colonel Thomas M. Stokes and the 24th MAU on November 1, 1982.

The Marine's mission was expanded on November 1, to authorize motorized and foot patrols. The mission was again extended, at the request of the Lebanese president, on November 11, to permit the Marines to train the LAF. The authority for this change was spelled out in NSDD 64, which authorized limited noncombat-related support (training and supplies) and directed the MAU to begin patrols in Christian-dominated East Beirut.[24] Training in general military subjects, physical fitness training, live-fire exercises, and antimechanized operations, began on December 13. Some students of the Marine deployment have noted that this seemingly sensible training mission inadvertently compromised the neutrality the Marines strived so hard to maintain.[25]

The MAU was relieved in place by the 22nd MAU, with Colonel Mead returning once again to Lebanon on February 15, 1983. Diplomatic efforts proceeded apace, that is, at a slow pace. The terrorist threat was gauged higher as factional violence in the area increased, and appropriate precautions were taken. The Marines felt exposed and knew that their vulnerabilities were apparent to the local Moslems. "The Marines continued to perceive that their best defense was their posture of neutrality," so that the Moslem perception of U.S. neutrality was actively sought.[26]

The Ides of March were not kind to the MNF. An Italian foot patrol was attacked on March 15. A hand grenade was thrown at a Marine patrol on the 16th, and the Italian command post fired on the 17th. A French paratrooper was wounded that same day. Random attacks continued through early April. A sense of doom rose, but no one accurately predicted the next step. A light van, previously stolen from the U.S. embassy, was returned on April 18 by an unknown assailant who slipped past a sleeping Lebanese guard outside the building. The van was parked immediately in front of the embassy. It contained a 2,000-pound gas-enhanced bomb which demolished and collapsed the front portion of the eight-floor structure. The explosion killed 63 occupants, including 17 Americans. Four of the dead were U.S. Marines and several were CIA representatives. The MAU immediately sent its quick reaction force for security around the devastated embassy building.

The 24th MAU, commanded by Colonel Tim Geraghty arrived a month later, on May 30 1983. The relief in place went smoothly, and the new MAU immediately began mobile and foot patrols. The 24th MAU moved into the same general buildings and cantonment arrangement as the 32nd MAU. It did not merely accept the defensive arrangements of the preceding command, however, and industriously applied itself to improving local defensive measures by filling 500,000 sandbags and laying 10,000 feet of wire to enhance its security.[27]

The MAU continued an active patrolling schedule, and Colonel Geraghty proposed to the MNF Military Committee on June 20 that LAF personnel accompany his patrols.[28] This step was approved and initiated the same week, indicating the erroneous assumption that the LAF was multi-factional and confessionally neutral remained. The program of cross training with the LAF and other contingents of the MNF continued as the remainder of the month passed quietly.

This period of quiet was rudely shattered in mid-July by rocket and mortar shelling from Druze elements believed under the control of Walid Jumblatt's Progressive Socialist Party (PSP). A total of twelve shells or rockets landed inside the Marine perimeter at the BIA on July 22, wounding two Marines. Foot patrols in the Hay es Salaam area were subjected to verbal taunts, and shots were fired at the Marines from beyond the fence surrounding the airport area.

The remainder of the month of August should have dispelled any concept of neutrality that remained in Beirut. The MAU received rocket fire on August 8 and on August 10. Later that day the entire airport was subjected to a rocket barrage, and the airport was closed. The MAU fired 81mm illumination rounds over the suspected locations of the firing sites to warn off the attackers.

Outside the BIA area, fierce fighting between Christians and Druze, Druze and LAF, LAF and Amal militia was raging. Everyone was preparing to scramble for advantage as the IDF prepared to pull out. Fighting in around Beirut continued to escalate. In a single two-day period over 100 rounds of 82mm mortar and 122mm rocket fire landed in or around the airport. Marines returned fire only when targets were readily identifiable, only in self-defense, and ceased firing when the threat stopped directing fire at them per their rules of engagement.

Still, by late August a concerted effort was being made to target the Marine force. Druze mortar fire killed two Marines and wounded another twelve in a single day. Later that day, "Marine artillery fired in anger for the first time."[29] For the last several days of August, Marine positions were under intermittent attack and harassing rifle and rocket-propelled grenade fire. On August 31 Marines fired 155mm fire on a suspected PSP position that was shelling the Ministry of Defense, where the American Office of Military Cooperation (OMC) was situated. Violence was breaking out everywhere in Beirut. To preclude casualties, Colonel Geraghty stopped foot patrols in the surrounding area, trading off the intelligence and initiative for a reduced exposure.

During the first week of September the LAF assembled forces to seize areas that the IDF would withdraw from. As the IDF withdrew, the Druze prepared to seize the crucial Shouf mountain spur overlooking Beirut and the Marines. The LAF did not do well in its first efforts, and remained on the defense in a small garrison at Suq al Gharb. The Marines continued to get hit, and a rocket barrage on September 5 killed two and wounded two Marines. According to the official Marine history, a total of 120 rounds of various ordnance had exploded at the airport during early September.[30]

On the seventh of September, after three rounds impacted inside the Marine lines, the MAU returned fire with a battery sheaf of six rounds of 155mm howitzer fire. The next day Marines answered in earnest again with artillery and naval gunfire when three rockets landed within 200 meters of two visiting Marine generals.

These events preceded what many military observers consider to be the crucial event, and the precursor to the tragic barracks bombing. Special Envoy McFarlane had gone back to Washington and engineered another change to the Marine mission that authorized the use of naval gunfire to support the LAF at Suq al Gharb. The authority, however, was delegated solely to the MAU commander based on his assessment as to whether the LAF could hold the garrison.

McFarlane and his military advisor, BGen Stiner, pressured Geraghty to authorize the naval gunfire. The MAU Commander resisted for several days, fully cognizant that the gunfire would expose his troops to any retaliation. He reportedly had several acrimonious exchanges with McFarlane. "We'll pay the price," said the MAU Commander prophetically during one such argument, "We'll get slaughtered down here."[31]

Though opposed by Weinberger, Mr. Reagan had authorized use of naval gunfire to fire upon non-Lebanese forces attacking Suq al Gharb. The Suq al Gharb had been redefined as essential to the Marine's own defense, but the real purpose was to support the Lebanese with a show of solidarity. But the authority to employ the Navy's guns was conditional because it delegated the decision to the MAU commander if he felt the post was in imminent danger of falling.[32] The change in the rules of engagement was not written solely to give the commander in the field greater authority. It was colored by attempts on the House floor to get the War Powers Act invoked. The language in the NSDD was a cover story designed to avoid triggering any Congressional interference, and a compromise between the NSC and the Pentagon.[33]

Colonel Geraghty resisted entreaties by Mr. McFarlane and the Lebanese to provide gunfire support for over a week. Eventually, he relented when he heard that the Syrians had moved up some armor to assist the Druze. The Navy fired a total of 360 five-inch shells into the Shouf. The shaky LAF held their ground. Many have attempted to paint this incident as the watershed event in the expansion of the Marines mission from one of pure "presence" and neutral peacekeeping to an engaged ally of the Christian Gemayel government. Geraghty himself is the originator of this argument; "The firing we did in support of the LAF up at Suq al Gharb, that clearly changed our role. It's a milestone, no question about it in my opinion."[34]

This ignores the earlier artillery missions and a major naval gunfire mission executed on the night of September 16. That night, in response to Druze shelling of the Ministry of Defense and the American ambassador's residence, the frigates *Bowen* and *Rogers* fired a total of 72 rounds in six separate fire missions. The Navy fired an additional 150 rounds over two days, September 20 and 21, at other suspected Druze positions.

One of the few clear points raised by the admittedly lengthy historical narrative preceding this point is to show that the Druze and Amal militia had been targeting the Marines for some time at this point. The Marines had received several hundred rounds of incoming mortar and rocket fire. Furthermore, the Marines had responded in kind several times and were credited for several successful fire missions resulting in PSP or Amal casualties. Additionally, in the aftermath of the battles in the Shouf, there was an increase in sniper activity around BIA early in October. The Marines countered with specially trained snipers, and publicly displayed their capabilities to the press on October 15.[35] The Marines were passive observers no longer.

### Bombing Aftermath

Little more than a week later, the Reagan Lebanese policy literally went up in smoke in a funeral pyre. Once again, American troops paid the price for poor decisions and bureaucratic politics manufactured in Washington. To many it was a very familiar and almost predictable tragedy. "The peacekeeping operation in Lebanon was doomed from the start," notes a typical observer, "Plagued by murky objectives and restrictive rules of engagement, failure was almost inevitable, placing the Marines in such an ambiguous and vulnerable position certainly invited trouble."[36]

In the aftermath of the bombing, Weinberger proposed establishing a commission to study the tragedy. He appointed four military officers and one civilian defense expert to what became known as the Long Commission named after its Chairman, Admiral Robert Long, USN (retired). The Commission was not restricted with a narrow charter, and made several careful observations regarding the mission, supervision, chain of command, and local security procedures. The group was chartered on November 7, and had a classified report prepared for the President by December 20. A carefully worded 143-page unclassified version was ultimately released. While the Commission's report could hardly be considered a whitewash, it supported Weinberger's major points regarding the vague "presence" mission assigned to the Marines, and the lack of a vigorously prosecuted diplomatic effort.[37]

Naturally, George Shultz was not happy with the Commission's report, a thinly veiled attack on the foreign policy process.[38] The sparing between the Defense Department and Foggy Bottom continued. Eventually, Weinberger, with the advice of several senior military officers, reduced the Pentagon's lessons from both Vietnam and Beirut into a set of criteria to guide future uses of America's combat force. This criteria eventually became widely known as the Weinberger doctrine.

Mr. Weinberger's criteria on when force should be used were reduced to six relatively simple steps. Force should be used only:

1. In support of vital U.S. interests.
2. With the full and wholehearted intent of "winning."
3. With clearly defined political and military objectives.
4. When circumstances change, reassessments must determine if force is still required.
5. With "reasonable assurance" of public and Congressional support.
6. Only as a last resort, when all other means have failed.

The doctrine reflected the Pentagon's view of the American Way of War, and the collective lessons of both Vietnam and Beirut. The doctrine was not acceptable to the State Department and Mr. Shultz countered with several speeches and articles about matching force to diplomacy.[39] Both Shultz and Weinberger continued to debate the necessary conditions for successful military interventions in the public domain. While couched in generalized terms, the debate was really over whose hands were bloody over the disaster in Lebanon.

## CLARITY OF PURPOSE

As distilled and absorbed by the military, the overarching lesson from Beirut involves the necessity of clearly defining political and military objectives. The military, particularly the Marine leadership, took a defensive attitude after the tragic bombing. The primary reason for the tragedy was shifted from one of poor military security to the ill-defined mission of "presence." In his Congressional testimony, General Kelley noted that this was not really a military mission and one not found in military doctrine or taught in the Service's schools.[40]

The collective memory of the Pentagon, as represented in its formal investigation and findings of the disastrous bombing, established this view. However, this lesson is too convenient. This view shields the local commander in Lebanon, but also shifts blame well away from the senior military leadership at OSD and EUCOM, which molded the parameters under which they were deployed. The collective embodiment of the Defense Department's lessons learned from Lebanon is found in the statements of Secretary of Defense and the Commandant of the Marine Corps General P. X. Kelley. Weinberger leaves little doubt about the ongoing struggle between the NSC and the Defense Department over the employment of U.S. forces. Weinberger is especially critical over the NSC's "great eagerness to have a force even without any defined objective."[41]

The original proposal, developed by the NSC, was to have a large force composed of several divisions to physically separate all warring parties. Mr. Weinberger resisted this attempt, which he found consistent with "the passionate desire to use our military" on the part of the NSC staff.[42] He opposed the idea strenuously and was supported by the JCS. His reasons, in his memoirs, focus on the lack of specificity of the mission. "Its objectives were stated in the fuzziest possible terms, and then later, when that objective was "clarified" the newly defined objective was demonstrably unobtainable." The JCS also opposed a renewed MNF effort, "because without a clearly defined objective, determining the proper size and armament and rules of engagement for such a force is difficult at best."[43] Yet Mr. Weinberger was actually resisting sending *any* forces.

What Mr. Weinberger memoirs do not describe is any contributions he made to refining the mission statement to ensure the Pentagon understood what was required of them. Nor does he describe his own efforts to offer alternatives or risk assessments to assist the NSC in properly constituting a mission, or the proper size and guidelines for the intervention. Mr. Reagan and the NSC were aware of Pentagon resistance to the deployment, and saw both OSD and the Joint Staff as obstructionists saddled with the infamous Vietnam Syndrome. Thus, their voice in policy making circles was ignored because of the perception that they were not part of any solution. The objective remained clear to Mr. Reagan, the NSC, and the State Department, yet no one knew how to get there. The Pentagon's resistance did not ameliorate this problem.

After the decision was made to deploy the force, Mr. Weinberger continued efforts to define the mission in the narrowest of terms, limiting the size and the capability of the force.

What was the mission? The Reagan administration, contrary to critics, had defined a political objective and end state in Lebanon. A sovereign and peaceful Lebanon, secure within its own borders, without either civil war or foreign forces, was the objective.[44]  The NSC failed to translate that objective into a strategy comprised of ways and means that would contribute to the desired end state.  No one matched the political objective to the various efforts being executed in the Nation's name.

The Marines on the ground in Lebanon perceived their mission as one of presence.  However, "presence" is not assigned as the mission or the intent.  The action verb and overall intent is to "establish an environment" in which the government of Lebanon could reconstitute itself and assert rule and order over Beirut and eventually the rest of the country.  A key element of the mission statement called for reestablishing the LAF.  This implies a function of "nation building" and security assistance, which the military disdained since Vietnam.

For many reasons, the Marines defined their role in both neutral and passive terms as one of "presence."  In his testimony after the bombing, General Kelley stated, "Our basic mission is presence, and the logical question is how do you define presence. It is not a classic military mission."  This term was interpreted by the Marines to mean that they had to be visible to provide "a backdrop which would be conducive to the stability of Lebanon, we had to be seen by the people."[45]  To be seen, the Marines had established patrols and regular contacts with various factions. They developed links to the communities through minor civic action projects and a medical assistance program.

The Marines imply that the "presence" mission precluded massive fortifications to defend themselves.  The argument is that sealing off the airport from traffic, and isolating the Marines from the populace, was inconsistent with their assigned mission.  In his testimony, General Kelley claimed it was impossible to establish a hard point defense consistent with the mission statement as perceived, and the position of the BLT building poised as it was in the midst of a busy international airport, a facility "literally crawling with civilians."[46]

In retrospect, the excuse that fortifications were inconsistent with the mission, and the view that the Marines were expected to "tough it out" while exposed to mortar, rocket, and RPG fire seems lame.  The perception of presence and neutrality should have worn off after the bombing at the American embassy in April, and far greater efforts taken to protect the Marines as violence increased in August.  This perception of the mission is inconsistent with the other portions of the overall strategy in Lebanon, including the training and equipping of the LAF, which the Marines were aware of, and participating in.  The OMC was proving tanks, armored personnel carriers, and howitzers.  In retrospect, the delusion of neutrality was inconsistent with these other efforts.  Later, Colonel Fintel, who headed the security assistance project, noted, "In Lebanon, we had a peacekeeping mission and a force-building mission and the two were inherently contradictory."[47]

Other observers point to the training program initiated at the Marine request as the key point where the contradictions began.  Eric Hammel notes that the December training program was "among the most crucial decisions taken during the entire experience in Beirut, for it inextricably linked the intentionally visible Marines to the fate of the LAF, and by extensions identified the Marines and their government completely with the fate of the Gemayel government."[48]

Others still point to McFarlane's insistence of providing naval gunfire support to the LAF in the Suq al Gharb on September 19. John Lehman, the Secretary of the Navy at that time points out that naval gunfire had already been employed on September 16, and that it would be impossible for the many Moselm positions to have been able to distinguish between gunfire intended for self-defense and that intended to support the LAF. "There were those who claimed that these actions cost us the protection of our neutral status," noted Lehman, but the Marines were seen by all factions as combatants and therefore "fair game" long before September. "As for the policy of neutrality," Lehman adds, "it was difficult to understand what our mission could be, if it was not to support the legal Lebanese government, however hopeless."[49]

In sum, it was not that the purpose of the deployment was not clear. The military resisted being integrated with the other instruments of national power, in a subordinate position, in an operational environment inconsistent with its preferred paradigm. The Pentagon did not agree with the policy, at best just misinterpreted it, and at worst provided half-hearted support.

## PLAYING TO WIN

The U.S. military was not permitted to carry out its mission in Lebanon in accordance with its historical and deeply rooted preference for "carrying the war to the enemy," and seeking "the destruction of the enemy's armed forces and his ability to wage war."[50] Offensive operations against an opposing force, playing by the sort of rules the Pentagon's military culture understands, was not appropriate in Lebanon. This should not have ruled out an effective role for the Marines in support of the diplomatic mission and the MNF.

However, many within the U.S. military did not walk away with that as a lesson. The lesson heard from many is that the Marines should never have been sent. This is true, in the sense that the policy and strategy should have been developed prior to the deployment. In the military's eyes, they once again found themselves hamstrung by politicians and meddlers who failed to understand the inherent nature of war or military force. As detailed in the Weinberger doctrine, if you cannot enter into a situation with sufficient force, and with the clear intention of "winning," then the military should not be sent. The last thing the military wanted was another quagmire where they became shooting ducks while diplomats dallied. The military did not want to find itself in another swamp, incrementally adding firepower, to achieve some nebulous political objective.

Another aspect very reminiscent of Vietnam is the myth that the Marines had their "hands tied behind their backs" with restrictive rules of engagement. "Because of ROE restrictions, the sentries' weapons were not loaded," noted one military writer basing his assessment from the published Long Commission.[51] What does not come out in the record is the fact that the rules of engagement (ROE) were controlled by the military at EUCOM, not the diplomatic corps.  Furthermore, the ROE did not actually preclude insertion of magazines in weapons.  The ROE did not a preclude sufficient defensive measures, obstacles, or an alert guard force.  Much of this was locally controlled, or alterable within the military chain of command.  The Long Commission faulted the local commanders for adjusting their own security steps, despite the great tensions that existed in Beirut since August.[52]

Colonel Geraghty was asked by both the Long Commission and by Congressional investigators whether or not his rules of engagement were derived from his own perceptions of the mission, or forced down by an indifferent outside source such as the State Department.  The MAU commander admitted, "No sir, in all honesty, it was my own perception."[53]  However, many other writers continue to insist that the Marines were not permitted to defend themselves.  One Marine veteran recalled, "When asked to improve the position, the answer was: denied.  We requested to build tank ditches around the building, we were told no.  Officials didn't want to send the impression that we were hunkering down."[54]  Such comments do not square with Colonel Geraghty's testimony and have not been proven by anything in the historical record to date.

## CIVIL-MILITARY RELATIONS

The term civil-military relations in this book goes beyond the more traditional view of the proper relationship between civilian policy makers and military leaders who execute policy.  While civilian control of the military is a given under our system, effective policy making and implementation goes past just a simple dominance of policy over the military.  A proper civil-military working relationship makes policy implementation feasible.  An honest and candid exchange of viewpoints is needed before the statesman and the general make that first supreme judgment.

It is during the course of the interaction between policy and military considerations that the ground is set for success.  Good decisions are neither the result of a purely political or purely military viewpoint.  Bad policy dooms the conduct of military operations.  In fact, a brilliant military strategy will rarely salvage a poorly defined objective or an inappropriate policy.

Within the context of this effort, civil-military relations addresses the broader scope of the management of the inherent tensions between political considerations and the military instrument.  It includes the provision for an adequate voice for military considerations during the development of policy.  Additionally, it also addresses the proper interaction of political and military considerations, since "policy cannot be a tyrant" and may have to be radically changed in light of military factors.[55]

Civil-military relations in this country have been tenuous during our major conflicts.  Lebanon was not a major conflict, but the seeds of discontent and mistrust planted during Vietnam were in full bloom.  The degree of mistrust between the

Pentagon's military leadership and the White House threatened effective civilian control and the proper integration of military viewpoints during the development of policy aims and the corresponding strategy in this case. This is not the first time that ineffective communications or mistrust at senior strategy levels has hampered military operations in the field. We should assume that it will not be the last.

The concept of civilian control of the military is taken for granted in the United States, and it is not even defined in the American military literature. In fact, some naively believe that "the absence of a definition has served us well."[56] Yet, the specter of Vietnam was a large hangover on the U.S. military, and the absence of any concrete perspective on the proper consideration of civilian and military viewpoints is something that cannot ever be taken for granted. The debacle of Beirut was, in large part, a product of poor relationships established after Vietnam.

By 1983, a decade had passed since most troops had pulled out of Vietnam, but the hangover remained. The American military's reluctance to use force in anything less than a clear-cut situation was a stolid orthodoxy, and the Army was more extreme and cautionary of the Services.[57] Weinberger parroted the "never again" attitude of his military subordinates.[58] This significantly contributed to the manifest failure to develop an adequate matching of policy and strategy during the ill-fated Lebanon intervention.

The Reagan Presidency was marred by a management style that failed to decisively resolve viewpoints from various departments prior to implementation. The Defense Department was well represented in this discussions by Mr. Weinberger, who was a "civilian front man" for the Joint Chiefs and shared their bitterness over Vietnam and their reluctance to get entangled. Mr. Weinberger's perspectives on the use of force were very much out of step with the active interventionist attitudes of the President and his symmetric interpretations of containment. Accordingly, he found himself cut out of some national security decisions.[59]

Mr. Reagan's management style emphasized a Cabinet-oriented approach, which left his principal deputies to design and implement programs to satisfy policy decisions.[60] Any lack of consensus was overlooked, and Mr. Reagan appears to have been reluctant to make clear decisions. Thus, his NSC harmonized decision memoranda into overly negotiated compromises. In the end "the lowest common denominator prevailed."[61]

The military leadership should not have accepted the lowest common denominator as the precondition for inserting the sons of American taxpayers into Lebanon as the "honest brokers" of Hades. The military leaders did not stand up, just like in Vietnam. The Joint Chiefs were all opposed to the reintroduction of the Marines, but doubted their opposition would have changed the President's mind. General Vessey, the Chairman of the JCS, eventually relented to dispatching the Marines. "It's not that we decided to go along with it," he said later, "we obeyed our orders."[62] Such a lame excuse reflects the seriously flawed nature of civil-military relations of the times.

## POPULAR SUPPORT

The issue of popular support was much more subtle during the Marine deployment in Beirut. In complete contradiction to Vietnam, the press got along well with the Marines and public support was high.[63] Declaring war or mobilizing the Reserves were not appropriate or germane either.

Yet, the intervention into Lebanon once again initiated the age-old tug-of-war between the Executive and Legislative branches over primacy in national security. The clash over the Congressional power to declare war versus the Executive power to initiate action in defense of national interests is older than the Republic itself. The Congress was slow to flex its constitutional muscle over the deployment of the Marines. The PLO evacuation was successful, and the horrible refugee camp massacres required some response. As the deployment extended into 1983, however, a partisan debate ensued. Congressional Democrats were quick to compare the extension of the Marine mission as "the first step towards another Vietnam."[64]

Opponents of the Administration threatened to impose provisions of the War Powers resolution instituted in 1973 over President Nixon's veto.[65] The War Powers Act in many ways represents the Congressional version of the Vietnam Syndrome.[66] The act represents the lessons Congress learned from the conflict in Southeast Asia. "Never again" will they be duped into another war or permit the country to drift into any quagmires.

Several policy experts, with Pentagon, NSC, and State Department experience, have challenged the myth that Congress was somehow duped into supporting the Vietnam War and never had any say in either its scope or duration. One, Dr. R. Turner, a former official at both State and OSD, finds the statute "essentially a fraud designed to absolve Congress of responsibility" for Vietnam.[67]

Yet ignoring the Congress only builds problems on the domestic front, while the President and his staff should be focusing on the troops they have placed in harm's way. Unfortunately, Congressional input into the policy making process in Lebanon was next to nil. The Administration attempted to placate the Legislature and took steps to characterize the Marine mission as benignly as possible to preclude interference. Former Secretary of the Navy, Mr. John Lehman, is sharply critical of the Administration's approach in trying to walk a tight rope between Congressional interference and its desire to play a role in Lebanon. In his view the Administration was trapped by verbal acrobatics it had undertaken to avoid congressional restrictions:

Though everyone knew that the Marines were never neutral, in attempting to avoid the strictures of the War Powers Act and satisfy the delusions of the State Department, the military chain of command institutionally forgot the reality of the Marine's true status as combatants, whatever the political rhetoric. Catastrophe was sure to result.[68]

Both Turner and Lehman have written extensively on the War Powers Act and its influence in Lebanon. They are both especially critical of Congress's callous disregard for creating incentives for terrorists to pegging timelines to troop deployment. Both underscore that Congress was warned by several officials including the Commandant of the Marines that imposing deadlines on the Marines would stimulate more attacks. General Kelley's testimony was ignored and Congress, in effect, put a bounty on the lives of the Marines. "The tragic loss of the 241 Marines in Beirut," Turner writes, "ought to serve as evidence of this predictable consequence and Congressional respect for their memory ought to lead to prompt revision of this unconstitutional and dangerous statute."[69]

Out of this experience, the U.S. military relearned that popular support is necessary to maintain freedom of action in difficult circumstances, but Congressional interference can be fatal. To preclude this, support should be gained in advance.

## ASSESSMENT

Lessons learned about Lebanon and the tragedy of the Marine unit have turned into a "round robin of recrimination."[70] The only clear record seems to be that once again the wrong lessons, if any, have been learned from the debacle. The intervention in Lebanon did have many similar factors between it and the dismal experience of Vietnam.[71] But not all of these were correctly sensed or applied.

The false lesson about the clarity of purpose and the vagueness of the "presence mission" masks the real lesson that there was a lack of congruence between what we were trying to accomplish in terms of a political end state and the role and tasks assigned to the military. The clarity of purpose issue also hides the failure of the policy making apparatus to evaluate, and direct adjustments to if necessary, the proposed military actions taken by the Defense Department.

With respect to the establishment of clear objectives, both political and military, the Pentagon bears a great burden. Both the Secretary of Defense and the Joint Chiefs resisted the deployment of the Marines as part of the MNF. The President overruled the military advice rendered by the Pentagon, without really ever getting a full hearing for their position. Rather than providing full support after the President's decision had been rendered, the JCS resisted the task further. The Pentagon defined a narrow mission for the Marines, ensured they were deployed in inappropriate size or capability, and limited their freedom of action in support of the policy objectives sought by the Administration.

Had the military been able to throw off the Vietnam syndrome and taken energetic steps to deploy a force properly sized and equipped to the mission dictated by the political situation, the ultimate tragedy of October, 1983 *might* have been avoided. Rather than see the Marines employed decisively in support of the Lebanese government, the Defense establishment sought to preserve an illusion of neutrality that permitted the Marine unit to "hunker down" in BIA and wait for a window of opportunity to withdraw them. Waiting out the situation also exposed the Marines to the risk that some pro-Syrian or Iranian group would exploit the opportunity.

Ultimately, the failure in Lebanon belongs in Washington, and should be shared by the full membership of the NSC. The military prefers to define the problem as simply a matter of fuzzy objectives or an improper use of military force to support diplomacy. Actually, as shown earlier, the political objective is clear. The problem lies in developing a military strategy that could buy sufficient time to generate a viable Lebanese government, with the necessary supporting institutions (which includes a vastly improved LAF) to govern the greater Beirut area. Such a task should not have been perceived as requiring a neutral stance. In fact, an activist stance to establish a satisfactory environment for both the Lebanese government and the LAF to assert itself was the mission. The military failed to sense this or carry it out.

Much of the handwashing over the bombing places great store over the need for the perception of neutrality. It is true that such perceptions were crucial in the first phase of the deployment during the PLO evacuation. However, the situation during the second phase in Lebanon is dramatically different and called for a different strategy. The Pentagon failed to recognize the political implications of the massacres at the refugee camps and the resulting resentment generated by those factions sympathetic to the Palestinians.

The illusion of neutrality, which clearly influenced both Colonel Geraghty's tactical dispositions and General Kelley's defense of his decisions, goes past Shabra and Shatila. Over the course of the previous year, the U.S. military was providing substantial amounts of training, ammunition, and equipment for the LAF. The LAF was long seen as an instrument of Christian political control in Lebanon. The American support provided by the OMC identified the United States with the present regime in power. The Marines contributed to the reduction of their own perceptions of neutrality by conducting training of the LAF, by collocating fighting positions with LAF units, by the sharing of intelligence, and by providing the LAF with vast quantities of ammunition.

In sum, there is little credence to be given to the charge that the mission was poorly defined or an inevitable failure. A solution was feasible, if the proper means were placed at the disposal of the commander on the scene. What had happened though was something in between. One Representative hit the nail on the head: "If we are there to keep peace, we are far too few. If we are there to die, then we are far too many."[72] Since the local tactical commander accurately sensed that he had insufficient forces to accomplish anything reasonably approaching a solution to the political environment he found himself in, he was reduced to limiting his vulnerabilities. The "illusion of neutrality" was his answer, and the loss of 241 souls the result.

The Pentagon's lessons are found in Mr. Weinberger's six criteria. Force is only to be used as a last resort, for vital interests, for clear political and military objectives, when the conditions permit the military to be deployed with the wholehearted intent of winning, and with some expectation of support from Congress and the American people. Beirut met none of these. The U.S. military collectively agreed with Pulitzer Prize-winning journalist Thomas Friedman, who spent seven years in Lebanon and

Israel, and empathized with the beleaguered Marines "sent to Lebanon by politicians who put them in an impossible situation and then blamed them when things went badly wrong."[73]

## NOTES

1. Robert C. McFarlane, "Lessons of the Beirut Bombing," unpublished article, dated October 23, 1993.  Mr. McFarlane, a retired Marine officer, served as Special Envoy to Lebanon, and later as National Security Advisor to President Reagan.  Mr. McFarlane wrote this paper for a symposium on Marine peacekeeping operations at the Marine Corps University, Quantico, Virginia.

2. Richard K. Betts, *Soldiers, Statesmen and Cold War Crises*, New York: Columbia University, Press, 1991,  p. 218.

3. Stephen E. Ambrose, *Rise to Globalism*, 7th ed., New York: Penguin, 1993, pp. 303–311; Lou Cannon, *President Reagan: The Role of a Lifetime*, New York: Simon & Schuster, 1991, pp. 390–395.

4. For some deeper background on U.S. interests in the region see Alexander Haig, *Caveat*, New York: Macmillan, 1984, pp. 317–352.  A very good overview of the history and policy objectives of the Reagan Administration during this time period is also found in George P. Shultz, *Turmoil and Triumph, My Six Years As Secretary of State*, New York: Scribner's, 1993, pp. 43–115.

5. Roy Gutman, "Battle Over Lebanon," *Foreign Service Journal*, June 1984, p. 28. Also Ralph Hallenbeck, *The Use of Military Force as an Instrument of U.S. Foreign Policy*, New York: Praegar, 1991, p. 14.  Hallenbeck was in the operations directorate of the U.S. European Command during the Marine intervention.  He describes the argument between the NSC and the Pentagon as a prelude to the Weinberger doctrine.  The Pentagon insisted that if a declaration of war was not warranted, then forces were not warranted citing the drift into Vietnam.

6. Hallenbeck, *Military Force*, p. 15.

7. Ibid., p. 15.

8. Benis Frank, *U.S. Marines in Lebanon, 1982–1984*, Washington, DC: U.S. Marine Corps, Government Printing Office, 1987, p. 10.

9. Message from Commandant of the Marine General Robert H. Barrow to the 32nd MAU, cited in Frank, *Marines in Lebanon*, p. 13.

10. Frank, p. 35.

11. Battalion Landing Team 1/8, After Action Report, September, 1982, p. 2.  See also Frank,  p. 21.

12. Betts, *Soldiers, Statesmen and Cold War Crises*, p. 218.  Caspar W. Weinberger, *Fighting for Peace*, New York: Warner Books, 1990, pp. 150–152; Hallenbeck, p. 16. Hallenbeck states the decision came in a surprise speech by the President on September 1. Colonel McFarlane asserts that a formal decision had never been achieved and that Mr. Weinberger issued the order to withdraw the Marines by himself, McFarlane, "Lessons of the Beirut Bombing," p. 3.  A formal documented decision does not appear to exist.

13. Frank, p. 35.

14. The importance of these assurances has been largely overlooked. Failure to comply with the agreement weakened U.S. credibility and generated mistrust over the U.S.'s alleged neutral stance. Perry, *Four Stars*, p. 307; Hallenbeck, *Military Force*, p. 21; Shultz, *Turmoil and Triumph*, pp. 102–103; Eric Hammel, *The Root,* Pacifica, CA: Pacifica Press, 1985, pp. 15–16.

15. Hammel, *The Root*, p. 34; Daniel P. Bolger, *Americans at War 1975–1986: An Era of Violent Peace*, Novato, CA: Presidio, 1988, p. 195.

16. Perry, *Four Stars*, p. 309.

17. An option to send a force of approximately 15,000 American troops similar to the American intervention in Lebanon in 1958 was developed and rejected. As Dr. Hallenbeck describes the decision, "The lessons of Vietnam were too fresh in the minds of all concerned." Hallenbeck, *Military Force*, p. 29. See also Gutman, "Battle Over Lebanon," p. 31; John Prados, *Keepers of the Keys: A History of the National Security Council From Truman to Bush*, New York: William Morrow, 1990, p. 471; and by Weinberger, *Fighting for Peace*, p. 151.

18. Roy Gutman, "Battle Over Lebanon," p. 31.

19. Shultz, *Turmoil and Triumph*, p. 107. Shultz criticized the Pentagon for placing inordinate conditions on its participation to drag out the debate. "When you don't want to do something, agree to do it, but with such an impossible set of conditions and on such a preposterously gigantic scale that the outcome will be to do nothing."

20. Hallenbeck, *Military Force*, p. 30.

21. Ibid, pp. 30–33.

22. Department of Defense Commission on Beirut International Terrorist Attack, October 23, 1983 (Hereafter referred to as Long Commission Report), Washington, DC: December 20, 1983, p. 35; Hallenbeck, *Military Force*, p. 30.

23. Hammel, *The Root,* p. 36.

24. Hallenbeck, *Military Force*, p. 41.

25. Bolger, *Americans at War: An Era of Violent Peace*, p. 200.

26. Frank, p. 55. The "presence" mission became a tactic designed to minimize the Marine's exposure. This is not the result of shirking. The mission required an engaged posture, but the factional violence, small Marine force, and the nature of the positions around the airport imposed a greater degree of vulnerability than perceived in Washington.

27. Ibid., p. 72.

28. Hallenbeck, p. 77; Frank, p. 73.

29. Hallenbeck, p. 77; Frank, p. 78.

30. Frank, p. 83.

31. Quoted in Hammel, p. 220. The background over the development of NSDD 103 that authorized naval gunfire support on behalf of the LAF is found in Prados, *Keepers of the Keys*, p. 473. See also Hallenbeck, pp. 81–83.

32. Hammel, p. 218. Hallenbeck, p. 87.

33. Gutman, "Battle Over Lebanon," p. 32.

34. Frank, p. 89.

35. Frank, pp. 92–93; Hammel, pp. 276–277.

36. Donald M. Snow and Dennis M. Drew, *From Lexington to Desert Storm: War and Politics in the American Experience*, Armonk, NY: M. E. Sharpe, 1994, pp. 323–324.

37. Long Commission Report, p. 8. A condensed version of the Long Commission's conclusions and recommendations can be found in the appendices to Frank, pp. 172–177.

38. Shultz, *Turmoil and Triumph*, pp. 231–232.

39. Weinberger's doctrine was originally promulgated at the National Press Club, on November 28, 1984 in an address titled "The Uses of Military Power." The background and text of the speech can be found in Weinberger, *Fighting for Peace*, pp. 159–160, 445–457. Mr. Shultz criticized the inflexibility of the criteria in general terms in several speeches; George P. Shultz, "Diplomacy and Strength," Department of State Bulletin, October 1984, pp. 18–20, George P. Shultz, "Terrorism and the Modern World," Department of State Bulletin, December 1984, pp. 12–15; See also Shultz, *Turmoil and Triumph*, p. 345. For an overview of the advantages and disadvantages of the doctrine, see Alan N. Sabrosky and Robert L. Sloane, The Recourse to War: An Appraisal of the Weinberger Doctrine, Carlisle, PA: Strategic Studies Institute, U.S. Army War College, 1988.

40. General Kelley's Congressional statement is found as an appendix in Frank, *Marines In Lebanon*, pp. 163–171. See also Betts, p. 218. See also Mark Perry, *Four Stars*, pp. 325–326.

41. Weinberger, *Fighting for Peace*, pp. 152–159.

42. Weinberger, p. 151. Mr. Shultz also described the NSC staff as militaristic, but he also found the Pentagon far too reluctant to employ force effectively in hand with other instruments of national power, *Turmoil and Triumph*, p. 225.

43. Weinberger, p. 152.

44. Hallenbeck, pp. 36-37; Willis, pp. 101–102.

45. Kelley testimony in Frank, p. 110.

46. Ibid., p. 111.

47. Thomas L. Friedman, "Fair Game," *New York Times*, May 30, 1993,   p. 50.

48. Hammel, *The Root*, p. 57. General Trainor made the same point. Interview with General B. E. Trainor, January 11, 1994.

49. John Lehman, *Command of the Seas: A Personal Story*, New York: Scribner's, 1988, pp. 318–319.

50. Weigley, *The American Way of War*, p. 467.

51. Jeffrey W. Wright, "Terrorism: A Mode of Warfare," *Military Review*, October 1984, p. 35.

52. Long Commission, pp. 48–51, 137; U.S. Congress, HASC staff report, "Adequacy of U.S. Marine Corps Security in Beirut," 98th Congress, 1st session, Washington, DC: GPO, Dec. 19, 1983, p. 78. The House report indicates that weapons were not loaded nor magazines inserted because of a rash of accidental discharges by the Marines. The House report, coupled with the Marine's own historical account, highlights the problem. The Marines had suffered seven wounded of their own from these incidents, had wounded a member of the press in another. Additionally, a Marine accidently shot two Lebanese soldiers. An anti-tank weapon was also inadvertently fired and hit an airport control tower. This information was pointed out in an interview with Colonel J. B. Matthews,  December 9, 1993.

53. Bolger, *Americans at War*, pp. 190–191. HASC Report, "Adequacy of Security in Beirut," p. 78.

54. Major Charles Dallachie, BLT staff officer and a survivor of the bombing, quoted by Chris Lawson, "Beirut: Ten Years of Sorrow," *Navy Times*, October 25, 1993, p. 10.

55. Clausewitz, *On War*, p. 87.

56. James Locher, *Defense Organization: The Need for Change*, Staff Report to the Senate Armed Services Committee, Washington, DC: Government Printing Office, October 16, 1985, p. 44.

57. Betts, *Solders, Statesman and Cold War Crises*, p. 214.

58. Ibid.

59. Prados, p. 471.

60. Hallenbeck, p. 149.

61. Gutman, "Battle Over Lebanon," p. 30; Cannon, pp. 401–402, 435–436.

62. Perry, p. 309; Cannon quotes Vessey's assessment that the Joint Chiefs thought that the Marines could be pulled out in 60 days, pp. 408–409.

63. Friedman, "Fair Game," p. 50.

64. Robert F. Turner, *Repealing the War Powers Resolution: Restoring the Rule of Law in U.S. Foreign Policy*, McLean, VA: Brassey's Inc, 1991, p. 141.

65. For a history and critique of the War Powers Act, in addition to Turner, see John Lehman, *Making War: The 200-Year-Old Battle Between the President and the Congress Over How America Goes to War*, New York: Scribner's, 1992; and David Locke Hall, *The Reagan Wars: A Constitutional Perspective on War Powers and the Presidency*, Boulder, CO: Westview Press, 1991.

66. This is Harry G. Summers' claim, *On Strategy II: A Critical Analysis of the Persian Gulf War*, New York: Dell, 1992, p. 30.

67. Turner, pp. 158–160.

68. Lehman, p. 105.

69. Turner, pp. 148–149.

70. Gutman, "Battle Over Lebanon," p. 28.

71. Hallenbeck, pp. xii–xiii.

72. Representative Sam M. Gibbons, D-FL, quoted in Larry Pintak, *Beirut Outtakes*, Lexington, MA: Lexington Books, 1988, p. 1.

73. Friedman, "Fair Game," p. 50.

# 4

# The Storming of Panama: Preferred Paradigm Tested

In October 1989, the Bush Administration had yet to define itself. Its new national security team remained untested, but problems in Panama were ready to boil over. Congress was irate when neither the White House nor the Pentagon took any risks during an attempted coup against Manuel Noriega in September 1989.[1] Noriega had resisted intense pressure to stand aside and let democracy have a chance. Economic sanctions had been applied for over year and were having a telling effect on the Panamanian economy. The United States had waged a war of nerves with Noriega since he had appointed himself President. Matters escalated in 1989 to the point where Noriega claimed that a "state of war" existed between Panama and the United States.

The Administration vowed to be better prepared the next time an opportunity rose to deal with Noriega. The Pentagon, particularly the new JCS Chairman, General Colin Powell, took deliberate steps to ensure that U.S. interests in the region were protected.[2] This included replacing the Southern Command (SOUTHCOM) commander, General Frederick Woerner, a Latin American area expert, with the more activist General Maxwell Thurman. Thurman reinvigorated contingency planning and the alert status in the region with a series of plans and exercises that prepared his troops for the eventual showdown with Noriega and his entrenched cronies in the Panama Defense Force (PDF).[3]

Noriega eventually taxed the President's patience and U.S. credibility. On December 16, 1989, a Marine officer, Lieutenant Robert Paz, was shot and killed at a Panamanian roadblock. The same night a Navy officer and his wife were detained and assaulted. The President believed he now had an actionable offense to justify a U.S. intervention. The President turned to his military advisors, who presented their plan for taking care of both Noriega and the PDF at one fell swoop. The operation was seen as an enormous and resounding military success to almost everyone.[4] While Panama was unique in its details, "it was exactly what Operation Desert Storm would later become: a distillation of nearly every lesson learned from the Vietnam War."[5]

Behind the backdrop of the success of 1989 was the lingering tensions of Vietnam and Beirut. Proposed actions for troop deployments in Panama put forward by the State Department in 1988 revealed the existence of the orthodoxy reviewed in the preceding chapter. A revealing *New York Times* article published in April 1988 reflected the great mistrust that existed in the military. The article underscored the emotional wariness of the military about ill-considered interventions, vague missions, and restraints that did not permit them to "win." "Why don't we want to go to Panama?" asked one general, "Because of Vietnam, pure and simple. We've been in that stuff before."[6] What the military wanted was feasible and attainable objectives set in clear terms with no hesitation to use military force in the manner in which the senior leadership felt it could be optimally used.

In the conduct of his research, the same reporter found that the military officers he spoke to, in case after case, referred to Weinberger's criteria. They all also insisted that "deploying combat troops to Panama met none of those criteria."[7] Yet, all added that if ordered to execute a feasible plan with clearly defined military missions, they would execute the orders of their superiors.

Operation Just Cause, designed by several Vietnam veterans, reflected everything they knew about war. The planning reflected the military's paradigm in every manner. There was no gradualism, passive "presence," signalling, or obtuse academic bargaining strategies. The invasion of Panama marked the post-Vietnam turning point in U.S. military strategy and the manifestation of its internalized operational code.[8]

## OPERATION JUST CAUSE

After receiving the recommendations of his senior foreign policy and military advisors at a two-hour meeting on Sunday, December 17, 1989, President Bush ordered the execution of Operation Just Cause. It was a highly complex operation involving the integrated use of hundreds of helicopters and several hundred fixed-wing aircraft, including the vaunted Stealth fighter, the F-117, which got its baptism in fire. The military offered a single plan, the "maximum option," which would decapitate Noriega and his military thugs from Panama forever.[9] Ultimately the National Command Authorities (NCA) approved the plan, almost unmodified except for the employment of the yet unveiled F-117 Stealth fighters.[10] The plan was daring and extremely intricate. It called for moving thousands of troops from the Continental United States and inserting them suddenly at night to have the greatest amount of surprise and shock. The plan put several hundred aircraft in motion at one time in a small air zone. A total of 27 separate targets, many of which were struck simultaneously, were planned and rehearsed in detail. More than 12,000 troops were to be airlifted into Panama to reinforce the 13,000 or more already there. The plan also called for massive applications of troops and firepower to overwhelm any resistance and to shock the PDF from further resistance.

The operation was conducted by a series of task forces coded by color that were assigned the major tasks and missions that comprised the operations order.[11]

Task Force Black was comprised of special operations forces who were poised to strike prior to H-Hour. The very first action of Operation Just Cause was a Delta Force strike against the Model Jail to extricate radio operator and CIA agent Kurt Muse. The special operations team grabbed Muse amid a hail of gunfire. The entire raid took little more than five minutes. The other raids were just as sudden and overwhelming.

Task Force Bayonet had three missions. The major task was to seize and secure the Commandancia, the walled PDF headquarters compound in El Chorillo defended by elements of the 6th and 7th PDF companies. Just prior to H-hour, the 193rd Brigade supported by Sheridan tanks from the 82nd Airborne arrived at the Commandancia. Sniper fire impeded the movement of the American forces, and numerous roadblocks had been hastily thrown up. AC-130 Spectre gunships and helicopter attack craft hovered over the area and supported the ground force. American tanks breached the compound, but the assault troops could not move forward. The Brigade commander called on the Spectres for direct support, who responded with a flurry of 105mm fire that destroyed the top floor of the 40-year-old brick building.    While this fight was progressing, another battalion from the 193rd, supported by Blackhawk helicopters, assaulted Fort Amador, where the 5th Company of the PDF was located. Fort Amador was near U.S. family housing, and the PDF had to be quickly stunned and overcome to prevent any hostages being taken. The American troops used Vulcan 20mm cannon and 105mm howitzers to stun the Panamanians, who immediately retreated.

The third element of this task force was required to secure the National Department of Investigation building and the headquarters of the transportation department. The PDF troops put up limited opposition but refused to surrender until taken under fire by 90mm recoilless rifle and machine gun fire. The direct use of firepower against Panamanian defenders was only used when the PDF refused to surrender immediately. This ably demonstrated the very effective but controlled employment of fire power as a psychological weapon to subdue the Panamanians.

Task Force Atlantic was assigned to deal with a PDF unit at Colon and some military units at Coco Solo. They rapidly overran the 8th PDF company located at Colon. "Light fighters" from the 7th Infantry Division and 82nd Airborne moved out against the Naval Infantry at Coco Solo, where they met some stiff resistance, losing a SOF helicopter to ground fire.[12]

Task Force Red was comprised of Rangers from two locations in CONUS (Ft. Lewis in Washington and Ft. Bragg in North Carolina), which came thousands of miles via airlift. Their mission was to attack and seize the Tocumen military airport, and the adjacent Omar Torrijos International Airport by a night airborne assault. The facilities were defended by roughly 350 Panamanians, including the 2nd Infantry Company of the PDF. Two AC-130s softened up Tocumen and destroyed the PDF barracks with 105mm fire just prior to the jump by 700 Rangers from the 1st Ranger

Battalion, which landed on schedule at 0103. Airport watch towers were sprayed with fire from AH-6s to eliminate PDF communications.

The Rangers met little resistance. The Spectres had done their job and stunned any real opposition. The Rangers needed to quickly secure the facilities for the follow-on jump of nearly 2,000 troops from the 82nd Airborne. A secure field for the airborne troops was required, and the Rangers had to be prepared to defend the field in the event that "Battalion 2000," an elite unit believed to be loyal to Noriega, and which was armed with V-300 light armored vehicles mounting 90mm cannon, moved down from Fort Cimarron only 16 miles away.

Charlie Company, 3rd Battalion/75th Rangers jumped into Torrijos with the mission of securing the terminal, prior to the follow-on landings. It met light resistance from the PDF troops there. At just before 0200 in the morning, a total of 28 C-141s dropped the armor and transportation assets of the 82nd Airborne Division. Many of the chutes and their heavy loads fell east of the runway into the tall elephant grass and swampy area southwest of the Torrijos terminal.

The last major assault of the operation was the airborne assault on Rio Hato, home of the 6th and 7th PDF companies. The defenders at this field were stunned by two 2,000-pound bombs delivered by the F-117s. The assault troops quickly followed in behind the air strike, parachuting in from only 500 feet up instead of the normal 800 feet, to reduce their exposure to enemy ground fire. This has been described as one of the sites of the hardest fighting during Just Cause.[13]

The last major element in the operation was Task Force Pacific. This task force was comprised of the Airborne troops who landed at Torrijos, and was assigned three separate air assault missions. The first was to assault Cerro Tinajitas, home to the 1st Company, PDF. Fort Cimarron, to the northeast of the airfield, was the second objective. Fort Cimarron was the base for the vaunted Battalion 2000. Last, the airborne troopers were to secure Panama Viejo, on the coastline. It was the barracks for the UESAT, a specially trained antiterrorist unit, roughly 250 strong, considered to be fiercely loyal to Noriega. These objectives were swiftly taken, despite some stiff but spotty resistance.[14]

## POST-INVASION ACTIONS

Security operations continued throughout the next day, including the defense of the American embassy. Forces were dispatched to secure the rescue of American civilians and other foreign nationals at the Marriott Hotel. During this phase, an intramural firefight between American forces resulted in the deaths of two foreign photographers.[15]

Forces moved to secondary objectives, such as securing almost all government buildings, setting up roadblocks, and trying to find Noriega. There was little interference from either the general population or the Dignity Battalions. Several Special Forces officers were successful in convincing Panamanian units in outlying areas to surrender over the phone. Organized resistance was gone, but the hunt for

Noriega continued unabated without success.

Four days later, Noriega slipped into the Papal Nuncio's residence and requested asylum. After a lengthy and public standoff, he surrendered to U.S. military authorities and was arrested and whisked away to Florida by the Drug Enforcement Administration.

In the aftermath of the conflict, however, serious deficiencies in the planning and coordination of the operation became apparent. As the fighting wound down, the disorder of a small Third World nation without a government or without any services was apparent.[16] Equally apparent was SOUTHCOM'S lack of preparedness to stabilize the rioting, looting, and public disorder occurring in the aftermath of the invasion. "In moving from combat operations to stability operations," writes a team of journalists, "the Army went from strength to weakness."[17]

In the aftermath of the operation, attention initially focused on the brighter side of the equation. The military was justifiably proud of the scope and speed of the intervention. From the President's approval on December 17, to the initiation of combat early on the 20th, the responsiveness of the armed forces was a remarkable feat. Brilliantly conceived, from a purely military perspective, the plan was executed despite the friction of war and accomplished its major objectives with crushing firepower and shock action. General Powell called it the most complex and best executed operation he was involved in.[18] The task force commander responsible for executing the plan, Lieutenant General Carl Stiner, called it so good there were no lessons to learn from it.[19]

Others have recognized that such an assertion is an overstretch and that there must be lessons learned from every conflict. Some reflect areas of improvement, while others just reinforce lessons learned earlier.

## CLARITY OF PURPOSE

According to military sources, the Pentagon and SOUTHCOM received clear political objectives from the President in approving its final plans for Just Cause. The president also used the same political objectives in explaining to the American public and their Congressional leaders why the United States was compelled to intervene in Panama. The express reasons offered were to:

1. Protect American lives,
2. Restore the democratic process,
3. Protect the integrity of the Canal treaties, and
4. Apprehend Noriega[20]

Translating the political objectives into military tasks was theoretically accomplished by General Powell and General Thurman during their planning sessions. Protecting American lives drove the planners to seek an overwhelming strike force to overcome any and all resistance quickly. Capturing Noriega was assigned as a specific task, and crushing the PDF was deemed necessary to ensure that a permanent solution could be sought. The military did not want to simply use a surgical strike to grab Noriega. As one participant put it, that would have just made a "promotion opportunity for another thug."[21] The PDF was a center of gravity as well as a source of continued annoyance.

Restoring the democratic process was also an assigned political objective. How the proposed operation plan was to achieve this was not clear. "Bringing about democracy" is not the sort of mission that readily lends itself to a military objective. President Bush's National Security Advisor, former Air Force Lieutenant General Brent Scowcroft, specifically asked how the plan served to achieve this explicit objective. He was informed that the plan was to secretly swear in President-elect Endara just before the invasion.[22] This apparently was the extent of the military's interpretation of what was necessary to restore the democratic process in Panama.

A Reserve officer on SOUTHCOM's staff, a specialist in civil-military operations, was a participant in the development of the early combat and restoration plans called Blue Spoon and Blind Logic, who had a different view. In a series of assessments after the campaign, this officer concluded that the strategic success of Just Cause was hampered by a planning process that never had a clear political objective.[23] While acknowledging that the President did annunciate a series of objectives, none of these were provided during the extensive planning process that drove SOUTHCOM's operational planning. They came after the plan. While taking down Noriega was always planned, what was supposed to replace him and the PDF was only thought of internally by a handful of staff officers and never was reduced to a formal, coordinated plan.

### PLAYING TO WIN

In Panama the military was finally allowed to plan and execute a military intervention consistent with every tenet of the American Way of War. The invasion was not a contest. It was a practice session on the application of overwhelming force, a scrimmage against an NCAA Division III opponent.

The senior officers were all Vietnam veterans, leery of piecemeal, tit-for-tat applications of force.[24] Instead of incremental applications of force and firepower, Noriega and his hapless PDF got the full dose. According to an officer who was involved in the planning, "time and again during the planning process, the idea of applying overwhelming combat power was espoused."[25] As the JTF commander stated to the press afterwards, "we came in here with the principle of overwhelming combat power." General Stiner stated his intention had been to crush the PDF and make any resistance useless, and that effect was largely successful.

The lesson was not lost on Congress either, including those scarred by their experience during Vietnam. Representative David McCurdy (D-Ok), a veteran of that conflict, noted:

The one lesson from Vietnam is clear and absolute, and that is the issue of decisive force. It may be a sledgehammer, but if we are going to be in conflict and going in on the heavy side saves American lives, then we ought to lean that way. I think that's the most significant lesson from Vietnam, in the Gulf and Panama we played to win.[26]

While instantly pointed to as a model for future interventions, some more objective observers noted the uniqueness of the conflict. We had several months to plan, were allowed to rehearse portions of the battle plan unimpeded on the actual objectives in some cases, most of the PDF's communications had been thoroughly tapped and monitored for months, and the U.S. armed services had been present for the better part of fifty years in the country. More than half the forces involved in the fighting were already on location. Such preconditions will not occur with frequency.

Because of this initial advantage, SOUTHCOM massed more than 25,000 troops against as little as 4,000 combat effectives and several thousand Dignity Battalion members. The results were preordained. The force struck with both surprise and an awesome display of air and ground firepower to shock the PDF. In comparison to Beirut, the rules of engagement were simple. According to one Battalion operations officer, "If you see anybody with a weapon, they are dead,"[27] In execution, however, the young and untested soldiers and Marines on the ground were much more disciplined and responsible than that sounds.[28]

A NATO ally captured the "playing to win" aspect of Just Cause better than anyone else. The lesson Panama will teach the American military is that if you're going to go in somewhere, go in with everything possible. This officer added :

After Grenada people started thinking about rapid and selective low profile operations, all that low-intensity stuff. But the truth is that nobody in the brass was keen on it. And the success of Panama will reinforce their prejudice: go in big.[29]

## CIVIL-MILITARY RELATIONS

The inputs into the campaign planning, and the concept of operations, for Just Cause were almost exclusively from the Pentagon and military leaders. Accordingly, the military was satisfied with the plan, and feels that the relationship between civilians and military was satisfactory during the build-up to the invasion of Panama. It was far different from Vietnam or Beirut, with little interaction and almost no political interference. The military developed a plan, pitched it to their superiors in general terms, and were authorized to execute it as designed. In the words of a retired military officer, Just Cause "showed what professional soldiers can accomplish when allowed to do their jobs without micro-management and second-guessing from on high."[30]

Relationships at the Pentagon were far from smooth, however. Mr. Cheney and General Powell had not yet worked out their working routines since Powell's appointment. The Chairman strove to isolate the information that Cheney received regarding operational information from the Joint Staff, and ensured that he got his operational information only from General Powell.[31] The personal interaction and trust level required for Huntington's subjective form of control had not yet matured.

The Chairman need not have been worried. Cheney felt that there was a tendency for people at the top to meddle needlessly and counter-productively in military matters.[32] Thus, the meeting at the White House to review the proposed plan for Just Cause was conducted at a strategic level, with little details offered. Mr. Cheney made no comments during Powell's brief. The decision was made by the President, supported by a small circle of advisors including Secretary of State James Baker. General Powell only presented the Blue Spoon plan; no other options or alternatives were presented.[33] Bush asked why they could not just get Noriega, and Powell explained that another corrupt thug from the PDF would merely rise to power, and the problem would not be decisively resolved. The President had reached a frustration level with problems in Panama and approved the Pentagon's plan.

The support of the President was instrumental in easing the Chief's mind about how Mr. Bush would react in crises. Army Chief of Staff Carl Vuono had "vivid memories of Vietnam, where the civilian leadership hadn't been willing to commit the force necessary to accomplish the military objectives."[34] Mr. Bush did not plan to interfere with operational details, and trusted his military experts to carry out their tasks.

Out of this experience, some generals concluded that the lack of involvement by civilian leadership in the detailed planning was instrumental to its success.[35] "We planned it, rehearsed it, and briefed the leadership—no one fiddled with it," in the words of Lieutenant General Carl Stiner, commander of the XVIII Airborne Corps.[36] Another Pentagon official reportedly told *Newsweek* that "Mr. Cheney's biggest contribution to the invasion was to get out of the way."[37] Obviously, this is an oversimplification of what occurred. Mr. Cheney had allegedly come to the Pentagon convinced that greater civilian control was necessary.[38] His lack of interference comes more from an assessment that the plan would meet the desired policy aim.

Had there been a willingness to bring in Pentagon policy experts or the State Department, and better civil-military relations, Mr. Cheney could have confirmed that assessment. Better relations would have allowed a more open exchange and analysis of the military's proposed plan, and offered constructive recommendations to ensure that force was being used in such a manner to guarantee that the political goals were being served. This could have prevented the disorder and looting problems, and would have at least precluded the clumsy Endara installation.

## POPULAR SUPPORT

In contrast to the Lebanon crisis, the War Powers Act (WPA) was not relevant in Panama since it was such a short and apparently successful operation. Congress was in recess for the Christmas holiday, and several members were already on record for more forceful actions. Despite his own inclinations towards a strong Executive in foreign policy matters, Mr. Bush did write letters to Congressional leaders, as required under the law, notifying them of his actions, but like all Presidents he did not request approval or invoke the WPA time clock.[39]

However, the issue of popular support did rear itself in this intervention. It was manifested by the military's conscious efforts to deny the media ready and uncontrolled access to the battlefield. The fallout from the resulting criticism proved that the relationship between the military as an institution and the media was a "troubled embrace" at best.[40] It revealed the lingering antipathy between the media and the military, and the military's preferred solution to handling a meddlesome press. It also showed that the adversarial relationship stemming from Vietnam was still very much alive and that "the clash of cultures between the press and the military is a constant."[41]

In many ways the problem was a repeat of Operation Urgent Fury. In this invasion of Grenada, reporters were denied access to the island by the task force commander. After that invasion, the Defense Department developed a compromise system to let the media send a pool of personnel to the next conflict. The Pentagon promised that they would notify media executives of pending operations and transport a group to the action if the media would designate reporters in advance and promise not to compromise military operations. The compromise offered access for first-hand accounts in exchange for preserving operational security for the lives of our young servicemen. The Defense Department did not fulfill the compromise during Just Cause, notifying the news agencies just hours before departure time for the pool aircraft.

From the media's perspective the pool was a "Keystone Kops operation" from the start.[42] Several members of the pool found themselves literally locked up and isolated from the action for their own safety. The only real action and civil disorder they saw was when their driver got lost. Fred Francis, who conducted an assessment of media matters after Just Cause found, "The pool was repeatedly denied or ignored when it asked for access to frontline troops, wounded soldiers, simple interviews." He added later, "The pool was a failure."[43] The Assistant Secretary of Defense for Public Affairs, Peter Williams, called it a mistake and blamed it on "incompetence" of his office and the staff at SOUTHCOM.[44] In essence, he confirmed allegations that the Pentagon had wanted pool coverage, the local commanders, Generals Thurman and Stiner, did not.

Fred Hoffman, former deputy press secretary at the Pentagon, and a defense correspondent for the Associated Press, wrote a report for Williams that blamed Cheney for excessive concerns with security and the late activation of the pool. The report was also critical of Williams's naivete in not supervising the public affairs plan and for failing to ensure that the media pool was supported upon arrival.[45]

What the public got to see was the Pentagon's version of a sanitized war with no glitches, no collateral damage, "a flawless feat of arms on an almost bloodless battlefield."[46] Instead of generating popular support in advance, the U.S. military learned a new lesson out of Panama. It could avoid the negative aspects of diminished popular support and the intrusive aspects of the media by executing a concise military victory where public support is secured by placing a veil over the execution of the operation and presenting the American public with a limited perception of what actually occurred.

Some veteran military officers with press experience traced the entire problem back to Vietnam, including retired Marine Lieutenant General Bernard Trainor, who later worked for the *New York Times* as their military correspondent. Trainor observed:

Although most officers no longer say the media stabbed them in the back in Vietnam, the military still smarts over the nation's humiliation in the Indochina and still blames TV and the print media for loss of public support for the war. Today the hostility manifests itself in complaints that the press will not keep a secret and that it endangers lives by revealing details of sensitive operations. The myth of the media as an unpatriotic, left-wing anti-military establishment is thus perpetuated.[47]

## SUMMING UP

Operation Just Cause is difficult to evaluate. The conflict was short, clear cut, and decisive in military terms. There is no doubt that the military felt that it had accomplished everything it was asked to do. Clearly, the military was permitted to execute the operation consistent with the paradigm it preferred and the model developing during the 1980s. Just as clearly, the military walked away feeling vindicated that this paradigm was the proper way to conduct ourselves in future situations. The circumstances surrounding the contingency, however, make the conflict a model only for that specific location and may not be applicable in another scenario where force or the threat of force is required.

Furthermore, little has been done to record useful lessons learned about some of the few shortfalls that do exist. Most of the literature has been produced by retired military officers who lack the objectivity to analyze this operation purely on the merits. Recent attempts to point out deficiencies in the operation by one Army officer who was present in Panama have been met with sharp ripostes.[48]

The president purportedly established clear objectives. Yet these seem to have been for public consumption to justify the operation. Clearly established policy aims were not put forward early enough to drive elements of the plan as it was being developed. The military translated its perceived objectives into a strategy and campaign plan for the takedown of Panama in purely military terms based largely on its operational perspectives about "playing to win." "Restoring democracy" was seen in simplistic terms. SOUTHCOM felt that removing the dictator and swearing in the properly elected official was all that was required.

The failure to coordinate this element of the plan with the State Department and other political-military experts is alarming. The new Ambassador found later that the State Department had been shut out, and he was completely dissatisfied with the obvious lack of planning inputs from other than military sources. He was also highly critical of the damaging implications of having had Endara sworn in at a U.S.

military base, with U.S. military personnel visibly present and the U.S. national color in the background.[49] Equally troubling was Endara's first formal communication as President, a letter to the Organization of American States, being promulgated on SOUTHCOM stationery.[50] Military expediency rather than policy drove many small details of the operation.

Not all observers feel that the scope and manner in which the operation was planned were consistent with the political objective or military necessity by all observers. It is one thing to agree with the conclusion that the overwhelming force approach ended the fighting as soon as possible with the least total amount of casualties to both sides. It is another thing to agree with the assessment that "it was an elegant work of operational art."[51] Few critical analyses of this operation have been conducted, yet it is often cited as a sterling performance worthy of emulation.

The essence of the operational art is linking and phasing military actions that contribute to the desired strategic end state. It is hard to find evidence that the policy objective drove all apsects of the operation plan in Panama. In fact, the size of the plan came very close to precluding the surprise needed to shock the PDF and preclude any counteractions. If Noriega had managed to escape, or if the PDF had prepared a standing counter-plan to grab civilian hostages from the Embassy or any of several dozen military posts, a prolonged stand-off was possible. "A closer examination of the Panama attack indicates that its large scale," writes one retired Marine general, "increased the number of civilian casualties and possibly forfeited the opportunity to seize General Noriega."[52] General Trainor, a former Deputy Chief of Staff for Plans and Operations for the Marine Corps, feels that the operation was just a virtual replay of the Army Concept. "The Army did what it knows how to do," he concludes, "It went in with heavy firepower and troops trained for a large-scale war on the plains of Europe, not the expeditionary wars of the Third World."[53]

It is crystal clear that SOUTHCOM was not prepared for follow-on actions that its own restoration plans and civil affairs experts had prepared for. The military found that policing the mess it created was just as complex a task as the military side of the problem. New unforeseen problems popped each for several weeks, which some planning and foresight could have prevented. One captain, tasked to regenerate a police force in a town, was reduced to have his wife read his college criminology textbook over the phone from Fort Ord, California.[54]

Actually, the disorder of the invasion had been anticipated by General Woerner, whose plans included an additional phase to the operation that would help restore the government of Panama.[55] This phase was documented in a civil-military operations plan that was developed in isolation from the battle plans developed by SOUTHCOM and suffered from the compartmentalization of the detailed planning effort undertaken at Quarry Heights. The planning was also handicapped by the lack of civil affairs expertise on the staff, augmented only by Reservists brought in on short tours. Their plan got short shrift until the invasion itself.

This shortfall has been attributed to numerous coordination problems. First was a coordination gap between SOUTHCOM and its Joint Task Force headquarters. Second, the plans were not coordinated with any civilian agencies such as the local embassy or the State Department. "Coordination with U.S. Embassy was critical but prohibited" since plans were closely held by the military.[56] The last problem was the new Commander-in-Chief, "On restoration, he gave no guidance. His entire focus and attention was devoted to Blue Spoon," his warfighting plan.[57]

So the military planned on the basis of "playing to win," which was fine from the purely military perspective, but could have been disastrous from a broader strategic level. The military should not have excluded political and civilian agencies from outside of the military. The strategic end state was of a very political nature, but the military planning focused solely on military aspects of the problem. The execution and follow up threatened public confidence in the government installed by U.S. forces, thus seriously threatening the overall objective of restoring democracy. Defense Department officials and SOUTHCOM failed to prepare the battlefield by bifurcating the planning process into political and military cells that were never integrated.[58]

The major complaint was that the military operation reflected a politically unsophisticated view of the strategic objective of restoring a democracy quickly and effectively. The operation did not eliminate TV and radio stations that could have rallied support to Noriega. Planners failed to protect the Embassy soon enough. An attack there could have had major ramifications. In addition, the task force did little to protect another potential hostage site at the Marriott Hotel.

Other critics believed the operation used an inappropriate amount of firepower, which contributed to civilian casualties (more than 300 civilians died) and collateral damage. Others were critical of the lack of interaction with the State Department and pointed to the clumsy handling of the swearing in of Noriega's successor. SOUTHCOM did not think through the delicate aspects of installing the Endara government without too much overt Yankee baggage. More importantly, the planners failed to realize that the economic costs of the disorder and looting would undercut the newly constituted government.[59]

Once again the paradox of public support appears. The military wants public support for its actions, but it brooks no interference and wants support to be unconditional, at least while the operation is ongoing. The military's preoccupation with operational security is completely understandable. However, the actions of both the Pentagon and the local SOUTHCOM bureaucracy went well past security issues. Even after the battle was over the military controlled access to soldiers back in the Continental United States for several days,[60] refused to answer questions regarding civilian casualties, and refused access to military combat camera footage taken during the war.

This post-battle abuse reduces the credibility of the excuses offered during the midst of the crisis. They lend additional credence to criticisms of the antipathy between the media and the military and the dangers to democracy if it is not checked. As General Trainor, now director of the National Security Program at the J.F. Kennedy School of Government at Harvard University, notes, "The antimedia attitude that has been fostered in young officers must be exorcised if both the military and media are to serve well the republic for which they stand."[61]

The military must learn to balance its concerns for security with the needs of the media. An adversarial relationship could be very damaging for the U.S. military over the long run. For its part, the press makes too much of trying to get information quickly and without detailed analysis or objectivity. Two competitive cultures will eventually have to settle on some sort of medium to balance the needs of military security with those of a pluralistic society that must reluctantly rely upon a free press to balance the temptations of ambition.

## CONCLUSION

In summary, the Pentagon's preferred paradigm was tested in Panama and found satisfactory by the military. Despite the unique circumstances surrounding this operation, the U.S. military walked away feeling good about its planning and execution of this battle laboratory. On the whole, the operation was a huge tactical success and achieved its major operational objectives. Yet the professed claims to clear objectives, use of overwhelming force, and oversimplified civilian-military policy making reflect the limitations of relying upon force to achieve lasting political outcomes. They specifically highlight the shortcomings of the American military and the need for continued interaction between policy makers and the military's leadership in crisis situations.

Panama reinforced the predisposition towards short and decisive operations using all the firepower and technology available to the American military. Quick and violent engagements result in minimal friendly casualties, ward off an inquisitive press, and preclude any seeds of doubt back at home. Short and conclusive military operations preclude opportunities for political oversight or civilian interference from either the White House or Capitol Hill. "Convinced that civilian micro-management ruined us in Vietnam, and that a willingness to give wide discretion to the military in Panama made that operation a success, the officer corps fears that sound military logic will go by the board if politicians begin to take too close an interest in the conduct of operations."[62]

Many of these same decision makers from Just Cause are still in place during the next major U.S. military intervention.

## NOTES

1. Bob Woodward, *The Commanders*, New York: Simon & Schuster, 1991, pp. 83–104, 127–128, 156–174.

2. Woodward, pp. 143–145. General Powell visited Fort Bragg before being confirmed as Chairman, JCS. He was briefed on the plans developed for Panama and recommended increasing the force build-up rate and the use of night operations.

3. Michael R. Gordon, "U.S. Drafted Invasion Plan Weeks Ago," *New York Times*, December 24, 1989, p. 1; George Wilson, "SOUTHCOM Commander Rewrote Contingency Plans for Action," *Washington Post*, January 7, 1990, p. 1.

4. Woodward, pp. 156–174. John M. Broder and Melissa Healy, "Panama Operation Hurt by Critical Intelligence Gaps," *Los Angeles Times*, December 24, 1989, p. 1.

5. Howard Means, *Colin Powell: A Biography*, New York: Ballantine, 1992, p. 246.

6. Richard Halloran, "What Terrifies the Toughest Soldiers?: A Civilian Military Plan," *New York Times*, April 14, 1988, p. B6.

7. Ibid.

8. Snow and Drew, *From Lexington to Desert Storm*, p. 318.

9. Molly Moore and George C. Wilson, "Bush Chose Pentagon's Maximum Option," *Washington Post*, December 21, 1989, p. 1.

10. Woodward, pp. 140–141.

11. The narrative history of the Panama operation has been drawn largely from Thomas Donnelly, Margaret Roth, and Caleb Baker, *Operation Just Cause: The Storming of Panama*, New York: Lexington, 1991; other sources include Edward M. Flanagan, *Battle for Panama: Inside Operation Just Cause*, McLean: Brassey's, 1993; Kevin Buckley, *Panama: The Whole Story*, New York: Simon & Schuster, 1991.

12. Lorenzo Crowell, "The Anatomy of Just Cause: The Forces Involved, the Adequacy of Intelligence, and Its Success as a Joint Operation," in Bruce W. Watson and Peter G. Tsouras, eds., *Operation Just Cause: The U.S. Intervention in Panama*, Boulder, CO: Westview Press, 1991, p. 8.

13. Ibid., p. 10.

14. For additional summarizations of Operation Just Cause from military officers, see William C. Bennett, "Just Cause and the Principles of War," *Military Review*, March 1991, pp. 2–13; Lyle G. Radebaugh, "Operation Just Cause: The Best Course of Action?" *Military Review*, March 1991, pp. 58–60.

15. Donnelly, et al, *The Storming of Panama*, p. 275.

16. Andrew Rosenthal, "American Troops Press Hunt for Noriega: Order Breaks Down; Looting Widespread," *New York Times*, December 22, 1989, p. 1.

17. Donnelly, et al, p. 375.

18. Eloy O. Aguilar, "U.S. Forces Still Seek 200 Noriega Backers," *Philadelphia Inquirer*, January 6, 1990, p. 4.

19. Donnelly, et al, p. 393.

20. Ann Devroy and Patrick E. Tyler, "U.S. Launches Military Operation in Panama to Seize Gen. Noriega," *Washington Post*, December 20, 1989, p. 1.

21. This remark is attributed to General Fred F. Woerner, former SOUTHCOM, in William C. Bennett, "Just Cause and the Principles of War," *Military Review*, March 1991, p. 3.

22. Woodward, p. 170.

23. John T. Fishel, *The Fog of Peace: Planning and Executing the Restoration of Panama*, Carlisle, PA: Strategic Studies Institute, U.S. Army War College, 1992, p. vii. Fisher is an Army Reserve Lieutenant Colonel, who served on active duty at SOUTHCOM.

24. Donnelly, p. 398.

25. Bennet, "Just Cause and the Principles of War," p. 6.

26. Means, p. 247.

27. Donnelly, p. 295.

28. Robert R. Ropelewski, "Planning, Precision, and Surprise Led to Panama Success," *Armed Forces Journal*, February, 1990, p. 32. While firepower was restrained, the employment of air support against the Commandancia did set off fires in Chorilla. Several blocks of the ghetto area were burnt to the ground.

29. John Barry and Evan Thomas, "Getting Ready for Future Wars," *Newsweek*, January 22, 1990, p. 25.

30. Benjamin F. Schemmer, "Panama and Just Cause: The Rebirth of Professional Soldiering," *Armed Forces Journal*, February, 1990, p. 5.

31. Woodward, p. 127 and p. 179.

32. Ibid., pp. 175–176.

33. Ibid., p. 168.

34. Ibid., p. 163.

35. Caleb Baker, "Army Officials Credit Success in Panama To Planning, Few Bureaucratic Obstacles," *Defense News*, March 5, 1990, p. 8.

36. Stiner quoted in Otto Kriesher, "Surprisingly Few Errors Committed in Panama Invasion," *San Diego Union*, January 7, 1990, p. A12.

37. "Inside the Invasion," *Newsweek*, June 25, 1990, p. 28.

38. Woodward, pp. 109–110.

39. Karen Hosler and Richard H. P. Sia, "Pentagon Says it Needs More Time, More Troops," *Baltimore Sun*, December 23, 1989, p. 1.

40. Bernard E. Trainor, "The Military and the Media: A Troubled Embrace," *Parameters*, December 1990, pp. 2–23.

41. Michael D. Mosettig, "Panama and the Press," *SAIS Review*, Summer/Fall 1990, p. 179.

42. Stanley W. Cloud, "How Reporters Missed the War," *Time*, January 11, 1990, p. 61.

43. Francis cited in Patrick J. Sloyan, "Candor Panama's 1st Casualty," *Long Island Newsday*, January 4, 1990, p. 3.

44. Cloud, p. 61.

45. Michael L. Gordon, "Cheney is Blamed in Muzzling Media," *New York Times*, March 20, 1990, p. 20.

46. Sloyan, p. 3.

47. Bernard E. Trainor, "The Military and the Media: A Troubled Embrace," pp. 2–3. Another journalist, believes that the younger military officer is even more fervent in his hostility towards the press, even though such attitudes are not directly reinforced by experience in Vietnam or any other conflict. See Mossetig, p. 187.

48. Tactitus [pseudo.]. "Few Lessons Were Learned in Panama Invasion," *Armed Forces Journal*, June 1993, pp. 54–56.

49. Donnelly, et al, *The Storming of Panama*, pp. 374–375.

50. Caleb Baker, "Army Officials Credit Success in Panama to Planning, Few Bureaucratic Obstacles," *Defense News*, March 5, 1990, p. 8.

51. Donnelly, et al, p. 400.

52. Bernard E. Trainor, "Flaws in Panama Attack," *New York Times*, January 2, 1990, p. 1.

53. Ibid., p. 1.

54. Donnelly, et al, p. 370.

55. John T. Fishel, "The Murky World of Conflict Termination: Planning and Executing the 1989–1990 Restoration of Panama," *Small Wars and Insurgencies*, Spring 1992, p. 60.

56. Ibid., p. 62.

57. Ibid., p. 63.

58. Richard H. Shultz, Jr. "The Post-Conflict Use of Military Forces: Lessons from Panama, 1989–1991, *The Journal of Strategic Studies*, June 1991, pp. 166–167. For additional criticisms regarding the failure to plan for the political side of the operation see Fishel, *The Fog of Peace*. This monograph is a detailed and critical assessment of civil-military operations and war termination planning during Just Cause. Also see Peter G. Gosselin, "Post-attack Plans Termed Inadequate," *Boston Globe*, December 24, 1989, p. 1.

59. In addition to General Trainor's review, see William Branigin, "U.S. Embassy Staff Attacks Security," *Washington Post*, December 31, 1989, p. 21; Bruce B. Auster, "Military Lessons of the Invasion," *U.S. News and World Report*, January 8, 1990, pp. 20–21; Edward N. Luttwak, "Just Cause: A Military Score Sheet," *Washington Post*, December 31, 1989, p. C4; David Evans, "Military Experts See Flaws in Attack Plan," *Chicago Tribune*, December 24, 1989, p. III-7.

60. Sloyan, p. 3.

61. Trainor, "A Troubled Embrace," p. 11.

62. Eliot A. Cohen, "How to Fight Iraq," *Commentary*, November, 1990, p. 23.

# 5

# Desert Storm: Preferred Paradigm Validated

"Nothing would better serve the interests of future Third World challengers," Jeffrey Record once observed, "than an American conclusion that, in the Gulf War, it had discovered a way of waging war without incurring war's traditional risks, pain and suffering."[1] Despite sound advice that the "first lesson of the Gulf War is to be very wary about drawing any so-called lessons from the Gulf War," the U.S. military has "learned" from its victory over the Iraqi Army.[2] It *is* useful and necessary to try to learn and adapt based on operational experience like Desert Storm. Unfortunately, good data and a bit of distance are required to objectively analyze any war.

Regrettably, few of the serious analyses produced since the war have focused on the major strategic issues of why, where, when, and how U.S. military force should be applied. Internal to the military, though, is a distinct and incontrovertible conclusion that the Gulf War repudiated the revisionists of Vietnam and validated the internal efforts of the military to revive itself as an institution.

The Vietnam experience was the touchstone for the senior military officers in the Gulf. Their decisions and conclusions about the Gulf War cannot be grasped without a feel for the deeply rooted and emotive conclusions that they drew from Southeast Asia. As Colonel Summers has observed, "If you would understand America's victory in the Persian Gulf you must first understand America's defeat in Vietnam. Combat experience in the jungles of Vietnam was the common thread that bound all the senior U.S. commanders" in the Persian Gulf war, from the Chairman of the Joint Chiefs to the Theater Commander and his Division commanders.[3]

While General Powell is frequently characterized as the "reluctant warrior" during the buildup, "in truth, they had all been reluctant warriors, badly scarred from Vietnam and wary of a fickle public that could cheer the armed forces off to war but turn venomous if things went badly."[4] General Powell was characteristic of his peer group since he "remembered Vietnam and the forlorn commitment, with little public support, to a badly planned military campaign whose objectives seemed murky at best.  There would never be another Vietnam as far as he was concerned."[5]

## DESERT STORM AND VIETNAM

It is understandable, but perhaps ironic, that the Vietnam analogy was raised so often by the military, the media, and the Congress during the prelude to the Gulf war. In many ways the entire strategic, operational, and tactical situations between Vietnam and Desert Storm are starkly dissimilar.  In fact, just a cursory review reveals far more dissimilarities than common elements.[6]

Arguably both crises occurred a great distance from the shores of America and were situated in a locale that the common American was hard-pressed to find on a map.  Just like Vietnam, the local governments were involved in a long-standing feud.  Likewise, the issues that generated the conflict were not entirely clear cut.  Our own interests were not crystal clear, given the nature of the regimes we sought to defend.  Our national interests in both conflicts were geopolitical in nature and hard to define to the average American in concrete terms.

The similarities end at this point.  What was different?  Just about everything that counts in military terms.  The nature of the terrain was a sharp contrast from the Central Highlands or Mekong Delta of Southeast Asia.  This war would be fought on an open, featureless terrain.  This war would have fronts, and clearly defined rear areas.  The "bad guys" wore uniforms and occupied military positions instead of hiding in villages.  This was a playing field far more conducive to the American Way of War.  It had goal posts and sidelines.  The equipment that we brought to the arena could be used to maximum effect.  The contest would be fought with jet aircraft, armor units up to Corps size, long-range reconnaissance and sensor systems, laser-designated weapons, sea-launched cruise missiles, and precision-guided munitions. This war would have targets.  The full panolopy of American technology and resource base could be, and would be, brought to bear.  In distinct contrast to the trauma of Vietnam, this war would be fought with our playbook and our rules.

At the strategic and operational levels, there are just as many dissimilarities, the major factor being that the nature of the war, the opponent, and the terrain combined to fit the American style of combat.  The end of the Cold War is often overlooked as a major distinction.  World opinion was far more united with the end of the superpower confrontation.  The Soviet Union could not materially interfere, and the United Nations could actually serve its purpose for once.  Iraq, again in a clear departure from Hanoi, found itself cut off from external support, isolated from the international community, and burdened with economic sanctions.

In the final analysis, despite the contrasts in analogy, the American military went to Southwest Asia with every intention of purging the Vietnam experience from its memory.  Ironically, Hussein operated on every level as if the United States had learned nothing.  He saw the same "paper tiger" and gave too much credence to the "straw giant" criticisms of a few reformers.[7]  Hussein was incapable of understanding that the United States would field a different team, coached by the Battalion commanders and company-grade officers of the last big war. He could not imagine that American public opinion could be massed against him, or that it could be sustained in the face of the casualties of a ground war. Hussein never understood that he had purchased a ticket to play in the ultimate Super Bowl and would face the 1960 Green Bay Packers.

## CLARITY OF PURPOSE

Consistent with the identification of Vietnam as the antithesis of the manner in which war was to be conducted, the American military sought to establish or receive clear guidance from their political masters. "If the Vietnam war had taught one ineluctable lesson," summarizes the staff of *U.S. News and World Report*, "it was that when the political objectives become muddy and politicians become generals, the cause is lost."[8] Not only must the objectives have clarity, but they must also be achievable. It is not enough to be able to see the prize, it must be within reach with the forces and capabilities assigned to the task.

For the American military the overarching lesson from Vietnam and Korea was the need for clear, immutable combat objectives. The Joint Chiefs, through Powell's oracular voice, insisted on a mission that was both finite and within the means of the forces at hand.[9]

The Administration did establish four major political goals relatively early in August, and stuck to them rather doggedly. The Bush policy circle seemed conscious of the need for consistency in political objectives. However, in trying to establish and maintain public support, the Administration struggled to find a sufficient rationale for the U.S. intervention, and hopped from rationale to rationale for five months.[10] With the same problem that LBJ had, Mr. Bush and his advisors employed a wide number of reasons, for a wide number of audiences. The definition of our vital interests changed from one press conference to the next, and the reasons for dispatching forces ranged from stopping aggression, enforcing international law, preparing for a "new world order," ensuring our economic stability, preventing Hussein from strangling or manipulating the world oil supply, and in more crass terms, the Secretary of State stated we were in the Gulf for "jobs."

The military does not seem to have noticed the lack of initial consistency. The Pentagon's own after action report on the Gulf war emphasized the establishment of clear political goals to drive the composition, purpose, and actions of the military. It even trotted out the questionable Kinnard results to support its report. In a form of backward reasoning, the U.S. military wants to think that it won because it had clear objectives, and thus, since the military performed so well, it must have been because the objectives were so clear and consistent.

A post-Vietnam survey of key military leaders who commanded relatively large forces during that conflict revealed many were, at times, unsure of the war's objectives. Those who commanded during the Gulf crisis did not suffer the same misgivings. Little confusion existed within Coalition military establishments as to what military force was expected to accomplish. Clear statements of goals helped instill confidence and eased the formulation of military objectives.[11]

The Bush policy team laid out four major policy objectives eventually, and they stuck to them pretty consistently. They were:

1. Unconditional withdrawal of all Iraqi forces from Kuwait
2. Restoration of Kuwait's legitimate government
3. Securing the safety and protection of American citizens abroad
4. Enhancing the security and stability of Saudi Arabia and the Persian Gulf[12]

The clarity of the last objective is not as pure as the others. As we will see later during the war termination phase of the conflict, this becomes a critical point. In his address to a Joint Session of Congress early in Desert Shield, the President stated that our goal was "assuring" regional stability in the Gulf.[13] Early on, "enhancing" security in Saudi Arabia and the Gulf region was the objective. In its Title V post-conflict report to Congress, the Pentagon stated that our national policy objective was simply the security and stability of the region.[14] Stability was not defined any further, and this distinction remains critical to assessing the real significance of the clear military victory achieved in the Gulf.

Following the establishment of clear national political objectives, the military could turn to defining a strategy and the means of achieving its military objectives. The detailing of clear military objectives is almost as important as finalizing the war's policy aim. The U.S. military believes that this was accomplished. "Clearly defined and articulated political objectives ensured development of equally clear military objectives and decisively contributed to success," according to DoD's report.[15]

The final assessment as to whether the United States achieved its policy or military objectives is not a crucial determination in this book. However, it is relevant to the validity of the lessons learned about clarity of purpose. It is also relevant when looking at exactly what the theater commander defined as his objectives. The liberation of Kuwait is clearly defined, as well as numerous steps leading to that objective. The nebulous political objective of enhancing or securing regional stability was also translated into specific military objectives. "Securing regional stability" was eventually defined as destroying the Republican Guard and eliminating Iraq's capacity for production or delivery of weapons of mass destruction.[16] The theater commander's goals resist the larger prize of toppling Saddam. While it may have been hoped for, changing the government in Baghdad was never a formal war aim.[17]

This becomes a critical element later in the assessment as to whether clear goals were really established, and as to whether a decisive victory was achieved or merely a "Pyrrhic Triumph."[18] To ascertain just how successful the U.S. military was, the assigned objectives should be examined. Central Command's objectives were:

1. Attack Iraqi political-military leadership
2. Gain and maintain air superiority
3. Sever Iraqi supply lines
4. Destroy known NBC production, storage, and delivery capability
5. Destroy the Republican Guard in the Kuwaiti Theater of Operations
6. Liberate Kuwait City[19]

The military is satisfied that they received explicit and clear policy aims, and that they were matched with equally clear military objectives.

## PLAYING TO WIN

In defining both the force size and manner of employment, the U.S. military desired to repeat the performance level established in Operation Just Cause. Panama was the dress rehearsal for overwhelming force, and Desert Storm was the real show. The ghosts of Vietnam would be entirely exorcised in one gigantic clash. The military would present a requirement for an overwhelming force that was to be carefully built and resourced. Political constraints on the use of the force and its firepower were to be minimized, and rules of engagement were to be kept sparse and crystal clear. The President reiterated repeatedly that it would not be "another Vietnam." This time the troops would have what they needed, "They will not be asked to fight with one hand tied behind their back."[20]

To accomplish its mission, the Joint Staff asked for and received nearly 500,000 American troops, in addition to the forces provided by 30 separate coalition partners. The force list authorized by the President exceeded the regional commander's request considerably. This force signalled U.S. resolve and commitment, but did not induce Iraq's leadership to withdraw. The military saw the President's rapid approval of its force request as a sign of decisive leadership and a commitment that the military would have the full support of the nation to carry out its assigned tasks.[21] The good guys would be allowed to win this one.

In its own report, DoD noted that the President's approval of the "enhanced option," in late October 1990, provided "an overwhelming offensive capability" to ensure that the United States would possess a "decisive force" capable of seizing the initiative and "avoid getting bogged down in a long, inconclusive war."[22] Desert Storm *was not* going to be another Vietnam.

Given the necessary tools and forces to accomplish its assigned objectives, the military turned to planning its war strategy. Vietnam remained the antithesis, firepower and mass would not be applied in a piecemeal fashion. "In order to achieve assigned goals quickly and with minimum coalition casualties," the DoD report notes, "U.S. defense planners applied the principle of decisive force. This contrasted with the incremental, attrition warfare which had characterized U.S. operations in Vietnam."[23]

The principle of decisive and overwhelming force can be seen in the force sizing of both air and ground campaigns, as well as in the actual conduct of both the air and ground phases of the CINC's campaign plan.

### Ground Phase

The ground force buildup was a direct counterpoint to the lack of mass and decisive force established in Vietnam. The commander's intent reinforced it. Firepower and attrition were employed to set up the battlefield not to signal or coerce but for a decisive blow. Mass, speed, and firepower were to be applied simultaneously. Gradual applications and incrementalism were eschewed; centers of gravity were to be targeted relentlessly until the enemy force was broken. There would be no pauses. The formal stated intent of the Commander-in-Chief, Central Command (CINCCENT) can be found in his Commander's intent statement:

Maximize friendly strength against Iraqi weakness and terminate offensive operations with the Republican Guard Force Command destroyed and major U.S. forces controlling critical lines of communication in the Kuwaiti Theater of Operations.[24]

General Schwarzkopf was fond of referring to the Battle of Cannae, the classic battle of annihilation. It was his favorite analogy before the war. He continued to emphasize that the Republican Guard was a center of gravity to Hussein, and thus must be targeted for decisive force and destruction. This is reflected in his campaign objective of "destroying" the Republican Guard and his commander's intent. The battle against the Guard was the main effort in the ground phase of the campaign. The CINC's intent was to initiate and complete a climatic battle of *die Schlacht*, the slaughter.[25] The CINC was "playing to win" in the finest tradition of the American Way of War.

The Chairman also reinforced the concept of overwhelming force and decisive results. In a much publicized (and apparently deliberately rehearsed) line, General Powell said, "Our strategy for going after this army is very simple. First we are going to cut it off. And then we are going to kill it."[26] This may have been purposeful posturing for Iraq to show that the United States had the will to engage in a ground offensive, at a time and manner of its own choosing, but it also set up certain expectations.

### Strategic Air Phase

The Air Force leadership, like its brethren on the ground, harbored great angst over limitations and constraints reminiscent of the air war over North Vietnam. Aerospace doctrine was built around technology, firepower, and overwhelming application just like the ground forces. The haunting memory of Vietnam was omnipresent. In a statement that could, and probably should, be seen as anti-Clausewitzian, the Air Force Component Commander in Southwest Asia, Lieutenant General Horner, observed:

Many of us here who are in this position now were in Vietnam, and that war left a profound impact on our feelings about how our nation ought to conduct its business. We will carry out any particular policy but as individuals we think that war is a very serious business and it should not be dragged out in an effort to achieve some political objective.[27]

As a Vietnam veteran, General Horner was speaking for a generation of aviators who remembered the frustrations of Rolling Thunder and the Linebacker campaigns. They also remember the loss of over 3,000 aircraft without any decisive results. As then Air Force Chief of Staff General Dugan stated before his relief, "Most Air Force officers believe to this day that if they had been allowed to bomb North Vietnam without limits the U.S. would have won the war."[28]

In direct contrast to the incrementalism of Vietnam, the chief air power strategists designed a strategic aerial bombardment program called Instant Thunder. The title impugns the many indignities dumped on air power proponents since the failures of Rolling Thunder. Rolling Thunder was "a prolonged, gradualistic approach." DoD's report notes that instead of "piecemeal attacks designed to send signals to enemy leaders, Instant Thunder was designed to destroy 84 strategic targets in Iraq in a single week."[29]

The CINC provided general guidance and direction but avoided micro-managing the air portion of the war. Some have accused him of providing insufficient direction, particularly with the targeting priorities. After the war, General Schwarzkopf noted that the Air Force was very sensitive to guidance and any controls that smacked of "straightjacket restrictions imposed during Vietnam."[30] He eventually placed his Deputy in charge of resolving the prioritization of targets.[31]

Air power proponents hold few inhibitions about the contributions the air phase made to the success of Desert Storm. The Air Force Chief of Staff, General Merrill A. McPeak, briefed journalists that it was his personal conviction that the Gulf air war "was the first time in history that a field army has been defeated by air power." Air Force doctrinal experts and historians quickly added Desert Storm clearly proved that "air power now dominates land warfare" and that "simply (if boldly) stated, air power won the Gulf War."[32]

In sum, the American military was successful in promoting the principle of decisive or overwhelming force in both its ground and air phases. More importantly, it was successful in advising its principal client. President Bush observed, "This will not be another Vietnam. This will not be a protracted, drawn out war. If one American soldier has to go into battle, that soldier will have enough force behind him to win and then get out."[33] The principle of decisive force was established, tested, and validated in Desert Storm. "Playing to win" had become national military policy.

The U.S. military derived a sense of closure from Vietnam to the Gulf war. Many veterans from Vietnam enjoyed the victory parades and accolades given to those returning from the Gulf war. General Powell told these veterans their honor and valor were never questioned, and that they too could claim a share of the credit. It was as if a generation had come full circle. As one special operations officer from Vietnam and the Gulf war noted, "The lessons of Vietnam were good ones, I didn't break faith with those lost, they did not die in vain."[34]

## CIVIL-MILITARY RELATIONS

As in the other categories, the U.S. military has come to see in both Operation Desert Shield and Desert Storm, the epitome of proper civil-military relations. Simply stated, the civilians provided the policy aims, the commitment to the requisite resources, and then stayed out of the way. "Virtually to a man," notes one journalistic team that conducted extensive post-war interviews, "every American commander in the Gulf conflict expressed gratitude and satisfaction over the fact that their President and Commander-in-Chief had allowed them to fight the war as they saw fit."[35]

Queried about his role in the initial formulation of U.S. policy objectives and the resulting decision to dispatch U.S. military forces, General Powell noted that the President and Secretary Cheney deliberately "allowed the military to participate in the decision making process from the very beginning, and allowed me as chairman to be a part of the inner sanctum."[36] He has since stressed that his input in the front end, not afterwards, was the key to properly integrating political issues and military considerations throughout the war.

It is clear from the record that the President was very hesitant to interfere with operational details. In addition, while there are situations during the crisis where it appears the President overruled General Powell's recommendations, there is little evidence the NCA did not seek out military perspectives at each and every turn. This is obviously an improvement over the Johnson and McNamara days. There were no Tuesday targeting lunches. Civilians from DoD, CIA, and State were involved in the policy development stage and the planning process. Battle plans were made by those who would execute them. The military as a whole had a seat at the table and a voice in all discussions. While General Powell's input was not accepted on a few key policy decisions, it is apparent that at no time did the NCA disapprove military advice on military matters.

## POPULAR SUPPORT

The establishment and maintenance of public support for U.S. policy objectives was critical to the overall success of Desert Storm. All three aspects of popular support; media policy, Reserve mobilization, and Congressional authorization, played a part in building and holding together an often tense equilibrium of Clausewitz's "remarkable trinity."

The media presented a major challenge in this specific theater of operations. The host nation was a closed society, with extreme sensitivity to Western cultural norms. The theater was far from the Continental United States, and the vast desert environment mandated detailed planning for transportation and logistics for public affairs teams. The horde of media personnel from around the world exacerbated the situation further. A total of 1,600 media representatives flooded Saudi Arabia and nearby military facilities. Their demands for access and support overran the capability of CENTCOM's Joint Information Bureau.

Because of these anticipated problems, DoD planned to employ the pool system employed in Panama and Grenada, and secured approval from the Saudis. The National Media Pool was notified on August 10, and a pool flew to Riyadh that week.

After the war, the media was extremely dissatisfied with the guidelines and restrictions imposed by the military. Pool coverage was considered poor, media escorts frequently interrupted or intimidated interviewers, security reviews were capricious and time consuming, and transportation assets and support were inadequate to get completed reports and imagery to their editors.[37] Probably the worst accusation was that several reporters were getting favorable treatment because they provided positive stories, while reporters who filed stories that the CINC found negative would lose interviews and other privileges.[38]

In their defense, DoD was really not obligated to provide the transportation, food, and logistics it did provide. CENTCOM made senior officers available for numerous public and private briefings. Division commanders took time out of pressing schedules to talk to the press, and their troops provided interviews for a multitude of human interest stories. Daily briefings were broadcast over the world. In many ways, in terms of quantity or volume, the war was extensively covered. Both the Secretary of Defense and his spokesperson, Assistant Secretary of Defense Pete Williams, would later defend DoD and describe the Gulf war as the best covered conflict of its kind.[39]

The military did not completely exonerate themselves; DoD's report on the war acknowledges that command support for the media effort was uneven. This would seem to support assertions that some generals, particularly senior Army officers who had served in Vietnam, did not resist the opportunity to repay reporters for the perceived "stab in the back" in Vietnam.[40] The Pentagon also admitted that several incidents of intimidation and inadvertent censorship had occurred through a lack of training and supervision. The Pentagon defended the security review process, but did admit transmission time must be greatly increased.

The major problem in the Gulf was retaining operational security in an age where technology permitted journalists to communicate live on a world-wide basis. Desert Storm was unique because it was the first modern war where news media personnel could broadcast instantaneously to the world, to include Baghdad. This was considered crucial in the psychological war being waged against Hussein, described by General Powell as "a CNN junkie."

Security did not turn out to be a major problem. Only five of 1,300 pool stories were restricted for security matters, and upon appeal, only one story was ever censored. The CINC was concerned about one or two stories that apparently had correctly speculated about VII Corps pending sweep around the left flank.[41] Apparently, Hussein got so much information and deliberate disinformation that he never was able to discern just what CENTCOM would do.

The media was quite upset after the war, and the major issue among many news organizations was what to do about it.  To many, the media was used to plant disinformation or doubt, and to shape U.S. domestic support for the war.  The pools, censorship, and "superficial and numbingly statistical" daily briefings came under extensive criticism.[42]  The most cynical of the crowd believes that the "lessons learned" from Vietnam, Grenada, and Panama focus solely on how to control the media.[43]  However, the American people awarded a lopsided victory to the brass.  A poll taken during the war reported that 80 percent of those polled agreed with the media restrictions imposed by DoD.  At the same time, over 78 percent reported great confidence in the U.S. military, but only 22 percent reported the same level in the press.  Even the Saturday Night Live television show spoofed the self-righteous antics of the press.[44]

After the war several major media representatives asked to meet with DoD officials and work towards constructive changes in meeting the conflicting requirements of operational security and informing the American people.[45]  This initiative will hopefully make several positive steps towards resolving the tensions and conflicts that occurred in Desert Storm.  This is important, as General Powell reiterates in speeches to senior officers at the National Defense University about the importance of good media relationships.  "Because you can win the battle but lose the war," he admonishes, "if you don't handle the story right."[46]  Exactly what General Powell means by "handling the story right" is the central point of difference between the media and the military.

The second issue relating to public support involves the activation of the Reserves.  A major element in the Army's post-Vietnam force planning process was the deliberate modularization of its active forces with Reserve forces to force civilian leaders to mobilize the Total Force and generate the concern and commitment of the American people.[47]  In Desert Storm the use of the Reserves was needed to support the deployment requirements of Operation Desert Shield, as well as the combat phase of Desert Storm.  A total of 245,000 Reservists were activated, and approximately 106,000 served in Southwest Asia.[48]

More important than the capabilities these Reserve units brought to the theater, however, was the powerful signal that the Nation was committed.  "One of the terrible mistakes we'd made during the Vietnam War was not mobilizing," noted CINCCENT, "Washington sent our soldiers into battle without calling on the American people to support them."[49]  While the National Guard experienced difficulty in getting some units to desired readiness levels, overall the Department is satisfied with the performance of the Reserves.

The third issue involved in generating popular support involves the Congressional authorization.  The Congress was not adequately involved in major policy decisions during the early stages of the conflict.  This sensitized key Congressional leaders early, and the Bush Administration took few steps to mend fences.

Contrary to the Constitutional perspective that the Congress should be asked to declare war, the President took sole responsibility for both the initial deployment of

250,000 Americans to Southwest Asia and the November decision to double it for offensive options. This was done on the basis of his executive authority and his statutory power as Commander-in-Chief. He did not invoke the provisions of the War Powers Resolution.

The Congress failed to take decisive action to rectify the situation. Numerous members made dutiful speeches referring to the Constitution and to the Vietnam war. Some members of the House of Representatives actually filed suit in Federal court to bar the President from preventing an offensive in the Gulf without a formal declaration of war from Congress. Hearings were conducted by the Senate Armed Services Committee, chaired by the powerful Senator Sam Nunn from Georgia, but little action was taken. The Democratic Caucus overwhelmingly passed a non-binding resolution calling on the President not to initiate war without Congressional approval.

While his staff strongly recommended he not seek such support, the President overrode their recommendations to gain a last chance degree of support to force Hussein's withdrawal. He requested Congressional authorization and the Administration also intervened to ensure the language of the resolution passed by the Hill would meet its requirements. Eventually, after several days of frequently eloquent and emotional debate, both Houses narrowly passed a resolution supporting "any means necessary" to liberate Kuwait.[50]

In the end, Congress could claim that it had not abdicated its Constitutional responsibilities. Second, George Bush could now claim he had asked Congress for their support, and received it. Military observers would note that Congress had put their own Vietnam Syndrome behind them now.[51]

The lessons of Vietnam were heeded, and building a solid home front was a key objective for the President and the military. National support was developed and maintained, but not through Reserve mobilization or the Congress. Public support was more a product of the President's and the military's ability to deal with populace through modern media, and the ability to talk over the heads of the pundits. They played to win that game too.

## ASSESSMENT

The preceding discussion has described the lessons perceived by the American military. The Defense Department is satisfied that it received clear political objectives and accomplished them very satisfactorily. Mission accomplishment was largely the result of the application of an overwhelming amount of force, applied decisively. Clear lines of authority existed from the President, through the Secretary of Defense to the Chairman, and then to the warfighting theater commander. These clear lines and relationships clarified authority and represented the proper division of labor between civilian superiors responsible for political direction, and a military singularly qualified to manage the military end of the conflict. Civilian authorities did not overrule military advice, and thus civil-military relations were smooth. Last, public support was maintained effectively, not through mobilization or Congressional support, but mainly through the military's ability to control the message put out through the mass media.

How do these lessons stack up? Are they valid, and can they serve as a useful template for future scenarios? Will we overlook the unique aspects of the contingency, and accept without question these institutional conclusions? As Dr. Eliot Cohen has observed, "The greatest test of our strategic maturity will be our willingness to view critically our performance in this rout." Victory can excuse a multitude of sins.[52]

It is difficult to challenge the conclusion that President Bush established four clear objectives during the crisis. To make this conclusion, though, it is necessary to accept the fourth objective, the establishment of regional stability in the Middle East, in narrow terms. Victory was not to be complete, or unlimited in scale or time. It is clear that the removal of Saddam Hussein, an unlimited and ambitious goal, was never formally established. However, in his rhetoric the President escalated expectations beyond narrow constructions. Few observers could expect a limited war with limited objectives given both the President's Hitler analogy for Hussein and the constant comparisons to Munich and appeasement.

Thus, Mr. Bush established a macro-level incongruity. Having identified Saddam as a Hitler, and massed an international army against him, victory was defined to a limited purpose. Having raised expectations that the military would not "fight with one hand tied behind its back," and after generating a level of international and domestic consensus not seen since the 1940s, Mr. Bush generated an implicit assumption that regional stability meant getting rid of the current leadership in Baghdad. As one Congressional defense expert writes, "This disparity between more limited formal objectives and ambitious, undeclared aims continues to hamper efforts at judging the war's ultimate success or failure."[53] This in turn has clouded efforts at evaluating whether or not the proper political objectives were established and how clear they really were articulated.

In addition to clear objectives, strategic success mandates clear and consistent strategic guidance to the military in general and the theater commander in particular. Here the record is a little more murky, and less positive. CENTCOM was not satisfied it knew what was going on in Washington and what planning efforts the Command should focus on. In October 1990, the CINC told the U.S. Ambassador to Saudi Arabia he was working "in the dark," and was assuming that a requirement for offensive operations would eventually be needed, but he had no idea if it was limited to freeing Kuwait or otherwise.[54]

In his memoirs after the war, the CINC included a draft message that he had prepared for the Joint Staff complaining of the "total vacuum of guidance" he sensed in theater.[55] The problem appears bigger than just the U.S. military. According to Schwarzkopf, even the British were unsure and asked for a written definition of coalition's strategic and political war aims. CENTCOM drafted a proposal and forwarded it, but it "disappeared without a trace."[56]

However, much of this confusion appears to have occurred in the late 1990 time frame when the President and his counselors were concentrating on the international diplomatic front, and on approving a large force deployment to undertake offensive operations. In context, the theater commander received both the guidance and the forces he needed, when he needed it.

The third element in assessing clarity of purpose involves the clarity of the military objectives. The CINC promulgated an overall intent and six specific military objectives.[57] These military objectives reinforce the narrow interpretation of the policy aims established by the White House. Ejecting the Iraqi forces from Kuwait and restoring its legitimate government was the primary objective. Ensuring regional stability was to be achieved through the destruction of the Republican Guard and the elimination of Hussein's offensive capabilities, particularly his NBC production and delivery potential.[58] The military objectives appear consistent with the political objectives, although once again, the establishment of regional stability is defined narrowly. Whether or not these were achieved is a matter for the next phase of the assessment.

General Schwarzkopf sought to achieve a decisive victory through the classic American Way of War. In this regard, he turned back to the most familiar icons of American military history for guidance. Perhaps indicative of the depth of mythology in the psyche of the American military, the CINC kept in his office a framed copy of Sherman's adage "War is the remedy our enemies have chosen. And I say let us give them all they want."[59]

The coalition gave Hussein all he could handle and more. Was a decisive victory achieved? Most observers readily accept that overwhelming force was concentrated in the theater, and that it was employed with few restraints. The American military was "allowed" to win this war, unlike its interpretation from Vietnam or Beirut. But did it achieve a decisive victory, and was the force employed decisively? The ultimate criteria for this determination must be based on the achievement of the stated political and military objectives.

As discussed earlier, the elimination of Saddam Hussein was not explicitly directed. It remained a political objective beyond the scope of the coalition's framework, and the degree of risk that both the political and military wanted to assume. We could live with Saddam without an Army, or the Iraqi Army without Saddam. We chose the former, and in the CINC's words "the option of going all the way to Baghdad was never considered."[60]

Thus, the war plan called for the use of a massive overwhelming force in a measured manner to achieve a straightforward, albeit limited, victory over the invading army. The theater campaign plan was not designed for the overthrow of the Iraqi government, consistent with the stated policy aims given to CENTCOM. While the means appeared unlimited, the goals were prescribed to more limited ends. While a battle of annihilation like Cannae was feasible, a strategy of annihilation culminating in unconditional surrender was not sought. This was not to be a war of annihilation culminating in surrender ceremonies on the teak decks of the USS *Missouri*. Thus, in several critical factors, the traditional American Way of War was not sought nor achieved in the Gulf.

This has created numerous criticisms of the Gulf war. Several major assessments have decried the war as a hollow victory. One major book called it a "triumph without victory," which presumes that we achieved only a tactical victory, meaningless in its relation to either strategic goals or the opportunities available. According to this view:

For a military operation prosecuted with such skill and vision, it was a tragic conclusion, one that no amount of post-war celebration could disguise. There could be no doubt America and its allies had triumphed over Iraq's army on the battlefield. But inasmuch as victory suggests the decisive defeat of an opponent, there was none. This triumph without victory was perhaps the most striking irony of the entire conflict.[61]

This brings up the cognitive incongruity raised by the military in the aftermath of the conflict. President Bush raised expectations with references to appeasement and Hitler, the U.S. military raised expectations with references to Cannae, and with pithy sound bites about "cutting off and killing" the Iraqi Army. Given the provision of the clear objectives, the overwhelming force, the lack of constraints on the application of power, under such ideal circumstances, much more was expected.

The argument about decisive victory relates back to the subject of war termination, and criticism regarding General Powell's recommendations to unilaterally cease hostilities. These recommendations, in retrospect, seem consistent with the "reluctant warrior" image captured by Bob Woodward in *The Commanders*. Even after the President decided that Iraq would withdraw or be forcibly ejected, the Chairman of the Joint Chiefs of Staff (CJCS) sought to keep war aims limited. Other reports suggest General Powell was "the loudest proponent for limited and militarily expedient war aims. He wanted no part of a war that required an extended American occupation or a protracted hunt for Saddam."[62] Some Pentagon officials questioned whether this view reflected his best advice based on a politically deft understanding of the geostrategic situation in the region or was merely "a convenient rationale for limited military involvement and entanglement in a messy situation."[63]

General Powell has no regrets since the war. Even a year later he was not the least bit defensive about his role in limiting the gains that could have been achieved, and criticizes counterarguments as senseless Monday morning quarterbacking.[64]

Like most conflicts, whether or not a truly decisive victory has been achieved cannot be determined immediately. The military's insistence that a decisive victory was achieved is understandable. It does not denigrate the valor of the military to question whether or not their victory achieved the political objectives set forth. However, given the "tactical victory, strategic defeat" school of thought that emanated from Vietnam, the acceptance of a merely overwhelming tactical victory is surprising. Instead of acting defensively, the military should accept the fact that decisive victories are the product of numerous political and military conditions, some beyond the control of the theater commander.

The sharp defensiveness points to the need to closely scrutinize the war termination aspects of this conflict. In fact, General Powell's advice at both the beginning and the end of the war deserves far more critical analysis than given to date. His primary job was to ensure the match between assigned political aims and military objectives. He appeared reluctant to recommend offensive combat to achieve those aims and then was very fast to stop the ground war and remove American troops. According to some reports, General Powell was a "brakeman" to the propensity for higher goals sought by civilian advisers around the President. Other reports have General Powell looking to end ground combat early as the second day of the ground phase.[65]

From the published record to date, it does not appear that the termination strategy had been thought out in detail. This undercuts the belief that clear objectives had been established. General Powell made an assessment that the political and military objectives had been accomplished, and the President accepted this conclusion. This view was based on limited information. The American military had not completed all of its assigned objectives, particularly the destruction of the Republican Guard. Some combination of poor communications, the fog of war, or faulty reporting permitted both the CJCS and the theater commander to believe they held more land, had destroyed more tanks, and greater amounts of the Guard than they really had.

After the war, Saddam Hussein's continued truculence, and the brutal crushing of internal dissension, leads many to think that the knockout victory of 1991 may being only temporary. The Phoenix will be hard to crush again if necessary, since the extremely favorable political conditions that existed in 1991 may not exist again. Thus, many believe a truly decisive victory had slipped away. Others go so far as to count the Gulf war as a major American political defeat given the immensity of the political and military effort marshalled against Saddam during and after the Gulf war.[66]

Such assessments presume far too much about what could have been achieved politically in Iraq, and what the risks and costs of continued combat would have been. There is no credible evidence that killing 5,000 Iraqis or destroying 500 more tanks would have contributed to a better state of peace.

But the premature decision to halt the ground offensive bears detailed review for future conflicts. Why did General Powell recommend halting the war? In post-conflict interviews, visual imagery from the "Highway of Death" was cited as a problem and that we were creating the impression that American pilots were engaging in wanton killing. However, several analyses have shown that no such images were presented on American networks or CNN.[67] Even if such reports were seen, the recommendation for a unilateral cease fire does not follow. Air attacks on retreating convoys in the kill zones could have been stopped, and the enveloping force could have blocked and captured the rabble as it proceeded towards VII Corps.

In retrospect it seems apparent the Administration was concerned about a "crisp and clean ending." Reportedly, planning conferences at the National Security Council deputy level made numerous references to long-term stalemates like Korea. The U.S. military wanted no part of any "ragged ending," nor did it desire a protracted presence and quagmire.[68] It was not only the military that was willing to accept a sharp, short, decisive win. President Bush stated, "we are not going to permit this to drag on in terms of a significant U.S. presence a la Korea."[69] The President's team did not want "victory fever" to take hold and escalate the stated policy aims like Truman's crossing the 38th parallel after Inchon.

To summarize, the campaign was decisive in military terms only. The results, from both the air and ground phases, were dramatically decisive at the tactical and operational levels of warfare. Raised expectations due to the exaggerated rhetoric of the President, the Chairman, and the CINC were not met. Furthermore, not all military objectives were satisfied. Substantial amounts of Iraqi armor escaped. The Republican Guard was not degraded during the air or ground phases to the degree specified before the war.[70] Additionally, after the war it was determined that Iraq's NBC capabilities were not degraded as much as desired.

The conclusion that the relationship between civilian policy makers and military experts the Gulf war represents a good model for future crisis management decisions should not be accepted at face value. Given the military's memory of LBJ on his hands and knees on the floor in the Oval Office picking bombing targets, President Bush was a major improvement. It is true that Mr. Bush religiously adhered to a strict chain of command running from Cheney to Powell to Schwarzkopf. Likewise, Mr. Bush was disinclined to disagree with the military, accepted the Pentagon's proposals and approved their requests, and made no major decisions that contradicted the military advice of his commanders. In the CINC's words, "his confidence in the military's ability to do its job was so unlike what we'd seen in Vietnam."[71]

However, even though the Oval Office refused to get down into operational minutia and never forced the military "to fight with one hand tied behind its back," it is an oversimplification to suggest that the war was a model for the future.

Both the manner in which the war began and was concluded really raise grave doubts about the level of trust that existed between the President and his major policy advisers. While the military was afforded access to policy councils, for some reason General Powell felt constrained in putting forth his position regarding economic strangulation over a military solution. The suggestion that the principal advisor to the President on military matters felt any hesitancy about giving his best advice reveals problems.[72]

*The Commanders* also reveals the absence of direct communications between the political leader and principal military advisor at a major juncture in the decision making process. According to this report, General Powell was surprised when the President made the decision and public announcement that Iraq's aggression would not stand and that it would be reversed. This was a major policy decision, and the failure to discuss and evaluate the costs of such a policy with one's principal military advisor is troubling.[73]

In addition to the problems in Washington, relations with the warfighting commander were tense. The CINC perceived a "lack of guidance," and at one point was relying on the text of UN resolutions to determine what actions he should be planning for.[74] Other details from CENTCOM bely the simple picture put forward by the Pentagon. CENTCOM was frustrated with constant changes in guidance with enforcing the naval blockade, having gotten four changes in four hours when an Iraqi tanker challenged the Navy. It was a "classic illustration of what happens when Washington tries to direct combat operations from afar" according to General Schwarzkopf.[75]

Relations between the Secretary of Defense Cheney and the Joint Staff are also less than sanguine. Several reports lead to the conclusion that General Powell sought to control information getting to the Secretary, and that Cheney used back-channel sources to "pulse the system" and not become dependent on just the Joint Staff for his information. Furthermore, Mr. Cheney felt forced to prod the Chairman to get the Joint Staff to prepare necessary military options for the President.[76] Later, in frustration, he began developing his own offensive operations and directing members of Joint Staff while Powell was out of town. This resulted in a plan called Operation Scorpion, a design for a very wide westward swing into Iraq. The CENTCOM staff ripped the proposal apart.[77]

Another indication of tension is seen in General Waller's public dispute with the White House. General Waller, the Deputy at CENTCOM, publicly disagreed with the President's January 15 date for the initiation of offensive operations. General Waller specifically told reporters that forces would not be ready, which undercut the White House's coercive diplomacy to make Saddam blink.[78] The entire incident reflects unfavorably on the military's acceptance of war as a political act. To make matters worse, on several occasions the CINC hinted he would resign rather than initiate the ground war early.[79]

One should not make too much of the sort of conflicts that appeared during the Gulf War. Such tensions are one of the timeless dimensions of warfare, inherent in the integration of political considerations and military perspectives during times of stress. However, this should not whitewash the problem, particularly since the situation favored the military's desired paradigm. Such problems could have been serious if several factors, such as the need for an early ground offensive, were changed.

Assessing the matter of popular support is a much clearer issue. With regard to Congressional support, the military relearned that Congress is of little help, and that partisan politics can play a stronger role than the Nation's best interests. The Congressional hearings in the fall of 1990 were insufficient and unbalanced, and Congress's late authorization was more of a product of the President's deft political maneuvering than Congressional leadership.[80] Congress did not regain any respect or authority in regard to the ultimate decision of war.

The belief that the media must be controlled is counterproductive for both the military and the country as a whole. The media is now prepared to resist any restrictions, and will go off on its own in the next war. Unreasonable constraints raise deep suspicions that the military has something to hide. A backlash could occur during the next war that will seriously undercut popular support. An adverse situation could arise, like the Amariyah bomb shelter bombing in Baghdad that inadvertently killed 400 Iraqi civilians.[81] Without any degree of mutual trust and credibility, the next incident could become a propaganda victory for our opponents.

Competent military officers have nothing to hide from the press, and attempts to handcuff the media as in Saudi Arabia will be futile and counterproductive.

## SUMMARY

After the war, Mr. Bush effusively declared, "By God, we've licked the Vietnam syndrome once and for all."[82] Like the military, Mr. Bush exorcised his own ghosts and fulfilled his promises. He pledged the war would not be "another Vietnam," that it would not be a halfway effort with a murky ending.

Implicit in this declaration, however, is the presumption that Desert Storm was a decisive victory. Such a conclusion remains debatable. However, the military has largely accepted it, despite the fact that indecisive wars are the rule rather than the exception. As Professor Weigley has shown, the history of warfare leans towards the conclusion of "recalcitrant indecisiveness" when assessing the utility of force as an instrument of statecraft.[83]

A "new" version of the American Way of War emerges in the aftermath of Desert Storm. Strategies of annihilation that seek the complete overthrow of an opponent and his government are now accepted as anomalies. The preference is now for the swift and massed application of overwhelming force for limited ends. The new preferred style acknowledges policy aims as the preceptor of strategy, but insists force is best employed for objectives that can be readily defined in military terms. Additionally, force should be used in those situations where it can be swift and decisive, where its use justifies the risks and resulting costs, and where the forces can be quickly withdrawn. Popular support is maintained by keeping conflict short, attainable, and by controlling the media message to the American taxpayer. Such a view leaves little to conclude other than to point out that this set of circumstances will rarely be satisfied, and that Upton's apolititcal ghost remains present.

The New American Way of War retains the old preferences for absolutism and autonomy during the conduct of military operations. What is sharply different is that such instances are now employed for more limited ends, in situations where military means can be optimally employed for narrower aims, and when both the objectives and the means will be popularly supported for a brief period instead of depending upon national mobilization and the slow building up of national will.

## NOTES

1. Jeffrey Record, *Hollow Victory: A Contrary View of the Gulf War*, McLean, VA: Brassey's, 1993, p. 153.

2. Bobby R. Inman, et al, "Lesson from the Gulf War," *Washington Quarterly*, Winter 1992, p. 57.

3. Summers, *On Strategy II*, p. 1.

4. Rick Atkinson, *Crusade: The Untold Story of the Persian Gulf War*, New York: Houghton Mifflin, 1993, p. 123.

5. U.S. News and World Report, *Triumph Without Victory: The Unreported History of the Persian Gulf War*, New York: Times Books, 1992, p. 71.

6. Guy Gugliotta, "Turning the Mistakes of Vietnam into Lessons for Desert Storm," *Washington Post*, December 23, 1990, p. A14; David H. Petraeus, The American Military and the Lessons of Vietnam; Summers, *On Strategy II*, pp. 7–57. Also Bob Woodward, *The Commanders*, New York: Simon & Schuster, 1991, pp. 229–230 and 306–307; *Triumph Without Victory*, p. 71; Richard P. Hallion, *Storm over Iraq: Air Power and the Gulf War*, Washington, DC: Smithsonian Institute Press, 1992, pp. 1–30; and H. Norman Schwarzkopf with Peter Petre, *It Doesn't Take a Hero*, New York: Bantam, 1992, pp. 145–173, 181–187, 379–380.

7. Despite many indicators of significant improvements in personnel, training, doctrine, and technological capabilities during the 1980s, the press and defense reform movement focused on perceived deficiencies in the U.S. military. Many of these criticisms would be proved baseless in the Gulf. For a sample of the reform school see Edward N. Luttwak, *The Pentagon and the Art of War: The Question of Military Reform*, New York: Simon & Schuster, 1985.

8. *Triumph Without Victory,* p. 71.

9. Atkinson, *Crusade*, p. 299.

10. Ibid., p. 193.

11. U.S. Department of Defense, *Conduct of the Persian Gulf War: Final Report to Congress*, Washington, DC: Government Printing Office, April 1992, p. 33.

12. The objectives were detailed in Mr. Bush's State of the Union address January 16, 1991; quoted in Summers, *On Strategy II*, p. 162; and in the Pentagon's Conduct of the Persian Gulf War report, p. 31.

13. George H. W. Bush, "Out of Troubled Times, A New World Order," *Washington Post*, September 12, 1990, p. 34.

14. *Conduct of the Persian Gulf War*, p. 31.

15. Ibid., p. 46.

16. Thomas A. Keaney and Eliot A. Cohen, *Gulf War Air Power Survey Summary Report*, Washington, DC: U.S. Air Force, Government Printing Office, 1993; Conduct of the Persian Gulf War, pp. 73–75. Atkinson, *Crusade*, p. 299.

17. Atkinson, *Crusade*, p. 298. Those who define the military achievements of CENTCOM and the Coalition as a "hollow victory" appear to jump to a conclusion that eliminating Hussein was an implicit political goal. For example, see Record, *Hollow Victory*, p. 8 and p. 156. Record believes that "American war aims manifestly encompassed Saddam Hussein's removal from power and the permanent elimination of Iraq's ability to threaten its neighbors, especially with ballistic missiles and hyperlethal munitions."

18. Record, *Hollow Victory*, p. 155.

19. *Conduct of the Persian Gulf War,* p. 74.

20. President Bush's Address to the Nation, January 16, 1991. Also cited in Summers, *On Strategy II,* p. 153.

21. *Conduct of the Persian Gulf War*, p. xix.

22. Ibid., p. xix.

23. Ibid., p. 70.

24. Ibid., p. 231.

25. Atkinson, *Crusade,* p. 112.

26. Means, p. 8; Summers, *On Strategy II*, p. 180.

27. Michael R. Gordon, "Generals Favor No Holds Barred by U.S. if Iraq Attacks the Saudis," *New York Times,* August 25, 1991, p. 1. Cited by Summers, *On Strategy II,* p. 112.

28. Dugan quoted in Summers, *On Strategy II,* pp. 112–114. The original statement was made in an article authored by John M. Broder, "U.S. War Plan in Iraq: Decapitate Leadership," *Los Angeles Times,* September 16, 1990, pp. A1, A6–7. This article and a similar piece in the *Washington Post* led to General Dugan's firing by Secretary of Defense Dick Cheney.

29. *Conduct of the Persian Gulf War,* p. 92. See also Atkinson, *Crusade,* pp. 56–65 for an overview of the aerial campaign plan and its direct contrast to Rolling Thunder. Record, *Hollow Victory,* has a good overview of the air war, pp. 103–118.

30. Atkinson, *Crusade,* p. 293.

31. Ibid., pp. 221–224. *Triumph Without Victory,* pp. 268–271.

32. General McPeak's statement was made in a briefing titled "The Air Campaign: Part of the Combined Arms Operation," U.S. Air Force, Washington, DC, March 15, 1991, p. 19. "Air power dominates" is a quote made by Colonel Dennis Drew, director of the Air Force Airpower Research Institute, Air University, Maxwell Air Force Base. Both McPeak and Drew quotes from Record, *Hollow Victory,* p. 103. "Air power won the war" is the conclusion of the Air Force official historian, Dr. Richard Hallion, *Storm Over Iraq,* p. 1.

33. *Triumph Without Victory,* p. 185.

34. Al Santoli, *Leading the Way: How Vietnam Veterans Rebuilt the U.S. Military,* New York: Ballantine, 1993, pp. 422–423.

35. *Triumph Without Victory,* p. 400.

36. Ibid., p. 95.

37. DoD acknowledges most of these complaints in their after action report. See Appendix S, Media Policy, *Conduct of the Persian Gulf War,* pp. 651–655.

38. James LeMoyne, "Pentagon's Strategy for the Press; Good News or No News," *New York Times,* May 5, 1991, p. D1. See also James Kellner, *The Persian Gulf TV War,* Boulder, CO: Westview Press, 1992, p. 83. John Fialka, a respected Wall Street Journal correspondent, also described how CENTCOM used interviews and access as leverage against reporters. See John Fialka, *Hotel Warriors,* Washington, DC: Woodrow Wilson Center Press, 1991, p. 33.

39. Pete Williams was quoted in one report stating that ""the press gave the American people the best war coverage they ever had." Quoted in Howard Kurtz, "News Chiefs Vote to Resist Pentagon War Coverage Rules in Future," *Washington Post,* May 14, 1991, p. 4. Also see Pete Williams, "View From the Pentagon," *Washington Post,* March 17, 1991, pp. D1 and D4. This article is essentially a distillation of his National Press Club speech of March 14, 1991, Reuters Transcript Service. See also Pete Williams, "The Press and the Persian Gulf War," *Parameters,* Summer 1991, pp. 2–9. Mr. Cheney's quote cited in Jason DeParle, "Keeping the News in Step: Are the Pentagon's Rules Here to Stay?" *New York Times,* May 6, 1991, p. 9.

40. Fialka, *Hotel Warriors,* p. 11.

41. David C. Morrison, "Weighing the Ground War in the Gulf," *National Journal,* February 2, 1991, p. 278. David Gergen, a communications director for the Reagan and Clinton administrations, wrote that *U.S. News and World Report* had two weeks notice about the ground campaign scheme of maneuver, but withheld disclosure. David Gergen, "Why America Hates the Press," *U.S. News and World Report,* March 11, 1991, p. 57. The security data is confirmed by Williams, p. 6.

42. Atkinson, *Crusade*, p. 160. Fialka's *Hotel Warriors* remains the best assessment to date. *Triumph Without Victory* is also critical of the "banality of antiseptic official briefings and the shackles of restrictive press pools," p. vi.

43. See Kellner, *The Persian Gulf TV War*, p. 45. Kellner's political views cloud his observations and recommendations. For more balanced assessments read Fialka's *Hotel Warriors*. For another critical review see John R. MacArthur, "The Other Defeat in the Gulf," *New York Times*, July 27, 1992, p. 17.

44. Georgie Anne Geyer, "Mediascape Littered with Gulf Losers: Journalism on the Fly," *Washington Times,* March 6, 1991, p. G3. Henry Allen, "The Gulf Between Media and Military," *Washington Post*, February 21, 1991, pp. D1–D2.

45. Howard Kurtz, "News Media Ask Freer Hand in Future Conflicts," *Washington Post,* July 1, 1991, p. 4. See also Kurtz's earlier "News Chiefs Vow to Resist Pentagon War Coverage Rules in Future," *Washington Post*, May 14, 1991, p. 4.

46. Atkinson, *Crusade,* p. 161.

47. Summers, *On Strategy II*, pp. 7–19; Lewis Sorley, "Creighton Abrams and Active-Reserve Integration in Wartime, *Parameters*, Summer 1991, pp. 37–39.

48. *Conduct of the Persian Gulf War,* p. 471.

49. Schwarzkopf, *It Doesn't Take a Hero,* p. 323.

50. Adam Clymer, "Congress Acts to Authorize War in Gulf: Margins Are 5 Votes in Senate, 67 in House," *New York Times,* January 14, 1991, p. 1; Michael Kinsley, "The War Powers War," *The New Republic*, December 31, 1990, p. 4; Woodward, *The Commanders*, pp. 355–358.

51. Summers, *On Strategy II,* p. 40.

52. Cohen, "After the Battle," p. 19.

53. Record, p. 2.

54. Schwarzkopf, *It Doesn't Take a Hero*, p. 355.

55. Ibid., p. 370.

56. Ibid., pp. 386–387.

57. See *Conduct of the Persian Gulf War*, p. 74. The same six objectives are listed in the Air Force *Gulf War Air Power Survey Summary Report* (hereafter referred to as the GWAPS report), by Thomas A. Keaney and Eliot A. Cohen, Washington, DC: Government Printing Office, October 1993, p. 39. The GWAPS report cites these objectives from the Central Command Operations Order USCINCCENT OPORD 91–001, January 16, 1991.

58. The destruction of the Republican Guard is listed in both the Commander's intent, and the theater objectives. The importance of this objective was also underscored in the GWAPS report, pp. 46–47, p. 106. Atkinson, *Crusade,* p. 299.

59. Schwarzkopf, *It Doesn't Take a Hero,* p. 430.

60. Ibid., p. 497.

61. *Triumph Without Victory,* p. 400.

62. Atkinson, p. 452.

63. Ibid.

64. Means, p. 276; See Cheney's comments to Charlie Gibson on Good Morning America, January 16, 1992 and Katherine Couric on *The Today Show*, also January 16, 1992. For General Powell's views see *CBS This Morning*, interview with Paula Zahn, Reuter Transcript Report, January. 16, 1992.

65. Atkinson, p. 449. General Schwarzkopf states that General Powell called him on February 27 about a cease fire. He also refers to TV imagery appearing on Monday night back in the U.S., and that General Powell told him the White House was nervous about wanton killing. Schwarzkopf, *It Doesn't Take A Hero,* p. 468.

66. Record, *Hollow Victory,* p. 8.

67. This issue is addressed in detail by the GWAPS report, p. 250. Several newspapers articles however did provide direct reports from pilots that they were "shooting fish in a barrel" and participating in a "turkey shoot." Richard Randall, "Like Fish in a Barrel US Pilots Say," *Washington Post,* February 27, 1991, p. A28.

68. Atkinson, *Crusade,* pp. 299–301, p. 491.

69. Ibid., p. 491.

70. CINCCENT wanted the Guard to be reduced 50 percent prior to the start of the ground campaign, and the GWAPS indicates that only 24 percent of the armor assets were attrited. By the end of the war, these units were reduced to 50 percent. The CINC's definition of success also required the three elite Guard Divisions (Tawakalna, Madinah, and Hammurabi divisions) to be incapable of mounting organized brigade level operations. Judging from the reports from the GWAPS, and from the March 1 fight between the 24th Mechanized Division and the Hammurabi, this objective was not achieved. See Keaney and Cohen, *GWAPS,* p. 27–54; Atkinson, *Crusade;* Record, *Hollow Victory,* p. 496.

71. Schwarzkopf, *It Doesn't Take a Hero,* p. 460.

72. Record, *Hollow Victory,* p. 120–127; Eliot A. Cohen, "In God We Trust," *The New Republic,* June 17, 1991, pp. 29–35. On the other hand, the fact that Cheney let Powell present his opinions before the President, speaks well of the Secretary and his subtle conception of civil-military relations. See Woodward, pp. 300–302.

73. Record, *Hollow Victory,* p. 123; Woodward, *The Commanders,* p. 125; Cohen, "In God We Trust," pp. 33–34.

74. Schwarzkopf, *It Doesn't Take a Hero,* p. 321.

75. Ibid., p. 322.

76. Woodward, *The Commanders,* pp. 230–234, 241.

77. This incident is covered in three major post-war books, including Schwarzkopf, *It Doesn't Take a Hero,* p. 368; *Triumph Without Victory,* p. 167; Atkinson, *Crusade,* p. 96.

78. Schwarzkopf, *It Doesn't Take a Hero,* pp. 394–395; *Triumph Without Victory,* p. 190.

79. Atkinson, *Crusade,* p. 270.

80. For an interesting critique of the Administration's view on the constitutionality of the war powers issue see Michael J. Glennon, "The Gulf War and the Constitution," *Foreign Affairs,* Spring 1992, pp. 84–101.

81. *Triumph Without Victory,* p. 272; Atkinson, *Crusade,* pp. 275, 288.

82. Quoted in Atkinson, *Crusade,* p. 493.

83. Russell F. Weigley, *The Age of Battles: The Quest for Decisive Warfare from Breitenfeld to Waterloo,* New York: Macmillan, 1991, p. 537.

# 6

# Decisive Force: The New American Way of War?

In the pleasant aftermath of Desert Storm, President Bush stated that "The specter of Vietnam has been buried forever in the desert sands of the Arabian peninsula."[1] Contrary to Mr. Bush's belief, the Vietnam Syndrome was not buried forever. It lives on, indelibly ingrained in the American military culture. One sharp 42-day campaign will not easily exorcise the trauma of Southeast Asia. Wars are always significant contributors to strategic culture, but great failures are more apt to result in rapid or substantive change. The Gulf war was obviously not a failure. Instead Desert Storm served to reinforce the trends of the preceding two decades in the American military culture.

The preceding chapters have traced the development of what the military learned from its operational experiences in four very different situations. The conflicts were very diverse, but the instructional points reflect common themes. These lessons have now been absorbed into the military culture, a culture arguably "enshrouded in mythology."[2] In addition to the difficulty of drawing lessons from history, such lessons are influenced, for better or worse, by organizational interests and perceptions.

Along with the apparitions of Vietnam, the heady success of Desert Storm is now reflected in a "new" American Way of War. The most distinctive element of this style of warfare is the principle of Decisive Force—the use of overwhelming force to achieve decisive military results without exposing American forces to protracted or indecisive conflict.[3] The concept succinctly sums up the military's perspective of a New American Way of War. The concept is a not-too-distant relative of the Weinberger Doctrine, and represents the distillation of the military's perspective from the four conflicts represented in this effort.[4]

The operational success of CENTCOM's crushing victory has brought the U.S. military full circle from Maxwell Taylor's frustration with Eisenhower's New Look and its reliance on massive retaliation. That frustration prompted him to write the

*Uncertain Trumpet*, the harbinger of "flexible response."[5]  Today, as a result of the Gulf campaign and the latent lessons from Vietnam, our military culture has come full circle and categorically rejects the limited war connotations of flexible response. The military insists on a more certain response for more clearly prescribed purposes. The U.S. military prefers the call of a "certain trumpet" and *inflexible* response.

This chapter will record the documentation of the New American Way of War and test the construct against postulated requirements for the use of military force. Criticisms of the Pentagon's approach will be matched against the requirements the Nation places on military power, and the efforts being made by the Defense Department to prepare for its role in the post-Cold War world.  The remainder of this book seeks answers to the following questions.

1. What is Decisive Force?
2. What are the advantages and disadvantages of the concept?
3. How does Decisive Force match our needs for military force in strategic terms?
4. How does Decisive Force match with future requirements?

## DECISIVE FORCE AND THE NATIONAL MILITARY STRATEGY

The military culture's interpretation of the proper employment of the military as an instrument of national policy has been reduced to the concept of Decisive Force. The concept was developed by the Joint Staff in the period immediately following the Gulf war.  It was persistently articulated by General Colin Powell during his final year in office as Chairman of the Joint Chiefs of Staff.  Numerous journalists and defense experts called it the Pentagon's post-Cold War warfighting doctrine.

The strategic principle of Decisive Force was included in the National Military Strategy (NMS) in 1992.  This was the first time the NMS was articulated in an open and unclassified format.  A public document was seen as a unique opportunity to explain the strategic rationale and framework for the Defense Department's post-Cold War force structure and fiscal requirements.  The strategy was produced in a top down process, unusual for Joint planning documents, and reflected the personal influence of General Powell.[6]

The new military strategy outlined several principles that build on traditional U.S. military strengths.  The purpose of detailing the principles was to capture the key lessons from Desert Storm and exploit weaknesses of those who might threaten U.S. interests.[7]  These strategic principles are recognizable as standard U.S. approaches, including forward presence, collective security, and technological superiority.  The only unique element was the concept of Decisive Force, defined as follows:

Once a decision for military action has been made, half-measures and confused objectives exact a severe price in the form of a protracted conflict which can cause needless waste of human lives and material resources, a divided nation at home, and defeat. Therefore one of the essential elements of our national military strategy is the ability to rapidly assemble the forces needed to win—the concept of applying decisive force to overwhelm our adversaries and thereby terminate conflicts swiftly with minimum loss of life.[8]

According to one of the principal drafters of the NMS, the concept is directly derived from Desert Storm, but it also seems to reflect the lessons of Vietnam and Beirut. In the definition the haunting specter of Vietnam lingers in the references to "protracted conflict" and the "divided nation at home." The military's lessons learned from Vietnam and Beirut are just as clearly demonstrated in the phrase "half-measures and confused objectives." Like the Weinberger Doctrine, an implicit foundation of the concept was a belief that force should only be used with the commitment of the Nation. Also included is the Weinberger criteria of "winning." Last, force should only be applied in such a manner as to ensure success quickly and decisively.[9]

The concept does not address the political decisions of *why* or *when* military force is used. The focus of the principle is on *how* military force should be applied. However, the requirement for clear objectives, for permitting the military to apply decisive force to win by overwhelming opponents, and for quickly terminating battle with a minimum of casualties reflects the essence of the New American Way of War. The concentrated use of offensive means, employing both mass and technology, remains consistent with the traditional strategy of annihilation.

The New American Way of War, though, does not assume that mass will be used to grind down an opponent through exhaustion. That takes too much time, protracts conflicts, and could lead to media-induced perceptions that sap public support. The limits of time, sensitivity to casualties, and popular support that influence our strategic culture no longer permit the older traditional approach. The emphasis has switched from slow and ponderous applications of resources in the tradition of U. S. Grant to a more focused and qualitatively improved style. As reflected in Decisive Force, the modern U.S. military seeks to use overwhelming force to rapidly overcome any opponent in as short a time period as possible, and with the least cost to us in terms of lives.

## THE CRITICS

The doctrine has been criticized in general for its insistence on the massive and unequivocal application of combat power. Critics of this approach include Mr. Les Aspin, then Chairman of the House Armed Services Committee, who sensed an "all or nothing" approach solidifying in the Nation's military leadership.[10] Mr. Aspin identified a common but narrow understanding within the Officer corps on the use of military force. In a speech made in late 1992, he evaluated this "new" school of military thought. He was critical of what he saw as a checklist approach, and its inapplicability to the challenges of maintaining peace in the post-Cold War world.

Mr. Aspin quite accurately predicted the dynamics of the uncertain, but chaotic, nature of this international security environment. He also accurately sensed that the U.S. military was not institutionally prepared or predisposed for the requirements of this environment.

Mr. Aspin found the emergence of this consensus among the Officer corps disturbing. He summarized his perception of this consensus in four propositions on when force is appropriate.

1.  Only as a last resort. Diplomatic and economic sanctions should be tried first.
2.  Only when there is a clear-cut military objective. Forces should not be sent to achieve vague political goals.
3.  Only when we can measure that the military objective can been achieved. We need to know when to bring the forces home.
4.  Only in an overwhelming fashion. We should get it done quickly and with little loss of life, by the use of overwhelming force.[11]

Mr. Aspin pejoratively termed this consensus with a bumper sticker slogan—the "all or nothing" school. From his view on the House Armed Services Committee, a "block of very expert opinion" existed that was unwilling to accept the wide variety of situations that exist where limited military force could be employed in the post-Cold War world. In essence, what he perceived was the return to an absolutist orientation in the U.S. military in the aftermath of Desert Storm. What he found unacceptable was the failure to accept that situations might exist where force be used prudently short of all out war. Mr. Aspin's view of the post-Cold War world reflected a Hobbesian world of fervent nationalism, terrorism, and ethnic conflict. An "all or nothing" absolutist school would be inconsistent with meeting challenges in this chaotic international security environment.

In direct contrast to the absolutist position, Mr. Aspin placed himself among a "limited objectives" school that finds the threat of military action and limited military operations as useful tools for preserving peace in an unstable world. Mr. Aspin concluded that the pragmatic application of force, and the coercive threat of force, served U.S. policy goals best in the post-Cold War world. His position was predicated on two basic assumptions. The first was that the demise of the Soviet Union permitted us to closely control the throttle and gear shift of any conflict without fear of escalation into a superpower Armageddon. Second, the American military technical revolution offered new tools in the form of precision munitions and advanced aerospace technology for compellence against rogue aggressors and challenges to the international community.

In Mr. Aspin's estimation, the end of the Cold War freed the United States from self-imposed limitations and from the fear of Third World conflicts escalating beyond control. Freed from the dangers of escalation, Mr. Aspin argued that we could opt for limited interventions without fear of sliding into quagmires and use force surgically with little risk to ourselves.[12]

Mr. Aspin was not alone. Others were equally critical of the generation of a "Beirut syndrome" as a substitute for the Vietnam syndrome. This Lebanese version made the Pentagon uneasy about handling less than ideal situations and made it resist involvement in sticky situations that did not fit its preferred paradigm and doctrine of overwhelming force.[13] The end result of this syndrome, the critics charged, was the failure to address serious challenges in Europe as the former Yugoslavia disintegrated.

The early criticisms of Decisive Force should be understood in the context of the domestic debate in the United States over intervention into Bosnia-Herzegovnia in 1992. In addition, the long suffering population of Somalia was ravaged by famine, and its government had completely collapsed into anarchy. Many critics wanted to mobilize the Pentagon to resolve these crises but found the military reluctant. The strategic backdrop to the entire debate was the role of America in the post-Cold War world. The options ranged from reverting to insular isolationism or mindless interventionism in the pursuit of idealistic humanitarian agendas.[14]

Proponents of a U.S. military intervention into the maelstrom that once was Yugoslavia were critical of the Pentagon's active resistance to intervention in Bosnia. One writer called the Pentagon's new attitude the "Invincible Force Doctrine," perceiving a reluctance to get involved in anything less than all-out conventional conflicts where our comparative advantages in technology could be put to use to.[15]

Some major newspapers were critical of what they saw as traditional absolutism from the Joint Chiefs of Staff stemming from Vietnam, noting that "the U.S. military continues to oppose limited intervention for limited goals."[16] The criticism was sometimes directed personally at General Powell, including a historically inaccurate and unfavorable comparison with General McClellan.[17] It was implied that the Pentagon was skewing policy choices with its professional advice and that its doctrine was predicated on maintaining a larger than necessary defense budget.[18] The *New York Times* opined that for roughly $280 billion the Pentagon should offer more than "no can do," and provide "a range of options more sophisticated than off or on, stay out completely or go in all the way to total victory."[19]

## COUNTERPOINTS

General Powell responded forthrightly to all his critics in numerous forums. Through these speeches, General Powell clarified and expanded the concept of Decisive Force. He admitted that he preferred decisive means instead of "surgical pin pricks" and limited bombings in situations like Bosnia. General Powell added:

Decisive means and results are always to be preferred, even if they are not always possible. We should always be skeptical when so-called experts suggest that all a particular crisis calls for is a little surgical bombing or a limited attack. History has not been kind to this approach to war-making.[20]

General Powell specifically responded to Mr. Aspin's speech in late 1992 in a major article that appeared in *Foreign Affairs*.  In this response, he rejected most of Mr. Aspin's distinctions between "limited war" and the "all-out war" schools as moot "academic niceties."  Somewhat ironically, Mr. Aspin became General Powell's immediate superior upon his confirmation as Secretary of Defense just a few months later.

However, in these rebuttals he further reinforced perceptions that the Pentagon was actively resisting involvement in limited conflicts.  During an interview with *The New York Times*, General Powell purportedly stated, "As soon as they tell me it is limited, it means they do not care whether you achieve a result or not.  As soon as they tell me it's surgical, I head for the bunker."[21]

Such statements also fed directly into the perceptions of critics who believed that the "all or nothing" school was the principal school of thought in the Pentagon.

General Powell eventually responded to these critics with a detailed description of what Decisive Force meant in terms of a process or guidelines for the determination of how military combat forces should be employed.  He had no qualms with the military being employed for nontraditional missions, and noted that Decisive Force was misinterpreted.  Making a major distinction, he distinguished between humanitarian operations and combat, or what he called "violent means," which was when he acknowledged that views began to differ about the use of force.[22]

He specifically rejected the insinuation that he or any other element of the Pentagon was advocating an absolutist approach or an insistence on "winning" in military terms.  "This is not to argue that the use of force is constrained to only those occurrences where the victory of American arms will be resounding, swift and overwhelming," he wrote.  But it does mean, he added, that force should be restricted to those situations where it can do some good, where the benefits outweigh the costs and risks that will accrue.[23]

General Powell's elucidations on the Decisive Force concept expanded it into a more generic decision making process than the singular operational doctrine that appeared in the National Military Strategy.  As he expounded on this set of guidelines, the so-called Powell Doctrine began to sound very much like the Weinberger Doctrine.  Force, according to General Powell, can be employed:

1. When the objective is important and clearly defined
2. When all nonviolent means have failed
3. When military force can achieve the desired political objective
4. When the costs and risks are acceptable, in terms of expected gains
5. When the consequences have been thought out[24]

These distinctions clarified the strategic concept, but at the same time, it extended his views past the professional purview about *how* force should be employed to a broader process or formula about *when* and *where* force is optimally used.  As his retirement approached in late 1993, General Powell's popularity and effectiveness as Chairman of the Joint Chiefs of Staff was recognized, but the legacy of his doctrine was consistently noted as a debatable issue born from the "indelible lessons from his generation's seminal conflict" in Vietnam as well as the failure of American policy in Lebanon. Even extremely favorable assessments pointed to General Powell as the author of a post-Cold War doctrine for American military force tied to the "deep emotional traditions of the American military." The most vocal critics, advocates of limited intervention in Europe, argued for a need for more flexibility from the Pentagon than "the reigning strategic doctrine of overwhelming force."[25]

Even when the military was tasked to provide forces for Somalia in late 1992, the so-called "Powell Doctrine" was raised. Critics focused on the massive size of the task force dispatched to Mogadishu, and its limited mission. Several critics noted the composition of the force reflected "the doctrine of decisive and overwhelming force championed by General Colin Powell," but wondered if the military acquiesced to the mission because it did not involve politics, there were few constraints, few risks, and a clear exit.[26] The use of excessive amounts of troops did not seem to raise any political concerns at the time, and provided the military commanders on the scene with sufficient force to provide a wide range of humanitarian missions in as secure an environment as could be created in famine torn Somalia.

The Somalia expedition demonstrably shows that the use of military force always incurs some risks and requires constant monitoring. The tragic debacle of October 3, 1993 when 18 U.S. Army Rangers were killed and another 75 injured in a firefight in Mogadishu has served to reinforce the concept of Decisive Force and its applicability to humanitarian missions as well. The example of Somalia, one could argue, vindicates the Decisive Force concept.[27] Both the senior envoy to Somalia, Ambassador Robert Oakley, and the Commanding General of the U.S. Central Command, Marine General Joseph Hoar, have concluded that Somalia supports the need for "overwhelming force" even in peacekeeping or humanitarian tasks.[28] However, it could be argued that the use of firepower and overwhelming force in Somalia was inappropriate for the task at hand.

The principle of Decisive Force has outlived General Powell's tenure as Chairman of the Joint Chiefs. It was reflected as a fundamental planning element in the Defense Department's final Persian Gulf conflict report to Congress in 1992, and has been retained as a basic strategic concept in revisions to the next iteration of the National Military Strategy.[29] The principle of Decisive Force is now firmly rooted in the U.S. military lexicon and culture. The remainder of this chapter will explore the advantages and disadvantages of this strategic concept.

## THE STRATEGIC USE OF POWER

The evaluation of the utility of decisive force as a declaratory policy or strategic principle hinges on how well its serves the use of power as an instrument of policy. Ultimately, the concept must be measured against what we want military power to do. The National Military Strategy is designed to address the "ways and means" that military force will contribute to desired ends. Decisive Force is a "way" of operating towards these ends or objectives. For analysis purposes, the Decisive Force concept will be matched and evaluated against four purposes served by military power. These are *deterrence, defense, decisive influence* when deterrence fails, and *diplomatic support.*[30] These four functions are detailed in Table 2.

### Deterrence

Deterrence is a difficult factor in defense theology. It cannot be predicted, nor can one even claim credit for success. Causation for something that does not occur, like deterring aggression, cannot be proven. Nonetheless, the concept of deterrence is universally accepted, and exists largely as a function of a state's credibility. Deterrence in its broadest sense means persuading an opponent not to initiate an action because of the perceived benefits and costs of doing so.[31] It presumes rationality on the part of the opposing state, since we are attempting to influence the antagonist to rationally compare the relative costs he will incur should he attempt to do something against us.

**Table 2**
**The Strategic Uses of Military Power**

| PURPOSE | DESCRIPTION |
|---|---|
| Deterrence | Strategic and conventional deterrence. Passive vice active use of force. |
| Defense | Defend CONUS and allies from external attack. Could include preventive war or preemptive employment. |
| Decisive Influence | Compellence via combat, or coercion via a specific threat of force. |
| Diplomatic Support | Peacekeeping, security assistance, and humanitarian tasks. |

The credibility factor is a function of both a country's assessed capabilities and perceived will. For the past several decades, other nations recognized that the United States had an enormous capacity in terms of raw military power, but our willingness to employ it decisively to advance stated policy aims was questioned.

Deterrence failed at the outset in preventing the invasion of Kuwait, but our decisive response should increase our credibility for future scenarios. Future opponents now have a new data set to calculate the costs of opposing the United States in conventional military conflict. With Iraq vanquished so decisively, Desert Storm "adds a powerful dimension to the ability of the United States to deter war."[32]

Of course this strategic credit account could be needlessly squandered by a feckless Administration that failed to employ diplomacy and force consistently.

The concept of deterrence is enhanced with the adoption of Decisive Force as a declaratory policy. Deterrence hinges upon perceptions about *capacity* and *will*. Around the world, nations have strategic "balance sheets" reflecting their overall credibility. Our stated intention of employing force decisively, with the full range of U.S. military and technological capabilities, improves deterrence and might minimize the number of opportunities whereby the U.S. strategic credit account is tapped.[33] This remains true as long as the perceived strategic balance sheet is not mindlessly debited on marginal accounts and expenditures.

### Defense

Likewise, military power is also used to defend the continental United States (CONUS), and our allies. The United States has numerous treaty obligations and collective defense arrangements. The credibility of these pacts is enhanced by the presumption that the U.S. government intends to and is fully capable of defending itself and its close friends. The defense literature normally includes the options of preventive war, or preemptive military operations, as legitimate means of maintaining a nation's defense. Such options are not consistent with American strategic culture or U.S. defense requirements.

Decisive Force remains supportive of the defensive employment of combat forces. The principle, as defined, minimizes any potential presumptions that America will fail to fully defend alliance members or U.S. possessions with anything less than a full response. This will contribute to situations such as North Korea that threaten a U.S. ally.

### Decisive Influence

The third purpose of military power is to achieve stated policy aims by decisively influencing another actors policies and/or behaviors. This is accomplished by coercion or compellence. Coercion involves the active threat of military force, as opposed to the more passive form of persuasion found in deterrence. Coercive diplomacy offers the possibility of achieving objectives economically, with little bloodshed, and fewer political costs and risk.[34] When employing coercive diplomacy, one tries to persuade another state to cease something by signalling, bargaining, or negotiating through an admixture of threats and "carrots."

Decisive Force provides real credibility to coercive diplomacy. A successful coercing power must create an image of urgency and unacceptable damage, and Decisive Force generates sufficient urgency and sense of risk in the opposing government's decision making process (assuming they are rational).

Coercive diplomacy is usually associated with crisis management and "brinkmanship." A fundamental component of coercive diplomacy is the perception that military force is a real and viable alternative. Diplomats can weaken this credibility by employing a "try and see" negotiating tactic or by bluffing.[35] An antagonist can call a bluff. This forces a subsequent decision or reaction on the part of the coercing power. If the coercing power finds it lacks the necessary will or means to carry out its threat, its credibility is reduced. A state may decide, for the purpose of credibility or prestige, that it needs to follow through on its threat, even if the original objective was not worth the costs and risks of combat. Techniques such as "try and see" can result in policy disasters and reduced credibility. Equally disastrous are situations when either diplomats or military figures make public statements that weaken the perception that military "sticks" are under active consideration and that the targeted power is not under the real risk of unacceptable damage. Thus, effective coercion requires the close coordination of diplomatic and military considerations before the fact.

The other form of decisive influence involves the active form of compellence. Compelling another government or group to change its goals or actions is normally accomplished by physically destroying its military capability or means to resist. This can also be done by the effective threat of force, when the target government changes its policy aims prior to the initiation of combat. Obviously, this purpose is consistent with the primary purpose for which military forces are trained and maintained. Decisive Force is completely consistent with the requirements of effective compellence.

### Diplomatic Support

The fourth and final purpose of military power is to provide necessary services, advice, and leverage to our diplomatic efforts. Military forces can provide a wide host of capabilities that enhance diplomacy or support international missions. International support in the form of security assistance, nation building, and peacekeeping are included in this category. Both the National Military Strategy and General Powell take support for such missions "as a given."[36] The historical record of the past several years in the Philippines, Iraq, Russia, Los Angeles, Florida, Bangladesh, and Somalia, strongly support the conclusion that the military is both capable and willing to execute these missions.

Decisive Force does not seem applicable here, but it is actually quite relevant. Diplomatic support includes "military operations short of war," which by definition could involve peacekeeping and peace-enforcement tasks.[37] Peacekeeping operations are defined as missions to separate two warring parties who have accepted the introduction of an interpositionary force and who show a willingness to end the conflict. The peacekeeping force remains in place to assure both parties that they are secure from the other side.

Peace-enforcement operations are fundamentally different. They lack the formal agreement by the parties regarding the introduction of the interpositionary force and lack any mutual consensus on terminating hostile activities. Thus, peace-enforcement missions require the introduction of an effective and robust military force to physically separate and maintain the separation of two hostile parties.[38]

While both peacekeeping and peace-enforcement operations fall under the umbrella of operations other than war, they do involve circumstances where the use of deadly force may be warranted. Under both types of missions, a large and actively engaged presence consistent with the principle of Decisive Force is useful. Intimidation of the local antagonists is an effective deterrent and a by-product of Decisive Force. This serves the overall mission by deterring factions from violating the peace, or by quickly establishing a peace where none existed. There is a historical tradition of employing lightly armed troops as peacekeepers and limiting their role to passive observers. Experience in recent operations suggests that the traditional approach is breaking down as a result of casualties absorbed by peacekeepers who found themselves restrained by inappropriate rules of engagement or governmental restrictions out of touch with conditions on the ground. Peacekeeping forces must remain neutral to execute their role, but neutral does not have to mean neutered.

However, there are other situations under diplomatic support (security assistance, Foreign Internal Defense, or nation building) where an extensive U.S. presence or where the unrestrained employment of American maneuver forces, firepower, or technology is inappropriate. It is possible that Decisive Force is not always overwhelming force in a strictly conventional military sense. This would include many situations under the umbrella of "operations other than war," such as counter-insurgency, where long-term social, political, and economic problems in areas of interest to the United States may require interventions of a politico-military nature, for a protracted period of time. In such scenarios (e.g., El Salvador), the introduction of Decisive Force to "overwhelm" the adversary may have little meaning, or may be counterproductive. In such scenarios, the meaning of decisive needs to be clarified and refined.

To summarize this section, the concept of Decisive Force supports the four purposes of military power. There is a need to differentiate between Decisive Force as it applies to warfighting or "violent means," and the sort of protracted and persistent involvement required in some low-intensity situations where tightly integrated politico-military operations are needed. The 1992 National Military Strategy did not adequately address this distinction, but subsequent revisions indicate that this has been noticed and rectified.

## MISINTERPRETATIONS AND MISAPPLICATIONS

In assessing the utility and viability of the principle of Decisive Force, a number of potential problems have been raised. These include problems associated with:

1. Prescriptive solutions
2. Misapplied precedents
3. Policy/Strategy inversion

## Prescriptive Solutions

Prescriptive approaches rarely fail to meet the tests of history, particularly in dynamic time periods. We certainly live in interesting times, disproving the overly simplistic notion of "endism."[39] The very breadth of the challenges facing the U.S. national security interests contradicts the simplistic notion that a single doctrine will provide the necessary guidance to deal constructively with the range of problems that might cause the introduction of U.S. military force.

The U.S. military discourages Jominian or Mahanian prescriptions in its military schools. This does not mean that Decisive Force could not creep into operational doctrines or exercises and be misapplied. There are indications its influence has been seen adversely in high-level wargames conducted at the National Defense University.[40]

Doctrine can be a convenient means of encapsulating history and lessons, but it can also be "the most frightful tyrants to which men ever are subject, because doctrines get inside of a man's own reason and betray him against himself."[41] Doctrine is defined as the "fundamental principles by which the military forces or elements thereof guide their actions in support of national objectives. It is authoritative but requires judgment in application."[42] Military commanders must have the mental agility to recognize distinctions between situations, avoid overestimating likenesses, and ignore key distinctions between scenarios. The U.S. military has not often demonstrated such strategic or doctrinal agility, and Vietnam reflects a relevant example.

General Powell is fully aware of the danger of prescriptive rules. He specifically noted that Decisive Force is not a fixed approach and that saying there was only one way to use force was similar to stating you should always use the elevator during a fire. Sure enough the next time there is a fire, the elevator is blocked. General Powell underscored his understanding that circumstances and the nature of a problem drive the response to it.[43] All doctrine and all principles can be misapplied if used inappropriately or out of context. Dogmatic or prescriptive applications are rarely effective, but this does not rule out the utility of doctrine. The challenge is to refine the judgment of military leaders to use strategies and operational doctrine as guidelines.

## Misapplied Precedents

The second theoretical issue involves the precedents that lie under the concept of Decisive Force. Precedents and historical analogies are important benchmarks in organizational cultures and learning. Great failures have historically been drivers of dramatic organizational change in military institutions, and great successes have contributed to complacency. We have reviewed the lessons that the U.S. military garnered from Vietnam and Beirut, and the vindication drawn from the desert in Kuwait. Yet, as Robert Jervis has warned, past success can be the cause of failure in future situations.[44]   A healthy measure of caution in accepting lessons and analogies is needed when developing and applying strategic concepts.

One problem with Decisive Force is the reverse logic of the precedents it has been drawn from.  Because Decisive Force is described as the antithesis of Vietnam, the logical reverse conclusion is that a massive and overwhelming application of ground forces and unconstrained airpower would have resulted in Hanoi's capitulation.  Hopefully this would be recognized by senior civilian and military leaders as an erroneous conclusion drawn from faulty logic.  As Professor Jay Luvaas from the U.S. Army War College notes, "there is a tendency not to appreciate that once removed from its unique context, a specific lesson loses much of its usefulness."[45]   Analogies are useful historical and analytical tools, but critical distinctions in analogies must be detailed.   "Desert Storm lessons do not automatically apply to Vietnam" should be a major conclusion to the Pentagon's Gulf War report.[46]

Equally unsettling is the application of the principle of overwhelming force to low-intensity situations such as El Salvador.  El Salvador represented a situation that many in the United States equated to a Vietnam-like quagmire.  However, the Reagan administration intervened in El Salvador with a long-term, low-cost (politically and in human lives), protracted involvement.  The strategy was limited by Congressional constraints, which probably elongated our commitment but forced us to draw on a cadre of core expertise left over from Vietnam.  To Latin American specialists, the U.S. intervention is an unqualified success, although our experience could be "forgotten before its significance can be fully absorbed."[47]

The issue of how the principle of Decisive Force relates to situations requiring the delicate integration of various instruments of national power needs to be addressed.  At this point it is merely noted that a potential conflict exists if the strategic concept evolves into a basic warfighting doctrine applied universally across the entire conflict spectrum as implied in the 1992 National Military Strategy.  It may not be applicable in situations short of war.  Decisive Force seems most relevant in those situations where the introduction of forces for combat is contemplated.

### Policy/Strategy Inversion

The impetus behind some critics of Decisive Force has been a perception the doctrine constitutes a restraint on the effective use of military power as an instrument of policy.  The same criticisms were thrown against the Weinberger Doctrine, because its criteria were seen by some as restrictive and only satisfied by a Soviet thrust through the Fulda Gap or another Pearl Harbor.[48]

Several critics have claimed that the purpose of the Decisive Force doctrine is to invert the subordination of military strategy to policy aims, by advocating a single and narrow strategic doctrine.  These critics have read into the doctrine all the post-World War II historical perspectives of American military culture—autonomy, apoliticism and absolutism.  Under this interpretation, the doctrine limits the use of military means to cases where political objectives that can be met with purely military means, in situations devoid of uncertainty, with little supervision and absolutely no restraints in terms of force size or firepower. Mr. Aspin's criticism's fall into this category.

Another pair of critics sees in the adoption of the New American Way of War an insistence that warfare "must follow a logic of its own, a logic in which all must be subordinated to complete military victory." Most critically, this "implies that government must effectively relinquish control over war's conduct in the name and for the sake of such victory."[49] Obviously, this is the reverse of what Clausewitz offered as the normal priority for affairs of state.

Such a pejorative interpretation cannot be taken by the doctrine when seen in the context of the National Military Strategy in its entirety, or upon review of General Powell's amplifying remarks. Admittedly, the professional ethic of the first 85 years of this century earned the U.S. military a reputation for apoliticism and technocracy. U.S. military history during World War II and in Vietnam revealed our marked inability to comprehend the deeper context of specific conflict situations. The result is "a lack of appreciation of the relationship between politics and war that makes the military a poor adviser to political authority on anything other than the technical side of military activity" and fails to provide the basis for an effective dialogue between military and civilian authorities.[50]

Such a harsh criticism of the U.S. military may no longer be valid. General Powell responds to such issues by pointing out that his statutory function as Chairman of the Joint Chiefs is to serve as the principal military advisor to the President. This role requires providing the National Command Authorities with his expert opinion regarding decisions that commit the Armed Forces of the United States to combat. His biggest interest is in defining what political outcome is desired, and matching military means to that end, when they are feasible. General Powell stresses that "this is not an abstract academic exercise."[51] He did not apologize for being reluctant to send troops into harm's way without a clear purpose in mind. Matching political objectives to the use of force in advance, instead of on the fly, is a valid function for the Chairman in fulfilling his role. In describing his role within the national security policy process, General Powell did not constrain his role to a purely functional or technical task:

My responsibility is to lay out to my political leaders the full range of military options, to let them know what we can do, to let them know how we can solve a political problem, to let them know where I do not believe military force will solve a political problem, and to make them understand all of the consequences of the use of military force.[52]

Instead of being blind to politics, or focusing purely on the technical aspects of military force, General Powell's input into policy matters reflects a greater degree of political sensitivity and "fusion" than seen in the past. This continues a trend evident since the mid-1980s to ensure that the decision making process includes a frank assessment of alternatives, costs, and risks. Such assessments are a part of the properly balanced pattern of civil-military relations that Dr. Huntington espoused. The last two decades have made the senior military leadership wary about civilian decision makers and the perspectives and opinions they bring to the table. Thus, the military insists on stronger representation and a greater consideration given to the consequences and limitations of military force. This should not be taken as a desire on the part of the U.S. military to break the linkage between policy goals and the tools of policy, or to make the application of force into something autonomous.

The concept of Decisive Force should be seen as the military's expert opinion on how military means can best contribute to meeting a policy objective. If it is seen as cautious, it accurately reflects the understanding of the military culture that not all situations can be satisfactorily met by military means. Such caution is not an attack on the primacy of civilian control in our political culture. Under any form of civil-military relations, such advice is proper and consistent with effective policy. It is only when such advice skews options, estimates, and recommendations that alarm is justified. Effective strategy is the product of retaining a degree of proportionality between ends and means. Decisive Force is designed, not to warp that relationship, but to ensure the risks and costs of intervention are kept in line with the value of the aim. Policy makers need to ensure that such a cost-benefit analysis is always conducted, even when the factors under consideration involve intangibles.

## FUTURE CONFLICT

Another useful test of the Decisive Force concept is comparing it against the projected employment requirements of the next decade. What kind of conflicts does the Pentagon anticipate facing, and what sort of preparations in terms of doctrine, force structure, or resources is the Defense Department making? Is the military planning to refight the last war by Decisive Force?

The U.S. military has conducted a thorough lessons-learned effort from the Gulf war. Most of these assessments have consistently underscored the unique aspects of the conflict, including political considerations, that contributed to the success of the coalition.[53] The professional literature is replete with indications that the military is aware of the potential for overlearning the lessons of Desert Storm, and the need to prepare for a wide range of threats and missions in the near term.[54]

As might be expected, the cultural orientation remains focused on the upper end of the conflict spectrum, and the ability to rapidly project overwhelming combat power from the United States for a regional conflict. The fundamental aspects of the Pentagon's warfighting strategy, although reoriented from a global strategy to a regional level, remain fixed on the application of firepower and technology against a conventional opponent in a major regional contingency. This should be seen in a broader context. The primary purpose of the Nation's armed forces remains deterring or winning wars. Regional scenarios as defined in the National Military Strategy and the Pentagon's follow up reviews represent an appropriate planning focus for the Pentagon.

The U.S. military is mindful of the criticism about refighting the last war. Fully aware that potential antagonists will conduct their own "lessons learned" effort from the Gulf war, the Pentagon recognizes that future opponents and future wars will be different.[55] The rest of the world now realizes that "pulling Uncle Sam's beard" can be hazardous to one's health.[56] Third World countries, particularly potential aggressor states, have concluded that they cannot compete with American military capabilities in the conventional sense, and that weapons of mass destruction offer a means of avoiding American intervention. To some regional powers, the conclusion from the Gulf war is summed up by the Indian Defense Chief of Staff, who when asked what was the most important lesson of the Gulf war, replied "Never fight the U.S. without nuclear weapons."[57]

The alternative approach could be a return to the employment of asymmetrical approaches to obviate areas of operational and technological superiority of the United States.[58] This would result in the adoption of more ambiguous situations and the use of terrorism, insurgency, and forms of low-intensity conflict. This is also supported by assessments indicating that ethnic conflict and cultural wars represent growing trends in international conflicts.[59] In *The Transformation of War*, noted Israeli historian Martin van Creveld points out that the trend in conflicts around the world leans not toward Desert Storm conflicts but towards non-conventional or paramilitary affairs, including terrorism, drug cartels, or insurgencies. Such a trend would suggest that future situations will not be clear-cut opportunities for the American Way of War.

The pattern of conflict, and the international lessons of Desert Storm, have combined to ensure that a strong probability exists that the U.S. military will be faced with future conflicts far more murky and frustrating.[60] The nature of the U.S. military's style of warfare, reinforced by Decisive Force, will place us at a disadvantage since we "historically had difficulty with prosecuting less conventional types of conflicts"[61]

Yet this may be a premature as well as a pessimistic conclusion. Critics tend to focus on the past historical record of the U.S. military and its cultural predispositions, and ignore the recent efforts by all the Services, and by the Department as a whole, to enhance the Pentagon's approach to low-intensity conflict situations, or as they are now called, "operations other than war."[62] Many still believe the Pentagon is institutionally unprepared or predisposed against effective involvement in such situations. As an example of a recent assessment by one pair of instructors:

The current preference of the U.S. military is captured in the Powell corollary to the Weinberger doctrine: the fast, overwhelming and decisive application of maximum force in the minimum time. Such an approach may produce effective, short-term results. It is irrelevant, probably even counterproductive, when matched against the very difficult internal problems that form the underlying problems in target countries.[63]

However, accepting this point of view requires one to ignore a large body of evidence of steps taken by DOD to ensure that force is used appropriately, depending upon the contingent circumstances faced in each unique situation. The military has taken numerous steps towards preparing for threats less challenging than the Soviets or another Gulf war.

The military fully recognizes the complexity of the future, the ambiguity of the challenges that might prompt military actions, and has crafted a military strategy and supporting capabilities to provide a range of deterrent options to support crisis management actions.[64] These actions are reflected in the development of the Adaptive Planning process articulated in the National Military Strategy, as well as the Flexible Deterrent Options (FDOs) that the Joint Staff and each Unified Command have prepared for each theater. FDOs provide a menu of preplanned options, including troop movements, exercises, and demonstrations, keyed to anticipated crisis and contingencies. The FDOs include a wide array of responses that integrate all instruments of national power to deter aggression, resolve conflict, position or deploy needed forces, or decisively fight and win.[65] However, the actual utility of these FDOs may be undercut by the ingrained mentality of senior military leaders against the use or movement of force for anything other than a purely military objective.[66]

The wide range of potential missions for the Armed Services can also be seen in the Defense Department's latest strategic assessment, the Bottom Up Review (BUR). The BUR addressed regional dangers, including proliferation of means of mass destruction, and opportunities where the use of military force can constructively contribute to reducing instability in situations short of armed combat. The options range from forward presence to deter conflicts, providing regional stability through visits and exercises, and conducting smaller scale intervention operations, such as peace-enforcement, peacekeeping, humanitarian assistance, and disaster relief to further U.S. interests and objectives.[67] The new strategy acknowledges that deterring regional aggression remains the most demanding scenario of the strategy, but that "our emphasis on engagement, prevention, and partnership, means that, in this new era, U.S. military forces are more likely to be involved in operations short of declared or intense warfare."[68]

If the military is adopting an "all or nothing" attitude, it is not apparent in doctrine published since Desert Storm. The Joint Staff, the U.S. Army, and the Air Force have all recently published major new doctrinal publications. None of these documents can be accused of advocating an "all or nothing" school. Quite to the contrary, each doctrinal document being developed includes a new chapter covering "operations other than war." These describe such missions as key operational environments requiring special skills and approaches that the U.S. military must be prepared for.[69] In the past, the issue of small or unconventional conflicts was relegated to separate and secondary publications.

While they have not published any major doctrinal publications, the Navy and Marine Corps have published a major policy White Paper called *"Forward. . . From the Sea"* which indicates a reorientation from large-scale operations at sea against a global threat and a refocusing towards smaller operations along the littorals and coastlines. The Navy has a long-standing history as an element of diplomacy and crisis response.[70]

Likewise, the Marine Corps has a historical reputation for service in expeditionary environments and in crises. Building on its experience in Latin America in the first few decades of this century, the Marines published the *Small Wars Manual* in 1940. The protracted and political nature of small wars is understood by the Marines, who republished the manual in 1987 anticipating the rise of instabilities around the world. The Marines recognize that small wars are "conceived in uncertainty, are conducted often with precarious responsibility and doubtful authority, under indeterminate orders, lacking specific instructions."[71] In fact, of all the Services, the Marine Corps is the one service most culturally predisposed towards small-scale conflicts requiring extensive amd delicate politico-military interaction.[72] The performance of the Marines in Somalia in late 1992 and early 1993 would reinforce this assessment.

There is one potential problem with Decisive Force and the pattern of conflict. The U.S. military acknowledges that the use of force must be tailored to its intended purpose, and can be limited by the nature of the conflict or the desired policy aim. There are situations where the literal application of Decisive Force is inapplicable or counterproductive. The military's existing low-intensity conflict doctrine includes several supporting principles including "restraint" and "persistence."[73] In many low-intensity situations, the concepts of restraint and persistence are very applicable and in direct opposition to the concept of Decisive Force, with its swift and overwhelming application of force and rapid withdrawal. When do the principles of restraint and persistence apply, and when is overwhelming force more applicable?

Thus, all the Services seem prepared strategically and doctrinally for a wider and more variegated range of problems. Publishing policy and doctrine, though, is not the same as being able to execute. Changes in personnel policy, training and education, and equipment will have to follow if the U.S. military is serious. The decline in budget resources will result in competing interests for fewer resources. There have been debates about the substantial costs of nontraditional and peacekeeping missions in the professional literature, and the degradation of capabilities and readiness if too much emphasis is placed on such tasks.[74] Given the uncertainty of the DoD budget and the sharp decline in available forces as the U.S. military downsizes, such concerns are very legitimate.

What remains to be seen is how the Services execute their respective doctrines and if "overwhelming" or Decisive Force supersedes the contingent assessment that each scenario warrants. "Playing to win" in such conflicts will require a more sophisticated understanding of political conditions on the part of the U.S. Armed Forces than it has historically shown.

## CONCLUSIONS

Sir Michael Howard was once very pessimistic about the institutional ability of the military to draw upon history between periods of conflict to adapt its strategy, doctrine, and force structure to meet the next threat effectively. The U.S. military is in such a period today, and could fail to properly adapt itself appropriately for the twenty-first century. Still, he said,

It is the task of military science to prevent the doctrines from being too badly wrong. All scientific thought is a sustained attempt to separate out the constants in any situation from the variable, to explain what is of continuing validity and to discard what is ephemeral, to establish certain abiding principles and to reduce them to their briefest most elegant formulation.[75]

Overall, the principle of Decisive Force does not appear "too badly wrong" if accepted at face value. It is an abiding principle of continuing validity, but one that is not reduced yet to its most elegant formulation. It satisfies most, but not all, of the expected strategic uses of military power. As presently worded, it could lead to misinterpretations or misapplication. Issues such as the application of Decisive Force across the conflict spectrum must be addressed. The relationship between Decisive Force and political objectives should be delineated in greater detail. Military victory for the sake of military victory is not consistent with Clausewitz or sound policy. What is decisive in one conflict may not be applicable in another. In fact, "yesterday's solutions, no matter how well or dramatically executed, rarely address tomorrow's problems."[76] Finally, a warning about prescriptive applications and the contingent nature of warfare must be made. Future conflicts will most likely resemble Beirut, Panama, and Somalia. It would behoove the Pentagon to dust off the lessons learned files on these case histories. Better yet, it may need to rewrite them.

Sir Michael had good reason to be pessimistic about military organizations and their ability to adapt. The lessons learned by the four conflicts in this book would reinforce such pessimism. Strategic concepts cannot be accepted or evaluated at face value. They are, ultimately, the product of historical development, institutional interpretation, and bias. Subjected to numerous competing pressures in the 1990s, the U.S. military will be hard pressed to analyze conflicts and their political context with professional detachment. Failure to do so and render appropriate advice to elected policy makers would return civil-military relations in the United States to the early 1960s and early 1980s, when inflexibility or absolutism excluded a proper voice to military considerations in policy councils.

## NOTES

1. President Bush quoted in Robert W. Tucker and David C. Hendrickson, *The Imperial Temptation: The New World Order and America's Purpose*, New York: Council on Foreign Relations Press, 1992, p. 152; Also cited by Harry Summers, *On Strategy II*, p. 7.

2. Snow and Drew, *From Lexington to Desert Storm*, p. 327.

3. Chairman, Joint Chiefs of Staff, *National Military Strategy of the United States*, Washington, DC: Government Printing Office, January 1992, p. 10.

4. The concept of sending sufficient forces to win "and win overwhelmingly" is consistent with the Weinberger doctrine. Mr. Weinberger used the same language himself in his memoirs. Caspar W. Weinberger, *Fighting for Peace*, New York: Warner, pp. 159–160.

5. Maxwell D. Taylor, *The Uncertain Trumpet*, New York: Harper, 1959.

6. Robert J. Art, *Strategy and Management in the Post-Cold War Pentagon*, Carlisle, PA: Strategic Studies Institute, U.S. Army War College, June 22, 1992, p. 20; Harry E. Rothmann, *Forging a New National Miliary Strategy in a Post-Cold War World: A Perspective from the Joint Staff*, Carlisle, PA: Strategic Studies Institute, U.S. Army War College, February 1992, pp. 1, 16. Colonel Rothmann was head of the Strategy Applications Branch, J-5 during the development of the 1992 strategy.

7. *National Military Strategy*, pp. 8–9.

8. Ibid., p. 10. Original drafts of the strategy employed the phrase "overwhelming force" vice decisive which was the subject of debate between the Joint Staff and various Pentagon departments. Eventually, the term "decisive force" was selected to avoid negative connotations. The present author was an action officer at the Pentagon at this time and involved in preparing Service comments for the Marine Corps. Confirmed by General Powell in an interview January 11, 1994. The terms overwhelming and decisive continue to be used. See Colin Powell, "U.S. Forces: Challenges Ahead," *Foreign Affairs*, Winter 1992/93, pp. 32–45.

9. Rothmann, p. 6.

10. Les Aspin, "Role of U.S. Military in Post-Cold War World," address before the Jewish Institute for National Security Affairs, September 21, 1992, pp. 1–6. The "all or nothing" characterization is a common attribution applied to the U.S. military. It can be found in Samuel P. Huntington, "Playing to Win," *The National Interest*, Spring 1986, pp. 8–16.

11. Aspin, p. 2.

12. Ibid., p. 6.

13. Jim Hoagland, "Here's a New One: The Beirut Syndrome," *Washington Post*, April 14, 1991, p. B7.

14. For a critique of the liberal internationalist viewpoint see Stephen Stedman, "The New Interventionists," *Foreign Affairs*, 1992/1993, pp. 1–16.

15. Jim Hoagland, "How August's Guns Will Shape U.S. Policy," *Washington Post*, August 9, 1992, p. A35.

16. Editorial, "At Least Slow the Slaughter," *New York Times*, October 4, 1992, p. E16.

17. Ibid. Dr. Weigley explored the comparison in "The American Military and the Principle of Civilian Control from McClellan to Powell," *Journal of Military History*, October 1993, pp. 27–58.

18. Editorial, "A Chairman for Changing Times," *New York Times*, September 14, 1992, p. 18.

19. "At Least Slow the Slaughter," p. E16.

20. Powell, "Challenges Ahead," p. 40.

21. Powell quoted in *New York Times* editorial, "At Least Slow the Slaughter," October 4, 1992, p. E16.

22. Powell, "Challenges Ahead," p. 36.

23. Ibid., p. 40.

24. Ibid., p. 38.

25. Eric Schmitt, "Powell Retires, as Popular With the Public as With His Troops," *New York Times*, October 1, 1993, p. A12. "Reigning doctrine" quote from *New York Times* editorial, "A Chairman for Changing Times," September 14, 1993, p. 18. See also Brian Duffy, "The Rules of the Game: A New Chairman of the Joint Chiefs of Staff and New Questions About American Use of Force," *U.S. News and World Report*, August 23, 1993, pp. 22–24; and Barton Gellman, "Powell Resumes Civilian Life After 35 Years," *Washington Post*, October 1, 1993, p. A21. Gellman concluded: "Among Powell's most hotly debated legacies is a doctrine of what he calls "decisive force," an attempt to prevent the dispatch of U.S. troops into circumstances they do not have the means to control."

26. Eric Schmitt, "Somalia Role: Why?" *New York Times*, August 27, 1993, p. A10; Jim Hoagland, "On Somalia, A Mysterious Decision," *Washington Post*, December 3, 1992, p. A21; Henry Kissinger, "Somalia, Reservations," *Washington Post*, December 13, 1992, p. C7. Kissinger remarked that Operation Restore Hope reflected "the new Pentagon approach toward military intervention, which says that never again must American military power be vitiated by political restraint" and that "once employed American force must be overwhelming." Along the same lines is Sidney Blumenthal, "Why Are We in Somalia?" *The New Yorker*, October 25, 1993, pp. 48–54.

27. General Powell made this same point when interviewed and asked to evaluate the application of Decisive Force to both interventions in Somalia. The principle "did not apply" in the first intervention because "it was not a war," but that it was actually implemented and successful in the sense that the size and disposition of the original 28,000 Marine contingent was able to maintain control. Author's interview with General C. Powell, January 11, 1994.

28. Robert B. Oakley, "An Envoy's Perspective," *Joint Force Quarterly*, Autumn 1993, p. 55; General Joseph P. Hoar, "A CINC's Perspective," *Joint Force Quarterly*, Autumn 1993, p. 63. Both commentaries share a common definition of overwhelming force in terms of force size.

29. Joint Chiefs of Staff, *National Military Strategy*, unpublished draft, dated December 6, 1993. The first two drafts of the 1994 update to the NMS retitled the Decisive Force concept as the principle of *prevailing force*. Subsequent revisions returned to Decisive Force, with criteria regarding policy considerations for the effective use of military force. Interview with Joint Staff action officer, J-5, January 1994; *Inside the Navy*, January 3, 1994, pp. 6–8. The final published version of the NMS retained the phrase Decisive Force, but it falls in line with the final recommendations of this study and employs it only within the context of warfighting.

30. These four purposes have been derived from Robert J. Art's "The Four Functions of Force," in Robert J. Art and Kenneth N. Waltz, eds., *The Use of Force: Military Power and International Politics*, 3rd ed., Lanham, MD: University Press of America, 1988, pp. 3–11. Art detailed Defend, Deter, Compel, and Swagger as his four functions.

31. John J. Mearsheimer, *Conventional Deterrence*, Ithaca, NY: Cornell University Press, 1983, p. 14.

32. William J. Perry, "Desert Storm and Deterrence," *Foreign Affairs*, Fall 1991, p. 17.

33. For more specific assessments of influence on Hussein's strategic calculations see Janice Gross Stein, "Deterrence and Compellence in the Gulf, 1990-1991," *International Security*, Fall 1992, pp. 147–175. The most well recognized deterrence literature includes

Alexander L. George and Richard Smoke, *Deterrence in American Foreign Policy*, New York: Columbia University Press, 1974; Thomas Schelling, *Arms and Influence*, New Haven: Yale University Press, 1966; and Schelling's *The Strategy of Conflict*, New York: Oxford University Press, 1960.

34. Alexander L. George, "Crisis Management: The Interaction of Political and Military Considerations," *Survival*, Vol. 26, September-October, 1984, p. 225.

35. Gordon A. Craig and Alexander L. George, *Force and Statecraft: Diplomatic Problems of Our Times*, 2d ed., New York: Oxford University Press, p. 199. Mr. Aspin's approach to coercive diplomacy appeared to accept this as a valid technique. General Powell referred to this technique as the "huff and puff" school of coercive diplomacy. Advocates of this approach have frequently later recommended military intervention, in circumstances where earlier analysis had determined that major interests were not engaged, in order to preserve national credibility or prestige. Interview with General Powell, January 11, 1994.

36. Powell, "Challenges Ahead", p. 33.

37. Department of the Army Field Manual, *FM 100-5 Operations*, Washington, DC: Government Printing Office, June 1993, pp. 2-0 and G-6, defines Military Operations Short of War as "military activities during peacetime and conflict that do not necessarily involve armed clashes between two organized forces."

38. These definitions are drawn from Donald M. Snow, *Peacekeeping, Peacemaking, and Peace-enforcement: The U.S. Role in the New International Order*, Carlisle, PA: U.S. Army War College, February 1993, pp. 15–30. Snow believes that effective involvement in various humanitarian and U.N. operations will require that the U.S. military, and particularly the U.S. Army, abandon "post-Vietnam dogma." In particular Dr. Snow points to the Weinberger Doctrine and "General Powell's principle of massive and rapid application of overwhelming force" as inappropriate for peace-enforcement situations.

39. "Endism" is the moniker applied to Francis Fukyama's thesis that we have arrived at the end of history, and that liberal democracy's and free market economies are predominant. Francis Fukuyama, "The End of History," *The National Interest*, No. 16, Summer 1989, pp. 3–18.

40. Sam Gardiner, "Overwhelming Force: A Guide For Policy or a Strategic Principle for Historians?" unpublished article, dated January 5, 1994, pp. 1–5. Mr. Gardiner is a retired Air Force officer who has worked with wargaming and studies for RAND and the National Defense University. Gardiner's article indicates that a crisis management scenario escalated faster and farther than intended as players rapidly brought in forces seeking to establish an overwhelming force capability.

41. William Graham Summer, cited in I. M. Destler, Leslie H. Gelb, and Anthony Lake, *Our Own Worst Enemy: The Unmaking of American Foreign Policy*, New York: Simon and Schuster, 1984, p. 272.

42. Joint Chiefs of Staff, *JCS Pub 1-02, DOD Dictionary of Military and Associated Terms*, Washington, DC: Government Printing Office, December 1, 1989, p. 118.

43. Powell, "Challenges Ahead," p. 36.

44. Robert Jervis, *Perception and Misperception in International Politics*, Princeton: Princeton University Press, 1976, pp. 217–282.

45. Jay Luvaas, "Lessons and Lessons Learned, A Historical Perspective," in Robert E. Harkavy and Stephanie G. Neuman, eds., *The Lessons of Recent Wars in the Third World*, Lexington, MA: Lexington Books, 1985, p. 68.

46. Daniel W. Christman and Robert D. Walz, "Military Role in the Emerging National Security Policy," in Helms, Robert F., and Robert H. Dorff, eds., *The Persian Gulf Crisis: Power in the Post-Cold War World*, Westport, CT: Praeger, 1992, p. 138.

47. Victor M. Rosello, "Lessons From El Salvador," *Parameters*, Winter 1993/1994, p. 108. For a critical but early assessment of U.S. policy and lack of success in El Salvador see Andrew J. Bacevich, et al, *American Military Policy in Small Wars: The Case of El Salvador*, Washington, Pergamon-Brassey's, 1988. For a favorable perspective completed just recently see Michael J. Hennelly, "U.S. Policy in El Salvador: Creating Beauty or Beast?" *Parameters*, Spring 1993, pp. 60–66.

48. Betts, *Soldiers, Statesmen, and Cold War Crises*, p. 221.

49. Tucker and Hendrickson, *The Imperial Temptation*, p. 159.

50. Snow and Drew, *From Lexington to Desert Storm*, p. 330.

51. Quote from General Powell's speech before the National Press Club, September 28, 1993, Reuter Transcript Service, p. 5.

52. Green Berry Melton, "Sacred Honor: A Biography of Gen. Colin Powell," *Today's Officer*, October 1993, p. 17.

53. See Dick Cheney's comments in the Defense Department's *Conduct of the Persian Gulf War* report completed in April 1992, pp. xvi–xviii.

54. Drew Bennet, "Will the Next War Be Like the Last One," *Marine Corps Gazette*, March 1992, pp. 2–13; Joseph J. Collins, "Desert Storm and the Lessons of Learning," *Parameters*, Fall, 1992, pp. 83–95; Daniel P. Bolger, "The Ghosts of Omdurman," *Parameters*, Autumn 1991, pp. 30–39; R. Scott Moore, "Small War Lessons Learned," *Marine Corps Gazette*, February 1993, pp. 32–34.

55. Cheney, *Conduct of the Persian Gulf War*, p. xvi. Christman and Walz, "Military Role in the Emerging National Security Policy," p. 138.

56. Patrick J. Garrity, "Implications of the Persian Gulf War for Regional Powers," *The Washington Quarterly*, Summer 1993, p. 154.

57. Quoted in Thomas Mahnken, "America's Next War," *The Washington Quarterly*, Summer 1993, p. 177; See also Garrity, p. 159.

58. Mahnken, pp. 175–180. Another foreign officer warned that "Saddam Hussein and the Third World also has lessons learned. They learned not to take on the United States or any other major power in conventional warfare." Santoli, *Leading the Way*, p. 410.

59. Martin Van Creveld, *The Transformation of War*, New York: Free Press, 1991, pp. 192–223. For an opposing view from a serving military officer, see Major Kenneth F. McKenzie, Jr., "Elegant Irrelevance: Fourth General Warfare," *Parameters*, Autumn 1993, pp. 51–60. At a somewhat different level of analysis regarding the forms and basis for conflict in the next century see Samuel P. Huntington, "The Clash of Civilizations," *Foreign Affairs*, Summer 1993, pp. 22–49.

60. Donald M. Snow, *Third World Conflicts and American Response in the Post-Cold War World*, Carlisle, PA: Strategic Studies Institute, U.S. Army War College, March 1991, p. 50.

61. Mahnken, p. 174; Cohen, "Constraints on the Conduct of Small Wars," pp. 280–307; Carnes Lord, "America's Strategic Culture and Small Wars," pp. 269–277; Sam Sarkesian, "The Myth of U.S. Capability in Unconventional Conflicts," *Military Review*, September 1988, pp. 2–17.

62. Joint publications and the Army's doctrinal publications have redefined the conflict spectrum into three areas; peacetime, operations other than war, and war. Under the area of operations other than war are missions that involve combat, and other tasks that are fulfilled short of the use of violent means. Joint Publication 3-0, *Doctrine for Joint*

*Operations*, Washington, DC, Joint Chiefs of Staff, September 1993, p. I-3; U.S. Army Field Manual 100-5, *Operations*, Headquarters, U.S. Army, Washington, DC, June 1993, p. 2-1.

63. Snow and Drew, *From Lexington to Desert Storm*, pp. 325–326

64. Christman and Walz, "Military Role in the Emerging National Security Policy," pp. 137–138.

65. See the *National Military Strategy*, p. 12; U.S. Armed Forces Staff College, *Joint Officer Guide*, Armed Forces Staff College, 1993, pp. 6-11 to 6-16.

66. The author attended a major military wargame in the summer of 1995, and a senior military official acknowledged in a public forum that he viewed FDOs "from a warrior's perspective." The same flag grade officer, representing the Joint Staff, also added that military forces should not be used to signal resolve, commitment, or interest. The explicit impression was to view FDOs, not as political instruments, but as a means of enhancing force posture in the event a crisis turned towards conflict.

67. Les Aspin, *Report of the Bottom Up Review*, Washington, DC: Department of Defense, October 1993, p. 7.

68. Ibid., p. 8.

69. Joint Chiefs of Staff, *JCS 3-0, Doctrine for Joint Operations*, pp. V-1 to V-16; U.S. Army, *FM100-5 Operations*, pp. 13-1 to 13-8; U.S. Air Force, *AFM 1-1 Basic Aerospace Doctrine of the United States Air Force*, vol. 2, March 1992, pp. 55–62.

70. Department of the Navy, ". . . *From the Sea: Preparing the Naval Service for the 21st Century*," Washington, DC: Government Printing Office, undated but published in 1992. For Navy participation in crises see Thomas P. Barnett and Linda D. Lancaster, "Answering the 911 Call: U.S. Military and Naval Crisis Response Activity, 1977–1991," Alexandria, VA: Center for Naval Analyses, August 1992, p. 7. This study shows that the U.S. Navy has been employed in over 86 percent of all crises over a fourteen year period covered in the report.

71. U.S. Marine Corps, *Small Wars Manual*, Washington, DC: Government Printing Office, 1940 (reprinted in 1987).

72. This point was suggested by General Trainor, Director, National Security Programs, Harvard University. Interview with the author, January 11, 1994.

73. The principles of low-intensity conflict include: objective, unity of effort, security, legitimacy, persistence, and restraint. The latter two are in direct contrast with the concept of Decisive Force. These principles were originally contained in FM 100-20, Low Intensity Conflict. The principles have now been included in the Joint Staff and Army principal operational doctrines. See Joint Chiefs of Staff, *JCS 3-0 Doctrine for Joint Operations*, Washington, DC: September 1993, pp. V-2 to V-4; and U. S. Army, *FM 100-5 Operations*, pp. 13-3 to 13-4.

74. Concerns about politicizing the military and diluting its capabilities by employing it in non-traditional domestic and international missions are the essential arguments of Charles J. Dunlap, "The Origins of the American Miliary Coup of 2012," *Parameters*, Winter 1992/1993, pp. 2–20; Charles J. Dunlap, "The Last American Warrior: Non-Traditional Missions and the Decline of the U.S. Armed Forces," *The Fletcher Forum*, Winter/Spring 1994, pp. 75–92; John F. Hillen, "Peacekeeping is Hell: America Unlearns the Lessons of Vietnam," *Policy Review*, Fall 1993, pp. 36–39; Seth Cropsey, "The Hard Truth About Soft Missions," *Wall Street Journal*, January 19, 1993, p. 14. Dunlap's argument has been widely distributed and cited. Hillen goes much further than Dunlap in criticizing peacekeeping missions, comparing them to Vietnam and wars of attrition. The goals and limitations of such tasks do not seek "decisive victory through overwhelming force. It is

complete anathema to the American military, evoking memories of Vietnam," p. 38. For an opposing view see Admiral Paul D. Miller, "In the Absence of War: Employing America's Military Capabilities in the 1990s," *The Fletcher Forum*, Winter/Spring 1994, pp. 5–16.

75. Michael Howard, "Military Science in an Age of Peace," *Journal of Royal United Services Institute*, March 1979, p. 4.

76. Bolger, "Ghosts of Omdurman," p. 31.

# 7

# Conclusions

It has been written that an army's doctrine is inseparable from its past and, therefore, rigorous study of the past is crucial to evaluating any given doctrine.[1] Likewise, strategies are the product of the accretion of experience and the interpretations of that experience. Understanding a given strategy requires an equally rigorous study of its strategic culture and the history within it. "To understand a strategy," one scholar has observed, "it is not sufficient simply to understand the facts on which it ostensibly is based. One must also understand the origins of the guiding principles and opinions that rendered the strategy."[2] To really understand a military strategy one must dig below the hidden assumptions, below the institutional interpretations, and into the sources of the strategy. The foregoing project has dug below the assumptions and organizational views underlying a new strategic concept.

The strategic concept of Decisive Force is consistent with the past experiences of the U.S. military and the American Way of War. It also consistent with the subjective lessons that institution has taken from recent conflicts. An appreciation of its antecedents helps to assess its potential utility and its liabilities. An inescapable concern from this review is the historical resistance and institutional inadequacy of the U.S. military in limited or unconventional conflict. Additionally, the U.S. military's separation of politics from military operations remains troubling despite what appears to have been a very tight correspondence during Desert Storm. A distinct preference for limited civilian oversight and control, and cynical views about maintaining public support, are equally alarming.

More alarming is the dangerous oversimplification of the complexity of war to a group of shibboleths. Calls to "set clear political objectives" and "don't tie the military hands behind their back" make both the decision to go to war and the conduct of war appear far easier than it really is. Similarly, other reductionisms abound. "Get out of the military's way," "protracted wars lose public support," and now, "use overwhelming force" are similar examples.

Such attitudes represent the inherent tensions of our strategic culture and the American Way of War. Our strategic culture does not fully accept the cold Clausewitzian rationalization of war as an instrument of policy. Yet the primacy of civilian control, and the subordination of the military to policy and to policy makers, remains a part of our political culture. This inherent tension goes back to the days of Upton. It is doubtful that Upton's Ghost will be laid to rest anytime soon.

## CLARITY OF PURPOSE

While a credible strategy and doctrine must meet the tests of "strategic acceptability" within the strategic culture, it must also ultimately serve the interests of that culture by being prepared to adequately counter expected threats. A pattern of smaller scale operations in future conflicts is fairly certain. The U.S. military must be prepared for engagements in situations of uncertainty and ambiguity, for such are the conditions of small wars.[3] In armed conflict, warns Dr. van Creveld, "no success is possible—or even conceivable—which is not grounded in an ability to tolerate uncertainty, cope with it, and make use of it."[4]

This does not excuse civilian leaders from seeking clarity of purpose when employing military force. The fog of war on the battlefield is bad enough and need not be worsened by confusion in the war council. Political goals and direction are required to ensure that military force serves the ends it is unleashed for. There is nothing heretical for military leaders to ask for, and insist on, such guidance. Nor is this guidance the sole purview of civilian policy makers. Under the form of civil-military relations operative in this country, the military should and must participate in an interaction with policy makers to effectively develop policy goals and corresponding strategies.

## PLAYING TO WIN

The U.S. military must guard against prescriptive approaches to the use of force. Our sense of professionalism must continue to include the proper integration of politics and military viewpoints. We cannot return to the faults of Vietnam, where a "disproportionate fascination with means at the expense of ends" produced a strategy at odds with the desired consequences.[5] Our inputs at the highest level of decision making must always focus on producing a strategy designed to produce a very precise correspondence between means and ends.

I am not arguing that force should be subject to the notion of "calibration." The history behind this concept is not very heartening.[6] We have become the world's sole superpower, and our use of military power should reflect this fact. We should pick our spots carefully, and then act decisively. We are a large, industrially advanced, technologically sophisticated, and often violent society. "Our military strategy," wrote Samuel Huntington, "should be, and indeed, must be built upon these facts. The way we fight necessarily will reflect the way we live."[7]

Still, this does not preclude ensuring that the means serve the desired end. The meaning of "decisive" and "victory" contain some degree of variation or imprecision. Defining success purely in terms of military victory will not always insure the desired outcome. "Playing to win" will require greater elasticity in concept and execution. The alternative is "the emergence of war not as the servant but as the master of politics."[8] The danger of military expediency evident in "overwhelming force" cannot be underscored enough.

While the Prussian Clausewitz would spin in his grave at some of the public statements made during Desert Storm by senior officers, there are indications that the Decisive Force doctrine is starting to be questioned throughout the U.S. military.[9] Lieutenant General Anthony Zinni, a Marine Corps officer, reflected a growing conclusion that, indeed, the U.S. military must do more than just deserts and Desert Storms, it must also "do windows" when he observed in a seminar that:

The missions we get certainly are nontraditional—I have trained and established police forces, judiciary committees and judges, and prison systems; I have resettled refugees, in massive numbers, twice: I've negotiated with warlords, tribal leaders, and clan elders; I have distributed food, provided medical assistance, worried about well-baby care, and put in place obstetrical clinics; I've run refugee camps; and I've managed newspapers and run radio stations to counter misinformation attempts. I'm an infantryman of 30 years standing. Nowhere in my infantry training did anybody prepare me for all this. We can say these things are not the matters that our armed forces should be involved in, but this is the direction that the new world disorder is going, and there isn't anybody else to call upon for help. And these are the kinds of operations we have to do better. We need to learn the nontraditional tasks required to accomplish our mission.[10]

Such a consensus, although much more common among the Naval Services than the other armed services, is sorely needed at present. The post-Cold War security environment offers a respite from a confrontation with another superpower, but not the end of conflict. The present era is replete with ethnic violence, local aggression, and humanitarian crises. These situations do not fit the neat guidelines of the Powell Doctrine. General Powell's doctrine of decisive force is "insufficient for many of the smoldering conflicts the United States faces today, where the military is called on not to win a decisive "victory" but to support diplomacy, protect peacekeepers, or carry out humanitarian tasks."[11] On balance, Richard Haass, a former NSC official has written, "the post-Cold War world promises to be a messy one where violence is common, where conflicts within and between nation-states abound, and where the question of U.S. military intervention becomes more rather than less commonplace and more rather than less complicated."[12] In such an environment, decision making on a case-by-case basis is all but unavoidable. One can develop guidelines to assist in analyzing cases, but "criteria established in the abstract can never anticipate particular contexts: the devil will always be in the details."[13] The present "professional orthodoxy" about using military force leaves something to be desired, especially when wrestling with the devil.[14]

## CIVIL-MILITARY RELATIONS

One of the most topical issues in the current security debate about the use of force involves the state of civil-military relations. To some observers, the military is "out of control" and a scandal exists because the military is vocally reluctant to employ force in pursuit of vague foreign policy objectives.[15] Other equally cogent observers have criticized the basis for these commentaries, and noted that civil-military relations and forms of civilian control need to adapt to new post-Cold War conditions.[16]

Overall, after looking through a number of case studies, it is apparent that civil-military relations, broadly defined, have been "undergoing long term deterioration" for many years and that the scars from these cases will not fade. This is not to conclude, however, that the blame should be placed entirely on the military, or even partly. While one can find scar tissue covering the organizational culture of the U.S. military, Eliot Cohen, an astute observer of the U.S. defense establishment, believes "the difficulty is much more on the other side, in the absence of a civilian class familiar with military people."[17]

Dr. Cohen, professor of strategic studies at Johns Hopkins University, acknowledges the major thrust of Kohn's and Luttwak's arguments, that the U.S. military is politically astute and bureaucratically powerful, but argues that the real problem is due to the "absence of a civilian class familiar with military matters and comfortable with military people."[18] Thus, twisting the debate around, it is the civilians, not the soldiers, who have abdicated their responsibilities. Both sides agree that a degree of tension exists.

The existence of tension between political leaders and military professionals is neither new or unexpected. Cohen even suggests such tension and conflict may even be an essential ingredient for victory.[19] However, a review of U.S. military history shows a long standing degree of tension since World War II, with little advantage. This would support a definitive conclusion that military conflict is most successfully conducted with healthy and open civil-military interaction and discourse. Such an open discourse does not occur in op-ed pieces in *The New York Times*, or public insistence by young Army officers that "Political strategies that aim to use armed force must accommodate the way in which that force is best used."[20]

In establishing a proper equilibrium in the relationship with civilian policy makers who are ultimately responsible for the decision to employ force to pursue political goals, the U.S. military must remain faithful to the "sacred trust" with the American people that General Marshall so jealously protected. There is no demand for a political military or one that substantially influences political decisions beyond its own expert advice.

That does not mean that the military must avoid any role in the political process or that the relationship is totally amicable. That would be an erroneous conclusion. The military has a legitimate role in providing advice and representing the military to both the Executive and Legislative branches of government, as well as to the American public. The primary role, however, is to provide clear and unequivocal estimates and recommendations to civilian policy makers when the use of force is considered. There will always be differences between the requirements of policy and the brutal realities of the battlefield. There is no way around this tension. General Matthew Ridgway once defined the ideal form of effective relations between civilian leaders and military professionals.

The statesman says to the soldier, "This is our national policy. What military means are required to support it?" The soldier studies the problem and replies with the means and costs. If the civilian authority finds the cost to be greater than the country can bear, then either the objectives themselves should be modified, or the responsibility for the risks involved should be forthrightly accepted. Under no circumstances, should the professional military man yield, or compromise his judgement. To do otherwise would be to destroy his usefulness.[21]

This should remain the ideal form, although it may be rarely attained.

## POPULAR SUPPORT

Keeping wars short and decisive will assuredly preclude the media from meddling in military affairs or reducing operational security. Trying to block out the media from access to future battlefields, however, is probably impossible, and could prove counterproductive. Pluralism, diversity, and public opinion are also all a part of our strategic culture, and thus, a part of the American Way of War too. Our political culture is fraught with tension, and the role of the media is an inherent and constant element of that friction. The American military might consider giving the American citizen greater credit for his or her ability to evaluate news information. Popular support remains more a product of success than a prerequisite for the effective conduct of military operations.

## CONCLUSIONS

This book has rigorously tested the principle of Decisive Force. The historical roots, development, and refinement of the concept over the past two decades have been documented. The concept has been tested against the requirements for military force, to include expected scenarios where military force might be employed in the decade ahead.

Based on this effort, the following conclusions have been drawn:

1. *Decisive Force is derived from the military's perceived lessons learned from the past two decades, particularly Vietnam, Lebanon, and Desert Storm.* While the lessons are not altogether accurate, they have served to focus attention on the principal considerations to be evaluated before employing violent force. Policy makers should be aware of the source, the strength, and the veracity of these lessons.

2. *Decisive Force is consistent with our strategic culture and the American Way of War.* While it appears well matched to the military's operational preference, it also reflects the limits of our political culture and our demographic form of government. In particular, it reflects the need to maintain popular support and preclude casualties endemic to the American political culture and the balances carefully drawn by the Founding Fathers in our public institutions. However, our public institutions were developed long ago, when the country's security interests were very different than today. It is not sufficient to argue what the Founding Father intended of a fledgling nation isolated by two large oceanic moats.

3. *Decisive Force is a very useful declaratory policy but does not enhance the use of military force as an instrument of diplomacy.* Decisive Force as a national strategic concept supports deterrence, defense, and decisive influence. At the same time, it prevents early use of military force to signal resolve or serve as a forceful deterrent during a crisis. This may limit military power as a tool during coercive diplomacy. Policy makers do not need to feel bound by military strategic concepts or declaratory policies, but could become hamstrung by domestic or international politics if the military takes a public stance.

4. *Decisive Force, while stated as an overarching strategic concept, is not universally applicable across the conflict spectrum and is inappropriate in the post-Cold War security environment.* It is applicable to almost all uses of force for violent means. Some situations, such as counterinsurgency, may require greater restraint and persistence, and less violent means. The pattern of conflict for the next decade or two will seriously challenge our capacity to handle ambiguous and hybrid forms of political warfare.

5. *Decisive Force does not represent a direct challenge to effective civil-military relations.* It does represent the considered judgment of the military about how combat forces should be employed, which must be noted. Ultimately, the judgment of when and how military forces are employed remains the purview of constituted civilian authority. Political leaders need to be aware of the nature of military affairs and of the military as a subset of the American strategic culture. Just as important, military officers need to engage their civilian counterparts in a detailed exchange on the issues raised in this book. An open dialogue is needed, and the military's professional military educational institutions offer an excellent venue for such an exchange. Regretfully, civil-military relations are not studied adequately at these institutions, and civilian policy makers do not spend enough time interacting with the professional military in forums where an honest and open debate can bring the issues involved to some resolution. Future research at our leading defense institutions should be directed at this problem, instead of refighting the military versus the media battle ad nauseum.

## SUMMARY

This book has addressed the development, advantages, and limitations of a strategic concept. Ultimately, the existence, benefits, and potential misapplication of this concept were shown. The major concern that motivated this endeavor was a perception about a trend in absolutism among the Officer corps stemming from the success of Desert Storm. The late Mr. Aspin obviously perceived the same trend. These attitudes could become insidiously inculcated into the institutional culture of the U.S. military and corrupt its professionalism and usefulness. Such attitudes would seriously impair the alloy of military and policy perspectives that produce effective strategic decisions.

These same attitudes could also ruin the proper balance between the roles of senior military officers and their civilian superiors in a democratic government. Our country has a limited conception of the proper relationships involved in civil-military relations in a democracy. Dr. Huntington has emphasized that civil-military relations are *the* principal institutional component of national security policy. However, the relationship is precarious and the principle of civilian control is too often taken for granted.[22]

Those who wield a sword in the service of the State must have a keen appreciation for the political and social context in which force is applied, domestically and externally. This mandates their interactive involvement in policy matters involving the use of the military instrument. Military leaders must be willing to tell their superiors what they *need* to hear, not what they want to tell them or what the civilian leader would like to hear.[23] The historical record to date suggests that General Powell met this test, but misinterpretation of Decisive Force puts this legacy at risk.

Military advice must be unvarnished, and at the same time it must not be colored by institutional preferences or biases. The most significant aspect of the professional ethos of the U.S. military is the obligation to the principle of civilian control. The opportunity to influence policy by the provision of sound professional military assessments is consistent with that obligation. Using opportunities when military intervention is under consideration to execute cultural predispositions is not. To compromise on the military advice they give would destroy their usefulness, as General Ridgway warned.

Civilian officials have obligations, too. The risks and costs incurred when the sword is employed are high. The costs of intervention must be measured against the value of the interests being advanced or defended. Civilian officials need to spend a greater amount of time studying the military, understanding its challenges as a profession, and wrestling with the intricacies of its employment. The strong attitudes, culture, and capabilities of the military must be fully understood by those elected to make policy decisions. Without such an understanding it is very doubtful that the "ultimate decision," the decision to send America's sons and daughters into armed conflict, will be wisely made.

The sword is drawn for a specific political objective, which controls the aim, magnitude, and duration of the effort.  Political leaders are ultimately responsible for meshing the military and political considerations and controlling this effort.  They alone define the aim and approve the means sought to procure it.  They must ensure that their aim is appropriate to the means, and that they have not ignored the risks, costs, and limitations of military force.  This requires listening to the professional advice of those who understand the limitations and blunt capabilities of military power.  Clausewitz warned that Statesmen need a grasp of military affairs so that the sword is not be used in a manner foreign to its nature.  A grasp of military affairs should include a feel for the military culture, and its relationship to our strategic culture as well.  If there is this is one single conclusion to draw from this analysis it is that those who forge the sword need to have a far keener appreciation for both the temper and edge of that instrument before drawing it.

## NOTES

1. Paul Hebert, *Deciding What Has to Be Done: General William E. DePuy and the 1976 Edition of FM 100-5, Operations*, Fort Leavenworth, KS: Combat Studies Institute, 1988, p. 107.

2. Yitzhak Klein, "A Theory of Strategic Culture," *Comparative Strategy*, Vol. 10, Fall 1991, p. 4.

3. Moore, "Small Wars Lessons Learned," p. 32.

4. Martin van Creveld, *Technology and War: From 2000 B.C. to the Present*, New York: Free Press, 1989, p. 316.

5. Gaddis, *Strategies of Containment*, p. 238.

6. Fry, Stone, and Wood, pp. 199–200.

7. Huntington, "Playing to Win," p. 13.

8. Russell F. Weigley quoted in Bacevich, "New Rules: Modern War and Military Professionalism," *Parameters*, December, 1990, p. 19.

9. Thomas E. Ricks, "Colin Powell's Doctrine on Use of Military Force Is Now Being Questioned by Senior U.S. Officers," *Wall Street Journal*, August 30, 1995, p. 12

10. Anthony Zinni, "It's Not Nice and Neat," *Naval Institute Proceedings*, August 1995, p. 29

11. Michael R. Gordon and Bernard E. Trainor, *The General's War: The Inside Story of the Conflict in the Gulf*, New York: Little Brown, 1995, p. 469

12. Richard N. Haass, *Intervention: The Use of American Force in the Post-Cold War World*, Washington, DC: Brookings Institution, 1994, p. 2

13. Ibid., p. 68

14. A. J. Bacevich, "The Use of Force in Our Time, *The Wilson Quarterly*, Winter 1995, pp. 52–61.  Bacevich has written that professional attitudes directly impact on public support for the military, and public expectations about force.  He goes on to suggest that public attitudes about the efficacy of force have been negatively impacted by public comments from serving officers over time.  "By coaxing American military leaders into becoming marginally more responsive to the world as it is, such changes in public attitudes might for a time enable the United States to use its military power more effectively.  But adjustments of this sort would provide at most a temporary palliative, merely postponing the final resolution of the

century-long crisis of military orthodoxy." p. 61.

15. The most cited examples are Richard H. Kohn, "Out of Control: The Crisis in Civil-Military Relations," *The National Interest*, Spring 1994, pp. 3–17; and Edward N. Luttwak, "Washington's Biggest Scandal," *Commentary*, May 1994, pp. 29–33. Kohn observes that the U.S. military is more alienated, more vocal and more partisan as a result of an erosion of relations. Luttwak is even more agitated by the military's vocal stance and resistance in developing options for the use of force.

16. See A. J. Bacevich, Civilian Control: A Useful Fiction?" *Joint Forces Quarterly*, Autumn/Winter 1994-95 pp. 76–79, and Mackubin T. Owens, "Civilian Control: A National Crisis?" *Joint Forces Quarterly*, Autumn/Winter 1994/95, pp. 80–83

17. Eliot A. Cohen, "What to Do About National Defense," *Commentary*, November 1994, p. 30.

18. Ibid, p. 31.

19. Eliot A. Cohen, "A War That Was Not Left to the Generals," *Joint Forces Quarterly*, Summer 1995, p. 49.

20. John F. Hillen, "The Backlash of Limited War," *Army*, January 1995, p. 6

21. Quoted in Summers, *On Strategy*, p. 99. Original source of this statement is from General Ridgway's memoirs, *Soldier: The Memoirs of Matthew B. Ridgway*, New York: Harper, 1956, pp. 271–272.

22. Bacevich, "Clinton's Military Problem—And Ours," pp. 37–38.

23. Richard Haney, "Politics and the Military: Lincoln to Aspin," *Washington Post*, December 4, 1993, p. 19.

# Selected Bibliography

## BOOKS

Allison, Graham. *Essence of Decision: Explaining the Cuban Missile Crisis*, Boston: Little Brown, 1971.

Ambrose, Stephen E. *Eisenhower: Soldier and President*, New York: Touchstone, 1990.

Atkinson, Rick. *Crusade: The Untold Story of the Persian Gulf War*, New York: Houghton Mifflin, 1993.

Bacevich, A. J., et al. *American Military Policy in Small Wars, The Case of El Salvador*, Washington, DC: Pergamon-Brassey's, 1988.

Betts, Richard K. *Soldiers, Statesmen and Cold War Crises*, New York: Columbia University Press, 1991.

Blackwell, James. *Thunder in the Desert*, New York: Bantam, 1991.

Blechman, Barry M., and Stephen S. Kaplan. *Force Without War: U.S. Armed Forces as a Political Instrument*, Washington, DC: Brookings Institution, 1978.

Bolger, Daniel P. *Americans at War 1975–1986: An Era of Violent Peace*, Novato, CA: Presidio Press, 1988.

Booth, Ken, and Moorhead Wright. *American Thinking About War and Peace: New Essays on American Thought and Attitude*, New York: Harvester Press, 1978.

Braestrup, Peter, ed., *Vietnam as History: Ten Years After the Paris Peace Accords*, Washington, DC: University Press of America, 1984.

Brodie, Bernard. *War and Politics*, New York: Macmillan, 1973.

Buckley, Kevin. *Panama: The Whole Story*, New York: Simon & Schuster, 1991.

Cable, Larry E. *Conflict of Myths: The Development of American Counterinsurgency Doctrine and the Vietnam War*, New York: New York University Press, 1986.

Clausewitz, Carl von. *On War*, edited and translated by Michael Howard and Peter Paret, Princeton: Princeton University Press, 1976.

Clodfelter, Mark A. *The Limits of Air Power: The American Bombing of North Vietnam*, New York: Free Press, 1989.

Cohen, Eliot A., and John Gooch. *Military Misfortunes: The Anatomy of Failure in War*, New York: Free Press, 1990.

Colby, William, with James McCargar. *Lost Victories: A Firsthand Account of America's Sixteen-Year Involvement in Vietnam*, New York: Contemporary Books, 1989.

Craig, Gordon A. *The Politics of the Prussian Army: 1640–1945*, New York: Oxford University Press, 1955.

Creveld, Martin van. *The Transformation of War*, New York: Free Press, 1991.

Davidson, Phillip B. *Vietnam At War: 1945–1975*, London: Sidgewick & Jackson, 1988.

Destler, I. M., Leslie H. Gelb, and Anthony Lake. *Our Own Worst Enemy: The Unmaking of American Foreign Policy*, New York: Simon and Schuster, 1984.

De Tocqueville, Alexis. *Democracy in America*, George Lawrence and J. B. Mayer, editors, New York: Doubleday, 1969.

Donnelly, Thomas, Margaret Roth and Caleb Baker. *Operation Just Cause: The Storming of Panama*, New York: Lexington, 1991.

Drew, Dennis M., and Donald M. Snow. *The Eagle's Talons—The American Experience at War*, Maxwell Air Force Base, AL: Air University Press, 1988.

Evans, Ernest. *Wars Without Splendor: The U.S. Military and Low-Level Conflict*, New York: Greenwood, 1984.

Fialka, John. *Hotel Warriors*, Washington, DC: Woodrow Wilson Center Press, 1991.

Finer, S. E. *The Man on Horseback*, Boulder CO: Westview Press, 1988.

Fishel, John T. *The Fog of Peace, Planning and Executing the Restoration of Panama*, Carlisle, PA: Strategic Studies Institute, U.S. Army War College, 1992.

Flanagan, Edward M. *Battle for Panama: Inside Operation Just Cause,* McLean: Brassey's, 1993.

Frank, Benis. *U.S. Marines in Lebanon, 1982–1984*, Washington, DC: U.S. Marine Corps, Government Printing Office, 1987.

Friedman, Norman. *Desert Victory: The War for Kuwait*, Annapolis, MD: Naval Institute Press, 1991.

Friedman, Thomas L. *From Beirut to Jerusalem*, New York: Doubleday, 1990.

Fry, Earl H., Stan A. Taylor, and Robert S. Wood. *America the Vincible: American Foreign Policy in the Twenty-First Century*, Englewood Cliffs, NJ: Prentice Hall,1994.

Gabriel, Richard. *Operation Peace for Galilee: The Israeli-PLO War in Lebanon*, New York: Hill and Wang, 1984.

Gacek, Christopher M. *The Logic of Force: The Dilemma of Limited War in American Foreign Policy*, New York: Columbia University Press, 1994.

Gaddis, John Lewis. *Strategies of Containment: A Critical Appraisal of Postwar American National Security Policy*, New York: Oxford University Press, 1986.

Gelb, Leslie H., and Richard K. Betts. *The Irony of Vietnam: The System Worked*, Washington, DC: Brookings Institution, 1979.

Gordon, Michael, and Bernard E. Trainor *The General's War: The Inside Story of the Conflict in the Gulf,* New York: Little Brown, 1995.

Grinter, Lawrence E., and Peter M. Dunn, eds. *The American War in Vietnam: Lessons, Legacies and Implications for Future Conflict*, Westport, CT: Greenwood, 1987.

Haass, Richard N. *Intervention: The Use of American Force in the Post-Cold War World*, Washington, DC: Brookings, 1994.

Hall, David Locke. *The Reagan Wars: A Constitutional Perspective on War Powers and the Presidency*, Boulder, CO: Westview Press, 1991.

Hallenbeck, Ralph., *The Use of Military Force as an Instrument of U.S. Foreign Policy,* New York: Praeger, 1991.

Hallion, Richard P. *Storm Over Iraq: Air Power and the Gulf War*, Washington, DC: Smithsonian Institute Press, 1992.

Hammel, Eric. *The Root*, Pacifica, CA: Pacifica Press, 1985.

Hartmann, Frederick H. *The Relations of Nations*, New York: MacMillan, 1983.

Helms, Robert F., and Robert H. Dorff, eds. *The Persian Gulf Crisis: Power in the Post-Cold War World*, Westport, CT: Praeger, 1992.

Herring, George C., *America's Longest War: The United States and Vietnam, 1950–1975*, New York: Wiley, 1979.

Huntington, Samuel P. *The Soldier and the State: The Theory and Politics of Civil-Military Relations*, Cambridge, MA: Belknap/Harvard University Press, 1957.

Janowitz, Morris. *The Professional Soldier: A Social and Political Portrait,* New York: Free Press, 1971.

Jervis, Robert. *Perception and Misperception in International Politics*, Princeton: Princeton University Press, 1976.

Karnow Stanley. *Vietnam A History*, New York: Viking, 1983.

Kellner, David. *The Persian Gulf TV War*, Boulder, CO: Westview Press, 1992.

Kinnard, Douglas. *The War Managers*, Hanover, NH: University Press of New England, 1977.

_____. *The Certain Trumpet: Maxwell Taylor and the American Experience in Vietnam*, Washington, DC: Brassey's, 1991.

Kitfield, James, *Prodigal Soldiers: How the Generation of Officers Born of Vietnam Revolutionized the American Style of War*, New York: Simon and Schuster, 1995.

Komer, Robert W. *Bureaucracy at War: U.S. Performance in the Vietnam Conflict,* Boulder, CO: Westview Press, 1986.

Krepinevich, Andrew F. *The Army and Vietnam*, Baltimore: Johns Hopkins University, 1986.

Larrabee, Eric. *Commander in Chief: FDR, His Lieutenants, and Their War*, NewYork: Touchstone, 1990.

Lehman, John. *Command of the Seas: A Personal Story*, New York: Scribner's, 1988.

_____. *Making War: The 200-Year-Old Battle Between the President and the Congress Over How America Goes to War*, New York: Scribner's, 1992.

Lewy, Guenter. *America in Vietnam*, New York: Oxford University Press, 1978.

Manwaring, Max G., ed., *Uncomfortable Wars: Toward a New Paradigm of Low Intensity Conflict*, Boulder, CO: Westview Press, 1991.

Matthews, Lloyd, J., ed., *Newsmen and National Defense: Is Conflict Inevitable?* Washington, DC: Brassey's, 1991.

Matthews, Lloyd J., and Dale E. Brown, eds., *Assessing the Vietnam War*, Washington, DC: Pergammon-Brassey's, 1987.

McNamara, Robert S. with Brian VanDeMark, *In Retrospect: The Tragedy and Lessons of Vietnam*, New York: Times Books, 1995.

Means, Howard. *Colin Powell: A Biography*, New York: Ballantine, 1992.

Millett, Allan R. *For the Common Defense: A Military History of the United States of America*, New York: Free Press, 1984.

Moore, Harold G., with Joseph L. Galloway. *We Were Soldiers Once . . . And Young*, New York: Random House, 1992.

Moore, Molly. *A Women At War: Storming Kuwait With the U.S. Marines*, New York: Scribner's, 1993.

Neustadt, Richard E. and Ernest May. *Thinking in Time: The Use of History for Decision Makers*, New York: Free Press, 1986.

Osborn, George, et al. *Democracy, Strategy and Vietnam: Implications for American Policy Making*, Lexington, MA: Heath & Co, 1987.

Osgood, Robert E. *Limited War Revisited*, Boulder, CO: Westview Press, 1979.

Palmer, Bruce. *The 25-Year War: American's Military Role in Vietnam*, Lexington, KY: University Press of Kentucky, 1984.

Palmer, Dave Richard. *Summons of the Trumpet: U.S.-Vietnam in Perspective*, San Rafael, CA: Presidio, 1978.

Petit, Michael. *Peacekeepers At War: A Marine's Account of the Beirut Catastrophe*, Boston: Faber and Faber, 1986.

Prados, John. *Keepers of the Keys: A History of the National Security Council From Truman to Bush*, New York: William Morrow, 1990.

Record, Jeffrey. *Hollow Victory: A Contrary View of the Gulf War*, McLean, VA: Brassey's, 1993.

Ritter, Gerhard. *The Sword and the Scepter: The Problem of Militarism in Germany*, Coral Gables: University of Miami Press, 1969.

Roth, David. *Sacred Honor: Colin Powell—The Inside Account of His Life and Triumphs*, New York: Harper Collins, 1993.

Rothmann, Harry E., *Forging a New National Military Strategy in a Post-Cold War World: A Perspective From the Joint Staff*, Carlisle, PA: Strategic Studies Institute, U.S. Army War College, February 26, 1992.

Sabrosky, Alan N., and Robert L. Sloane, eds., *The Recourse to War: An Appraisal of the Weinberger Doctrine*, Carlisle, PA: Strategic Studies Institute, U.S. Army War College, 1988.

Santoli, Al. *Leading the Way: How Vietnam Veterans Rebuilt the U.S. Military*, NewYork: Ballantine, 1993.

Sarkesian, Sam C. *The New Battlefield: The United States and Unconventional Conflicts*, New York: Greenwood, 1986.

Schelling, Thomas, C. *Arms and Influence*, New Haven: Yale University Press, 1966.

Schwarzkopf, H. Norman, with Peter Petre. *It Doesn't Take a Hero*, New York: Bantam, 1992.

Sharp, U.S. Grant. *Strategy for Defeat: Vietnam in Retrospect*, San Rafael: Presidio, 1978.

Sheehan, Neil. *A Bright Shining Lie: John Paul Vann and America in Vietnam*, New York: Random House, 1988.

Shultz, George P. *Turmoil and Triumph: My Six Years as Secretary of State*, New York: Scribner's, 1993.

Snow, Donald M. *National Security: Enduring Problems in A Changing Defense Environment*, New York: St. Martin's Press, 1991.

————. *Peacekeeping, Peacemaking and Peace-enforcement: The U.S. Role in the New International Order*, Carlisle, PA: U.S. Army War College, February 1993.

————, and Dennis M. Drew. *From Lexington to Desert Storm: War and Politics in the American Experience*, Armonk, NY: M. E. Sharpe, 1994.

Snyder, Jack. *The Ideology of the Offensive: Military Decision Making and the Disasters of 1914*, Ithaca: Cornell University Press, 1984.

Spanier, John W. *The Truman-MacArthur Controversy and the Korean War*, Cambridge: Harvard University Press, 1959.

Spector, Ronald H. *After Tet: The Bloodiest Year in Vietnam*, New York: Free Press, 1993.

Summers, Harry G. *On Strategy: A Critical Analysis of the Vietnam War,* New York: Presidio, 1982.

_____. *On Strategy II: A Critical Analysis of the Gulf War*, New York: Dell, 1992.

Taylor, Maxwell D. *The Uncertain Trumpet*, New York: Harper, 1959.

Thompson, W. Scott, and Donaldson D. Frizzell, eds. *The Lessons of the Vietnam War*, New York: Crane, Russak, 1977.

Tilford, Earl H. *Setup: What the Air Force Did in Vietnam and Why*, Maxwell Air Force Base, AL: Air University Press, 1991.

Tucker, Robert W., and David C. Hendrickson. *The Imperial Temptation: The New World Order and America's Purpose*, New York: Council on Foreign Relations Press, 1992.

Turner, Robert F. *Repealing the War Powers Resolution: Restoring the Rule of Law in U.S. Foreign Policy*, McLean, VA: Brassey's Inc, 1991.

U.S. News and World Report. *Triumph Without Victory: The Unreported History of the Persian Gulf War*, New York: Times Books, 1992.

Warden, John A. *The Air Campaign*, Washington, DC: National Defense University Press, 1988.

Watson, Bruce W., and Peter G. Tsouras, eds. *Operation Just Cause: The U.S. Intervention in Panama*, Boulder, CO: Westview Press, 1991.

Weigley, Russell F. *The American Way of War: A History of United States Military Strategy and Policy*, Bloomington: Indiana University Press, 1973.

_____. *Eisenhower's Lieutenants: The Campaign in France and Germany 1944—1945,* Bloomington: Indiana University Press, 1981.

_____. *The Age of Battles: The Quest for Decisive Warfare From Breitenfeld to Waterloo*, New York: Macmillan, 1991.

Weinberger, Caspar W. *Fighting for Peace*, New York: Warner Books, 1990.

Westmoreland, William C. *A Soldier Reports*, New York: De Capo, 1989.

Williams, Harry T. *The History of American Wars: From 1745 to 1918*, New York: Knopf, 1981.

Woodward, Bob. *The Commanders*, New York: Simon & Schuster, 1991.

## PERIODICALS AND ARTICLES

Art, Robert. "The Four Functions of Force" in the *The Use of Force: Military Power and International Politics,* Robert J. Art and Kenneth N. Waltz, 4th ed., Lanham: University Press of America, 1993.

"At Least Slow the Slaughter," *New York Times*, October 4, 1992, p. E16.

Auster, Bruce B. "Military Lessons of the Invasion," *U.S. News and World Report*, January 8, 1990, pp. 20–21.

Bacevich, Andrew J. "Old Myths, New Myths: Renewing American Military Thought," *Parameters*, March, 1988, pp. 15–25.

_____. "New Rules: Modern War and Military Professionalism," *Parameters,* December, 1990, pp. 12–23.

_____. "Clinton's Problem—and Ours," *National Review*, December 1993, pp. 36–40.

_____. "Civilian Control: A Useful Fiction?," *Joint Forces Quarterly*, Autumn/Winter 1994/95, pp. 76–79.

_____. "The Use of Force in Our Time," *The Wilson Quarterly*, Winter 1995, pp. 50–61.

Baker, Caleb. "Army Officials Credit Success in Panama To Planning, Few Bureaucratic Obstacles," *Defense News,* March 5, 1990, p. 8.

Barry, John, and Evan Thomas. "Getting Ready for Future Wars," *Newsweek*, January 22, 1990, p. 24.

Bennett, Drew A. "Will the Next War Be Like the Last One," *Marine Corps Gazette*, March, 1992, pp. 37–39.

Bennett, William C. "Just Cause and the Principles of War," *Military Review*, March 1991, pp. 2–13.

Bernstein, Alvin. "U.S. Has No Strategy for Intervention," *Wall Street Journal*, November 10, 1986, p. A24.

Bletz, Donald F. "The Modern Major General," *Parameters*, Vol. IV, No. 1, 1974, pp. 20–31.

Blumenthal, Sidney. "Why Are We in Somalia?" *The New Yorker*, October 25, 1993, pp. 48–54.

Boehlert, Eric. "Panama Coverage: One Big P.R. Job," *New York Times*, January 17, 1990, p. 25.

Branigin, William. "U.S. Embassy Staff Attacks Security," *Washington Post*, December 31, 1989, p. 21.

Broder, John M., and Melissa Healy. "Panama Operation Hurt by Critical Intelligence Gaps," *Los Angeles Times*, December 24, 1989, p. 1.

Bush, George. "When Force Makes Sense," *New York Times*, January 6, 1993, p. A6.

Caldwell, Jean. "Vietnam War Leader Analyzes Gulf War: Westmoreland Sees Few Similarities," *Boston Globe*, March 14, 1991, p. 9.

Cancian, Mark F. "Future Conflict and the Lessons of Vietnam," *Marine Corps Gazette*, January 1983, pp. 57–65.

Carr, Caleb. "American Military Leaders Have Bad Aim," *Long Island Newsday*, December 2, 1992, p. 91.

Christman, Daniel W., and Robert D. Walz. "Military Role in the Emerging National Security Policy," in Helms, Robert F., and Robert H. Dorff, eds. *The Persian Gulf Crisis: Power in the Post-Cold War World*, Westport, CT: Praeger, 1992, pp. 137–168.

Clarke, Jeffrey J. "On Strategy and the Vietnam War," *Parameters*, Vol. XVI, No.4, Winter, 1986, pp. 39–46.

Clodfelter, Mark. "Of Demons, Storms, and Thunder: A Preliminary Look at Vietnam's Impact on the Persian Gulf Air Campaign," *Air Power Journal*, Spring 1991, pp. 17–32.

Cohen, Eliot, A. "Constraints on America's Conduct of Small Wars," contained in *Conventional Forces and American Defense Policy*, Steven Miller, ed., Princeton, NJ: Princeton University Press, 1987, pp. 277–307.

_____. "How to Fight Iraq," *Commentary*, November 25, 1990, pp. 20–23.

_____. "The Mystique of U.S. Air Power," *Foreign Affairs*, January/February 1994, pp. 109–124.

_____. "What to Do About National Defense," *Commentary*, November, 1994, pp. 30–31.

_____. "Making Do With Less, Or Coping with Upton's Ghost," Carlisle, PA: Strategic Studies Institute, U.S. Army War College, May 1995.

_____. "A War That was Not Left to the Generals," *Joint Forces Quarterly*, Summer 1995, p. 49–52.

Cohen, Richard. "Summing Up the Bush Doctrine," *Washington Post*, January 7, 1993, p. A31.

Cordesman, Anthony H. "America's New Combat Culture," *New York Times*, February 28, 1991, p. A37.

Cropsey, Seth. "Barking Up a Fallen Tree: The Death of Low Intensity Conflict," *The National Interest*, Spring, 1992, pp. 53–60.

Davidson, Michael W. "Senior Officers and Vietnam Policymaking," *Parameters*, Spring, 1986, pp. 55–62.

Devroy, Ann, and Patrick E. Tyler. "U.S. Launches Military Operation in Panama to Seize Gen. Noriega," *Washington Post*, December 20, 1989, p. 1.

Downey, Frederick M., and Steven Metz. "The American Political Culture and Strategic Planning," *Parameters*, September 1988, pp. 34–42.

Duffy, Brian. "The Rules of the Game: A New Chairman of the Joint Chiefs of Staff and New Questions About American Use of Force," *U.S. News and World Report*, August 23, 1993, pp. 22–24.

Dunlap, Charles J. "The Origins of the American Military Coup of 2012," *Parameters*, Winter 1992-1993, pp. 2–20.

Evans, David. "Military Experts See Flaws in Attack Plan," *Chicago Tribune*, December 24, 1989, p. 7.

_____. "Questions From an Invasion: Panama and the Pentagon," *Chicago Tribune*, January 5, 1990, p. 17.

Fessenden, Ford. "Chain of Command, Generals Molded in a Common Crucible—Vietnam," *Long Island Newsday*, February 10, 1991, p. 4.

Fishel, John T. "The Murky World of Conflict Termination: Planning and Executing the 1989-1990 Restoration of Panama," *Small Wars and Insurgencies*, Spring 1992, pp. 58–71.

Friedman, Thomas L. "Fair Game," *New York Times*, May 30, 1993, p. 50.

Fromkin, David, and James Chace. "The Lessons of Vietnam?" *Foreign Affairs*, Spring 1985, pp. 722–746.

Garrity, Patrick J. "Implications of the Persian Gulf War for Regional Powers," *The Washington Quarterly*, Summer 1993, pp. 153–170.

Gates, John M. "Vietnam: The Debate Goes On," *Parameters*, Spring 1984, pp. 15–25.

George, Alexander L. "Crisis Management: The Interaction of Political and Military Considerations," *Survival*, Vol. 26, September/October 1984, p. 224.

Gordon, Michael R. "The Marine Corps in Lebanon," *National Journal*, November 12, 1983, pp. 23–67.

_____. "U.S. Drafted Invasion Plan Weeks Ago," *New York Times*, December 24, 1989, p. 1.

_____. "Cheney is Blamed in Muzzling Media: Report on Panama Coverage Cites Concern for Secrecy," *New York Times*, March 20, 1990, p. 20.

_____. "Powell Delivers a Resounding No on Using Limited Force on Bosnia," *New York Times*, September 28, 1992, p. A1.

Gordon, Michael R., and Bernard E. Trainor, "Beltway Warrior," *New York Times Magazine*, August 27, 1995, pp. 40–43.

Gosselin, Peter G. "Post-attack Plans Termed Inadequate," *Boston Globe*, December 24, 1989, p. 1.

Gugiotta, Guy. "Turning the Mistakes of Vietnam Into Lessons for Desert Shield," *Washington Post*, December 23, 1990, p. A14.

Gutman, Roy. "Battle Over Lebanon," *Foreign Service Journal*, June 1984, pp. 28–33.

Haass, Richard N. "Military Force: A User's Guide," *Foreign Policy*, Fall 1994, pp. 21–37.

Halloran, Richard. "For Military Leaders, the Shadow of Vietnam," *New York Times*, March 20, 1984, p. B10.

————. "What Terrifies the Toughest Soldiers?: A Civilian Military Plan," *New York Times*, April 14, 1988, p. B6.

Haney, Richard. "Politics and the Military: Lincoln to Aspin," *Washington Post*, December 4, 1993, p. 19.

Hennelly, Michael J. "U.S. Policy in El Salvador: Creating Beauty or Beast?" *Parameters*, Spring 1993, p. 66.

Herring, George C. "American Strategy in Vietnam: The Postwar Debate," *Military Affairs*, April 1982, pp. 57–63.

Hillen, John F. "Peacekeeping is Hell," *Policy Review*, Fall 1993, pp. 36–39.

————. "The Backlash of Limited War," *Army*, January 1995, p. 6.

Hoagland, Jim. "A National Consensus on Easy Little Wars," *Washington Post*, January 18, 1990, p. 33.

————. "Here's a New One: The Beirut Syndrome," *Washington Post*, April 14, 1991, p. B7.

————. "August Guns: How Sarajevo Will Reshape U.S. Strategy," *Washington Post*, August 9, 1992, pp. C1–C3.

————. "On Somalia, A Mysterious Decision," *Washington Post*, December 3, 1992, p. A21.

Hoar, Joseph P. "A CINC's Perspective," *Joint Forces Quarterly,* Autumn 1993, pp. 38–43.

Hoffman, Frank, G. "The Powell Doctrine: Inflexible or Prudent Response?" *Marine Corps Gazette*, February 1994, pp. 32–33.

————. "Decisive Force—A New American Way of War," *Strategic Review*, Winter 1995, pp. 23–34.

Hoffmann, Stanley, et al. "Vietnam Reappraised," *International Security*, Summer 1981, Vol. 6, No. 1, pp. 3–26.

Hosler, Karen and Richard H. Sia. "Pentagon Says It Needs More Time, More Troops," *Baltimore Sun*, December 23, 1989, p. 1.

Hunt, John, B. "Hostilities Short of War," *Military Review*, March 1993, pp. 41–50.

Huntington, Samuel, P. "Playing to Win," *The National Interest*. Spring 1986, pp. 13–20.

————. "New Contingencies, Old Roles," *Joint Force Quarterly*, Autumn 1993, pp. 38–43.

Johnson, Douglas and Steven Metz. "Civil-Military Relations in the United States: The State of the Debate," *Washington Quarterly*, Winter 1995, pp. 208–220.

Johnston, Alastair Iain. "Thinking About Strategic Culture," *International Security*, Spring 1995, pp. 32–64.

Kemp, Kenneth H., and Charles Hudlin. "Civil Supremacy Over the Military: Its Nature and Limits," *Armed Forces and Society*, Vol. 19, No. 1, Fall 1992, pp. 7–26.

Kier, Elizabeth "Culture and Military Doctrine-France Between the Wars," *International Security*, Spring 1995, pp. 65–93.

Kissinger, Henry. "Somalia: Reservations," *Washington Post,* December 13, 1992, p. C7.

Kohn, Richard H."Out of Control: The Crisis in Civil-Military Relations," *The National Interest*, Spring 1994, pp. 3–17.

Komarow, Steven. "Pooling Around in Panama," *Washington Journalism Review*, March, 1990, pp. 45–47.

Kozak, David C. "The Bureaucratic Politics Approach: The Evolution of the Paradigm," *Bureaucratic Politics and National Security*, David Kozak and James Keagel, eds., New York: Reinner Publishers, 1988, pp. 3–15.

Krauthammer, Charles. "Good Morning, Vietnam," *Washington Post*, April 19, 1991, p. A23.

Lewy, Guenter. "Some Political-Military Lessons of the Vietnam War," *Parameters*, Spring, 1984, pp. 2–14.

Lord, Carnes. "American Strategic Culture," *Comparative Strategy*, Vol. 5. No. 3., 1985, pp. 269–293.

_____. "American Strategic Culture in Small Wars," *Small Wars and Insurgencies*, Winter 1992, pp. 205–216.

Lowenthal, Abraham F. "Operation Just Cause Six Months Later," *Chicago Tribune*, July 10, 1990, p. 9.

Luttwak, Edward N. "Operation Just Cause—What Went Right, Wrong," *Army Times*, January 1, 1990, p. R7.

_____. "Just Cause—A Military Score Sheet," *Washington Post*, December 31, 1989, p. C4.

_____. "Washington's Biggest Scandal," *Commentary*, May 1994, pp. 29–33.

Luvaas, Jay. "Lessons and Lessons Learned, A Historical Perspective," in Robert E. Harkavy and Stephanie G. Neuman, eds., *The Lessons of Recent Wars in the Third World*, Lexington MA: Lexington Books, 1985.

Mahnken, Thomas G. "America's Next War," *The Washington Quarterly*, Summer 1993, pp. 171–184.

Maynard, Wayne, K. "The New American Way of War," *Military Review*, November, 1993, pp. 5–16.

McKenzie, Kenneth F. "Fourth General Warfare: Elegant Irrelevance," *Parameters*, Autumn 1993, pp. 51–61.

Mead, James M. "The Lebanon Experience," *Marine Corps Gazette*, February 1983, p. 33.

Moore, Molly and George C. Wilson. "Bush Chose Pentagon's Maximum Option," *Washington Post,* December 21, 1989, p. 1.

Moore, Molly, and Rick Atkinson. "Despite Glitches, Invasion Was a Military Success," *Washington Post*, December 29, 1989, p. 1.

Moore, Robert S. "Small War Lessons Learned," *Marine Corps Gazette*, February, 1993, pp. 32–34.

Mosettig, Michael D. "Panama and the Press," *SAIS Review*, Summer/Fall 1990, pp. 179–187.

Muravchik, Joshua. "Beyond Self-Defense," *Commentary*, December 1993, pp. 23–27.

Oakely, Robert B. "An Envoy's Perspective," *Joint Forces Quarterly*, Autumn, 1993, pp. 44–55.

Osgood, Robert. "The American Approach to War," in *U.S. National Security: A Framework for Analysis*, Daniel J. Kaufman, Jeffrey S. McKitrick, and Thomas J. Leney, eds., Lexington, MA: Lexington Books, 1991, pp. 98–109.

Owens, Mackubin T. "Civilian Control: A National Crisis?" *Joint Forces Quarterly*, Autumn/Winter 1994/95, pp. 80–83.

Powell, Colin L. "U.S. Forces: Challenges Ahead," *Foreign Affairs*, Winter, 1992/1993, pp. 32–45.

_____. "What Makes Generals Nervous," *New York Times*, October 8, 1992, p. A35.

Prosch, Geoffrey G., and Mitchell M. Zais. "American Will and the Vietnam War," *Military Review*, March 1990, pp. 71–80.

Radebaugh, Lyle G. "Operation Just Cause: The Best Course of Action?" *Military Review*, March 1991, pp. 58–60.

Richburg, Keith B. "Top Marine Calls Somalia Mission Done," *Washington Post*, January 30, 1993, p. A18.

Ropelewski, Robert R. "Planning, Precision, and Surprise Led to Panama Successes," *Armed Forces Journal International*, February, 1990, pp. 27–32.

Rosello, Victor M. "Lessons From El Salvador," *Parameters*, Winter 1993/1994, pp. 100–108. Rosen, Stephen P. "Vietnam and the American Theory of Limited War," in *American Defense Policy*, 6th ed., Schuyler Foerster and Edward N. Wright, eds., Baltimore:Johns Hopkins University Press, 1990, pp. 306–320.

Rosenfeld, Stephen S. "Colin Powell's Somalia Operation," *Washington Post*, December 11, 1992, p. A27.

Rosenthal, Andrew. "American Troops Press Hunt for Noriega: Order Breaks Down; Looting Widespread," *New York Times*, December 22, 1989, p. 1.

Schmitt, Eric. "Somalia Role: Why?" *New York Times*, August 27, 1993, p. A10.

Shultz, Richard H. "The Post-Conflict Use of Military Forces: Lessons from Panama, 1989–1991," *The Journal of Strategic Studies*, June 1991, pp. 145–172.

Sloyan, Patrick J. "Candor Panama's 1st Casualty," *Long Island Newsday*, January 14, 1990, p. 3.

Snider, Don M., and W. J. Taylor. "Needed—A Pentagon Prepared to Wage Peace," *Washington Post*, August 9, 1992, p. C1.

Snyder, Jack. "Civil Military Relations and the Cult of the Offensive, 1914 and 1984," *International Security*, Summer 1984, pp. 108–144.

Spector, Ronald H. "U.S. Army Strategy in the Vietnam War," *International Security*, Spring 1987, pp. 130–135.

Szafranski, Richard. "Thinking About Small Wars," *Parameters*, September, 1990, pp. 39–50.

Trainor, Bernard E. "Flaws in Panama Attack," *New York Times*, January 2, 1990, p. 1.

Twining, David T. "Vietnam and the Six Criteria for the Use of Military Force," *Parameters*, Vol. XV, No. 4, 1986, pp. 10–18.

Tyler, Patrick E. "Vietnam and Gulf Zone: Real Military Contrasts," *New York Times*, December 1, 1993, p. 8.

Waghelstein, John, D. "Some Thoughts on Operation Desert Storm and Future Wars," *Military Review*, February 1992, pp. 80–83.

Webb, James H. "An Appropriate Use of Force," *Naval War College Review*, Winter 1988, pp. 20–26.

Weigley, Russell F. "The American Military and the Principle of Civilian Control from McClellan to Powell," *The Journal of Military History*, October 1993, pp. 27–58.

Wilson, George C. "Tit-for-Tat in Vietnam is What the Brass Hated," *Washington Post*, March 30, 1986, pp. D1, D4.

_____. "SOUTHCOM Commander Rewrote Contingency Plans for Action," *Washington Post,* January 7, 1990, p. 1.

Zinni, Anthony. "It's Not Nice and Neat," *Naval Institute Proceedings*, August 1995, pp. 26–30.

## GOVERNMENT DOCUMENTS

U.S. Congress. *U.S. Low Intensity Conflicts 1899–1990*, Congressional Research Service, Library of Congress, Washington, DC: GPO, September 10, 1990.

U.S. Congress. House Armed Services Committee, *Report on the Adequacy of Security at the Marine Barracks*, Washington, DC: GPO, December 19, 1983.

U.S. Congress. House Armed Services Committee, *Defense for a New Era: Lessons of the Persian Gulf War*, Washington, DC: GPO, 1992.

U.S. Department of the Air Force. *Air Force Manual 1-1, Basic Aerospace Doctrine of the United States Air Force, Vol. II*, Washington, DC: GPO, March, 1992.

U.S. Department of the Air Force. *Gulf War Air Power Survey*, Washington, DC: GPO, October, 1993.

U.S. Department of the Army. *A Study of Strategic Lessons Learned in Vietnam*, 8 vols., McLean, VA: BDM Corporation, 1980.

U.S. Department of the Army. *Field Manual (FM) 100-5 Operations*, Washington, DC: Headquarters, U.S. Army, June, 1993.

U.S. Department of Defense. *The Pentagon Papers: The Defense Department History of the U.S. Decision-making on Vietnam*, Senator Gavel Edition, 5 vols., Boston: Beacon Press, 1971.

U.S. Department of Defense. *Commission on Beirut International Terrorist Attack, October 23, 1983 (Long Commission Report)*, Washington, DC: GPO, December 20, 1983.

U.S. Department of Defense. *Conduct of the Persian Gulf War: Final Report to Congress*, Washington, DC: GPO, April, 1992.

U.S. Department of Defense. *Annual Report to the President*, Washington, DC: GPO, January, 1993.

U.S. Department of State. *The United States and the Politics of Conflict in the Developing World*, Washington, DC: Center for the Study of Foreign Affairs, Foreign Service Institute, October, 1990.

U.S. Joint Chiefs of Staff. *JCS Pub 1-2: Dictionary of Military and Assciated Terms.* Washington, DC: GPO, 1989.

U.S. Joint Chiefs of Staff. *The National Military Strategy of the United States*, Washington, DC: GPO, February, 1992.

U.S. Joint Chiefs of Staff. *JCS Pub 3-0, Doctrine for Joint Operations*, Washington, DC: GPO, May, 1993.

U.S. Joint Chiefs of Staff. Draft *National Military Strategy*, mimeograph, December, 1993.

**UNPUBLISHED MATERIALS**

Aspin, Les. "The Use and Usefulness of Military Forces in the Post-Cold War, Post-Soviet World," address to the Jewish Institute for National Security Affairs, mimeograph, Washington, DC: September 21, 1992, pp. 1–6.

Brady, Michael J. "The Army and the Strategic Legacy of Vietnam," unpublished Master's Thesis, U.S. Army Command and General Staff College, Fort Leavenworth, KS, 1990.

McFarlane, Robert. "Lessons of the Beirut Bombing," unpublished article, Washington, DC: October 23, 1993.

Petraeus, David H. "The American Military and the Lessons of Vietnam: A Study of Military Influence and the Use of Force in the Post-Vietnam Era," PhD. dissertation, Princeton University, 1987.

Willis, Jeffrey R. "The Employment of U.S. Marines in Lebanon 1982-1984," unpublished Master's thesis, Fort Leavenworth, KS: U.S. Army Command and General Staff College, 1992.

# Index

**About the Author**

F. G. HOFFMAN is Historian, Studies and Analysis Division, Marine Corps Development Command, U.S. Marine Corps.